Advance Pr.

"We've reviewed dozens of personality profile approaches, and what I love about the Color Q method in this book is that it does what personality assessments rarely do well—it answers the great "So what?" question. It teaches what your personality means for your career and how to make the most of it. We coach with Color Q because it gets to this extremely important bottom line: finding a job that really fits and keeping it."
—**John Courtney, CEO, NextJob, Inc.**

"We all know that 'people skills' are important in one's career. Perhaps no one has defined those skills and their potential applications as well as Shoya Zichy in her book *Personality Power*. At last, the mysteries of successful, professional interactions are solved, laid out in plain English and organized to allow the reader to immediately understand difficult personality types. Even people who don't read this book will benefit—as others apply what they have learned from the book."
—**Ellen Reynolds, Senior Vice President and Chief People Officer, The Segal Group, Inc.**

"*Personality Power* opens the floodgates to improved profitability, productivity, and communication. Individuals who embrace the principles in this book are happier, more productive, and committed to their career choices, and organizations learn how to make internal and external meetings and conversations more successful and less stressful and ensure that the 'right people are in the right seats on the bus.'"
—**Jeannette Hobson, Senior Vice President, Eastern Division, Vistage International**

"I recommend *Personality Power*, a unique reading selection in today's crowded business literature. The ideas work; the suggestions are easy to remember. One can bring out the best in oneself and others while succeeding on the job. The key is to insightfully access and understand the personalities that surround us in our work environment, including most importantly one's own personality and style, its strengths and shortcomings."
—**Sergio I. de Araujo, Chairman, AnSer Latin American Opportunities Fund**

"Leadership is about bringing out the best in people or an organization. This book provides a unique framework, combining business experience and psychological insight."
—**Kathleen Waldron, President, William Paterson University**

"Zichy is masterful at boiling down into plain English the complex topics of career and personality. *Personality Power* is like a wise career adviser at your fingertips."
—**Nancy Ancowitz, business communication coach and author of Self-Promotion for Introverts®**

personality power

discover your unique profile— and unlock your potential for breakthrough success

SHOYA ZICHY
WITH ANN BIDOU

AMACOM AMERICAN MANAGEMENT ASSOCIATION
New York • Atlanta • Brussels • Chicago • Mexico City
San Francisco • Shanghai • Tokyo • Toronto • Washington, D.C.

Bulk discounts available. For details visit:
www.amacombooks.org/go/specialsales
Or contact special sales:
Phone: 800-250-5308 / E-mail: specialsls@amanet.org
View all AMACOM titles at: www.amacombooks.org
American Management Association: www.amanet.org

Library of Congress Cataloging-in-Publication Data has been applied for and is on file at the Library of Congress.

About AMA
American Management Association (www.amanet.org) is a world leader in talent development, advancing the skills of individuals to drive business success. Our mission is to support the goals of individuals and organizations through a complete range of products and services, including classroom and virtual seminars, webcasts, webinars, podcasts, conferences, corporate and government solutions, business books, and research. AMA's approach to improving performance combines experiential learning—learning through doing—with opportunities for ongoing professional growth at every step of one's career journey.

Printing number
10 9 8 7 6 5 4 3 2 1

CONTENTS

ACKNOWLEDGMENTS

We have been blessed to connect with many people who share our passion for the study of personality differences:

Peter and Katharine Myers, for continuing to support new applications of personality type.

David Keirsey, whose book *Please Understand Me* introduced us to temperaments, and Linda Berens, whose ongoing research continues to enrich our understanding of the model.

U.S. District Judge Paul Crotty for his generous introductions.

Linda Konner, our agent, for seeing the potential of the manuscript and providing steadfast focus, support, and wisdom.

The vibrant AMACOM team: Andrew Ambraziejus and Ellen Kadin for their professionalism and dedication to the publishing of this book; Louis Greenstein, Barry Richardson, and William Helms for their editing savvy and Jim Bessent for copyediting and production coordination; and the AMACOM publicity group for their creativity and enthusiasm.

Members of the APTi, FWA, and training communities for sharing anecdotes, tips, and insights, especially: Nancy Ancowitz, Suzanne Brue, Emily Christakis, Robert Cuddy, Juanita Davies, Mary Davis, Phyllis Weiss Haserot, Iris Jacobs, Craig Jennings, Laurie Lawson,

Ray Linder, Mary Lippitt, Jane Maloney, Susanne Mueller, Andrea Nierenberg, Jim Oher, Jeannette Paladino, Pamela Fox Rollin, Hile Rutledge, Jeri Sedlar, Cynthia Sefton, Jerry Solomons, Tanya Straker, Rob Toomey, Malachy Vance, and Kathryn Wankel.

Participants of Shoya's two mastermind groups for always being there to evaluate new ideas: Galit Ben-Joseph, Diane DiResta, Libby Dubick, Bonnie Halpern, Laura Hill, Kathryn Mayer, Maureen McCarthy, Lynne Morton, and Barbara Stein.

Our interns Olga Geletina, Brisejda Gjoka, Mina Hirsch, and Elena Shneider, for taking time from their studies to help with research and social media.

Brendan Newman, program director, Bike & Build, Inc., for allowing us to share stories of how Color Q was applied during their cross-country bicycle and building tours. Donation and participation information is available at www.bikeandbuild.org.

Greg Bidou, for his constant support, belief, patience, and encouragement.

And last but certainly not least, thanks to Shoya's family: Mother, Charles, Sheila, and Fiona, for always being the cheerleaders.

PEOPLE PROFILED

In Order of Appearance

Most of the following individuals have been personally assessed by Shoya Zichy, except where evaluated by the Myers-Briggs community as noted in their chapter.

Greens: Diane Sawyer, journalist and anchor, *ABC World News*; Dr. Mehmet Oz, cardiac surgeon, television personality, and author; Her Highness Sheika Hessa Salem Al Salman Al Sabah, chairperson of ATAMANA of Kuwait; Erik Detiger, managing director, Philanthropia, Inc.; Fiona Thompson, director of HR operations, Urban Land Institute; Dr. Mobarak Abdulhadi Aldosari, founder, Rowad Almaarefa Educational Consulting, Saudi Arabia; Carolyn Maloney, United States Congress; Katharine Myers, co-owner Myers-Briggs Type Indicator copyrights; Catherine Atwood, co-leader, Bike & Build cross-country bicycle trip.

Reds: Countess Editha Nemes, former designer and real estate broker; Donald Trump, chairman and president, The Trump Organization; Edward Koch, former mayor of New York City; Randolph A. Hogan, freelance writer/editor and former editor of the *New York Times Book Review*; Sheila L. Birnbaum, co-head, Skadden Arps Mass Torts and Insurance Litigation Group; Michael Naso, partner, FBN Securities, Inc.; Margaret Davis, president and CEO, Marine Corps Scholarship Foundation; Hugh Heisler, partner, Heisler, Feldman, McCormick & Garrow; Christopher L. Dutton, president and CEO, Vermont Electric Power Company; John Sawyer, web developer/computer technical support and owner, Chon Resources; Timothy R., vintage motorcycle restorer.

Blues: Hillary Rodham Clinton, United States secretary of state and former First Lady; Phyllis Haberman, senior managing director, Egret Capital Partners, LLC; Mark W. Smith, founder, Smith Valliere, PLLC; Mark Taylor, chair, Vistage International, Inc.; Vanessa A. McDermott, management consultant, MWH, Inc.; Matthew B. Alsted, vice president, channel marketing and brand strategy, Calvert Investments; James G. Squyres, owner, Buyside Research.

Golds: Sonia Sotomayor, associate justice of the Supreme Court of the United States; Warren Buffett, founder, Berkshire Hathaway; Martha Clark Goss, board member; Steven Brill, president and founder, The Lighting Design Group; Martha Sloane, certified nursing assistant; Dr. Silvester Lango, orthopedic surgeon; George Yarocki, author and Indian motorcycle restorer.

Approach to Innovation: Lily Klebanoff Blake, board member and emerging market specialist.

All other profiles are composites of author Shoya Zichy's clients and seminar attendees.

1

introduction

I SAT, STRANDED, in a muggy Asian airport. It had been a long, over-scheduled trip seeking new private banking clients. In the midst of a pile of debris left behind by the late-night floor sweepers, I noticed a dog-eared book. I picked it up and, from that moment, my view of the world was changed forever.

"If a man does not keep pace with others, perhaps it is because he hears a different drummer," it began with the frequently quoted Henry David Thoreau. The book, a since-discontinued presentation of the theories of Swiss psychologist Carl Jung, outlined new insights into the way people take in information and make decisions. The contents confirmed what I had long sensed intuitively, having observed people with fascination since I was a child. The information hinted of a new framework to use with clients and associates.

Settling back in my Hong Kong office the next morning, I decided to categorize each of my customers according to their Jungian behavioral profiles. I used four colors to create a simple system that could be used by the support staff during my frequent absences. Each file included brief instructions for handling personal interactions. "When a Gold comes in, make sure all statements are up-to-date and organized in date-sequential order. If a Blue makes an appointment, call our investment guys in New York and get three new ideas." There were four color groups of clients; each had its own service strategy.

Over the next few months our new business increased by 60 percent, primarily on word-of-mouth. My company benefited, but I did as well. I began to enjoy my clients more, my stress level went down, and, in time, my relationships outside of the office would improve as well.

For some ten years, I applied the same techniques to a growing and diverse client base: high-net-worth individuals in South America, white-robed sheiks in Abu Dhabi, shipping magnates in Athens, aristocratic landowners in Spain. No matter who or what, the color coding dotted their files and it worked—for men, women, young, old, and worldwide ethnicities, the results were universal.

Institutions reorganize and solid careers dematerialize overnight. With my firm in the throes of a major transition, I took some time off to go up to Maine and rethink my life direction. On the porch of my small seaside inn sat a man reading a book written by Isabel Myers, who had been deeply influenced by none other than Carl Jung. She had developed a new application for Jung's work called the Myers-Briggs Type Indicator (MBTI). It was the life direction I was looking for.

As I discovered a worldwide network of MBTI books, seminars, tapes, and people, a new and strong sense of internal direction unfolded. Suddenly, the right people and events began to materialize. Jung would have dubbed it "synchronicity."

Drawing on my corporate experience, I began pioneering unique ways of applying these ideas to workplace applications, such as team building, leadership development, and sales. And 35,000 attendees to my seminars later, my life is now completely focused on my coding system, which has evolved into a model called Color Q (www.ColorQPersonalities.com).

Evaluating people was key to survival during my unusual childhood; I was born a countess in Hungary. When my family fled the communists, we landed in the court of King Farouk of Egypt, where I played with his daughters in his 550-room palace. Later, we fled the horrifying bloodshed of Colonel Gamal Abdel Nasser's revolution.

I've turned what I learned then into a system that helps all of us define our unique strengths, pursue the best career, and reduce conflicts in key areas of our lives.

What Color Q Is Not

Color Q is not a labeling system denying the individuality of every person. It does not measure the impact of education, intelligence, mental health, special talents, economic status, motivation, drive, and environmental influences on the core personality type. There are billions of unique people on our planet and only four color groups. If you wonder what that leaves, I say the deepest and most important part of you—the part that always knows what it really wants and won't be happy until it gets respect!

The framework is not gender specific. It works equally well for males and females. Both men and women are found in each personality style, though in some groups the percentages differ.

What Color Q Is

Color Q is about categorizing people—ourselves and others. It is based on the extensive research of "personality type" experts who, for the past seven decades, have laid the intellectual groundwork that serves as the basis of this book. There are many systems for understanding others. This is the one that I have found probes most deeply into the core of human behavior. It confirms that each personality style is *natural, equal, observable, and predictable,* and that each can be equally effective at work. Once mastered, the system provides practical ways to maximize our natural talents, as well as those of others.

Truly exceptional people always do so much more than is required. The only way to do that without severe burnout is from passion born of confidence. You are the right person doing the right thing in the right place, and enjoying it! Sound impossible? Not at all, for those who are true to themselves in spite of naysayers, parental expectations, and societal pressures. Use this book to reveal your road to being exceptional.

Color Q is also a tool for understanding the sometimes-incomprehensible behaviors of colleagues, bosses, clients (and even friends, dates, mates, and children!). Since so much of success depends on "emotional intelligence," you'll find your increased ability to "read people" perhaps the most valuable outcome of reading this book. Enjoy your new journey!

the self-assessment test

THE DUAL EPIDEMICS of workplace conflict and employee disengagement have reached alarming levels and need to be addressed immediately. Modern Survey, a human capital measurement firm, reported a record-breaking 70 percent level of U.S. employee disengagement in 2011. CPP, a provider of products and services for individual and organizational development (including the Myers-Briggs Type Indicator), compiled a 2008 "Human Capital Report" of 5,000 workers in nine countries. The results revealed U.S. employees spend 2.8 hours a week dealing with conflict, which equals a staggering $359 billion in paid hours per year.

This book is a tool to reverse these numbers.

The theory behind the Color Q system has been tested for decades on millions of people worldwide. For many individuals, including both authors of this book, the system has been career and life changing. The following self-assessment test is your key to this very powerful (and actually rather fun) professional and personal tool.

There are four parts to the Color Q assessment and one supplemental section. Together, they will take you about ten minutes to complete. Part I will test you for your Color Q primary personality color. This is who you are at your core, when no one's looking.

Note: In the self-assessment you will be asked to select your preferences. A preference is not "I generally work with piles, but I'd prefer if I kept my desk clean." What you generally choose to do is what you prefer. Slight or strong, there is always a preference.

Part I: Instructions

Part I has three sections. To begin, select one of the two choices in *each* line according to your first impulse, which is usually correct. There are no "right" or "wrong" answers, just like being right-handed or left-handed is neither right nor wrong. While you can use both, you use the preferred hand with less effort and better results. If you are truly torn between the two choices, it typically means you feel pressured to function in a certain way. Right now, set the guilt and pressure aside.

Choose your answer from either Column A or Column B. Each choice must be filled in, choosing the statement that describes you at least 51 percent of the time. You should wind up with a total of nine checkmarks in each of the sections (I, II, and III).

For example, the first set of choices reads: At least 51 percent of the time I tend to:

Column A		Column B
❏ value accuracy more	-OR-	❏ value insights more

Which do you prefer most of the time? Accuracy or insights? Put a checkmark in the box next to "accuracy" or "insights" and move on to the second set of choices below it. You may not check off both boxes; check only the box where you have a slight or strong preference.

Section I

Be sure to answer every question. Total each column, and then follow the instructions to Sections II *OR* III.

At least 51 percent of the time I tend to:

Column A		Column B
❏ value accuracy more	-OR-	❏ value insights more
❏ be interested in concrete issues	-OR-	❏ be interested in abstract ideas
❏ prefer people who speak plainly	-OR-	❏ prefer unusual ways of expression
❏ remember many details	-OR-	❏ be vague about details
❏ be down to earth	-OR-	❏ be complex
❏ focus on the present	-OR-	❏ focus on future possibilities
❏ be valued for my common sense	-OR-	❏ be valued for seeing new trends
❏ be realistic and pragmatic	-OR-	❏ be theoretical and imaginative
❏ be trusting of facts	-OR-	❏ be trusting of my intuition

If you have chosen more items in Column A, please _go directly to Section III_. If you have chosen more items in Column B, _please go directly to Section II_.

Section II

At least 51 percent of the time I tend to be *more*:

Column 1		Column 2
❏ frank and direct	-OR-	❏ tactful and diplomatic
❏ skeptical at first	-OR-	❏ accepting at first
❏ won over by logic	-OR-	❏ won over by appeal to values
❏ analytical	-OR-	❏ empathetic
❏ apt to meet conflict head-on	-OR-	❏ apt to avoid conflict where possible
❏ interested in fairness	-OR-	❏ sympathetic
❏ objective when criticized	-OR-	❏ apt to take things personally
❏ impartial	-OR-	❏ compassionate
❏ competitive	-OR-	❏ supportive

If you have chosen more items in the left Column 1, _you are a Blue_.
If you answered more items in the right Column 2, _you are a Green_.

Section III

At least 51 percent of the time I tend to:

Column @		Column #
❏ meet deadlines early	-OR-	meet deadlines at the last minute

❏ make detailed plans before start	-OR-	❏ handle problems as they arise
❏ be punctual and sometimes early	-OR-	❏ be leisurely, sometimes late
❏ like to be scheduled	-OR-	❏ prefer to be spontaneous
❏ like clear guidelines	-OR-	❏ like flexibility
❏ feel settled	-OR-	❏ often feel restless
❏ have a tidy workplace	-OR-	❏ have a workplace with many piles/papers
❏ be deliberate	-OR-	❏ be carefree
❏ like to make plans	-OR-	❏ like to wait and see

If you have chosen more items in the left Column @, _you are a Gold_.
If you answered more items in the right Column #, _you are a Red_.

Part II: Instructions

Now read the short overview of your primary color. Does it ring true? If yes, continue to Part III to determine your backup style. If not, skip down to the section on "What to Do If This Doesn't Ring True for You."

GOLDS (46% of population)

Grounded, realistic, and accountable, Golds are the backbone of institutions of all kinds—corporate and public. They are society's protectors and administrators who value procedures, respect the chain of command, and have finely tuned systems for everything. From raising children to running large divisions, Golds get involved in details and are known for following through and mobilizing others to achieve concrete goals. They are most interested in making lists, planning in advance, and dealing with what has worked in the past.

BLUES (10% of the population)

Theoretical, competitive, and always driven to acquire more knowledge and competence, Blues are unequaled when it comes to dealing with complex, theoretical issues and designing new systems. As natural skeptics, their first reaction is to criticize and set their benchmarks against which they measure everyone and everything. They are highly precise in thought and language, trusting only logic, not the rules or procedures of the past. Blues are future-oriented visionaries who do best in positions requiring strategic thinking. Then they move on with little interest in maintenance.

REDS (27% of the population)

Action-oriented, spontaneous, and focused on "now," Reds need freedom to follow their impulses, which they trust over the judgment of others. Cool-headed and ever courageous, they get things done and handle a crisis better than most. Found in careers that provide freedom, action, variety, and the unexpected, they bring excitement and a sense of expediency. Work must be fun and the environment collegial. Reds resist schedules and hierarchies. Long-term planning is a low priority as each day brings its own agenda.

GREENS (17% of the population)

Creative, empathetic, and humanistic, Greens need an environment that is idea-oriented and egalitarian and that provides the chance to impact the lives of others. Gifted in their understanding of people's motivations, they have an unusual ability to influence and draw the best out of others. They also excel in verbal and written communications and in the ability to position ideas. Greens are enthusiastic spokespersons for the organizations of their choice, and have a unique, charismatic quality that sweeps others into their causes.

Part III: Instructions

Now that you have determined your primary style, go back to the assessment and fill out the section you originally left out (that is, Section II or Section III). This exercise will provide you with your backup style. You should share about 40 percent to 50 percent of the characteristics of your backup style. The backup style refines your primary style.

If your primary is Gold or Red, *your backup would be either Blue or Green.*

If your primary is Blue or Green, *your backup would be either Gold or Red.*

My primary style is _____. My backup style is _____.

Part IV: Instructions

From each pair of statements, choose one statement from the left or right column. You should wind up with seven checkmarks in this section.

At least 51 percent of the time I tend to:

Column (e)		Column (i)
❏ like to talk	-OR-	❏ prefer to listen
❏ become bored when alone too much	-OR-	❏ need time alone to recharge batteries
❏ prefer to work in a group	-OR-	❏ prefer to work alone or with one other
❏ speak first—then reflect	-OR-	❏ reflect first—then speak
❏ be more interactive and energetic	-OR-	❏ be more reflective and thoughtful
❏ know a little about many topics	-OR-	❏ know a few topics in-depth
❏ initiate conversations at social gatherings	-OR-	❏ wait to be approached at social gatherings

If you answered more items on the left, you are an Extrovert (drawing energy from group activity).

> **If you answered more items on the right, you are an Introvert (drawing energy from your own inner resources).**
>
> Note your full style here:
>
> **Primary:** _____ **Backup:** _____ **Extrovert or Introvert:** _____

More About the Introvert and Extrovert

The Extrovert/Introvert dimension is often misunderstood. That's because it appears to be a biologically based preference for recharging one's batteries. It has nothing to do with being socially adept—there are Introverts with wonderful people skills and Extroverts who turn people off.

Extroverts (which the Myers-Briggs community spells as "extraverts") get their energy from being with people and doing group activities. If they have to spend too much time alone or doing tasks in solitude, they become tired, bored, and dispirited. Conversely, Introverts get energized from spending time alone to recharge their internal batteries. Even if they like being with people, which most Introverts do, too much interaction drains their energy.

The population divides fairly equally between Extroverts and Introverts, and many people hide their natural preference well. An Introvert who needs to socialize for business can appear Extroverted. Also, as your score will indicate, you may be mild or pronounced in this dimension. Relationships between Introverts and Extroverts are often tense, until this dimension is understood and valued.

Next Step

Familiarize yourself with all the Color Q personalities, then focus on you: Greens are covered in Chapter 5, Reds in Chapter 10, Blues in Chapter 15, and Golds in Chapter 20. Go next to your individual chapter, which is one of the four chapters after your primary color.

What to Do If This Test Doesn't Ring True for You

Your Color Q personality is simply who you really are when you are not being pressured by family, friends, or work/life demands. But if the majority of characteristics do not ring true, it's likely you belong to another group.

Reexamine the section of the self-assessment where you had close scores. Did you answer as other people need you to be? Or as you feel you ought (instead of prefer) to be? That creates false results. Choose the opposite column choice and follow instructions to a new color. If that fits better, return to Section III and continue.

Or see if a family member or friend who knows you well agrees with your self-assessment. You might be surprised, as one lawyer was when her friend of thirty years completely corrected her answers! The lawyer didn't want to admit to her real preferences for piles on her desk and last-minute deadline rushes. Remember, no one is judging you or suggesting that you need to change. What you categorize as a "weakness" is probably a strength—the lawyer was effective and innovative under chaotic circumstances.

If you currently are going through catastrophic life changes, or have been dissatisfied with your life for some time, scores may reflect your survival skills and not your real preferences. You may have "forgotten" your real preferences (unhappiness is a signal they're being denied). Try answering as if, right now, you lived in the world of your choice. If your personality color still seems wrong, wait until things have stabilized and retest yourself.

how to use this book for fast results

MOST OF US HAVE mentally disengaged during work hours because of conflict, stress, or frustration. An alarming 33 percent of us are disengaged permanently, costing $300 billion in lost productivity annually. According to a 2011 *New York Times* article, "Do Happier People Work Harder?" progress in meaningful work is the greatest professional motivator, ahead of raises and bonuses.[1]

Conflict occurs when people are required to spend long periods of time together, physically or virtually; but that's also the time when creativity and accomplishment occur. The trick is to recognize and harness everyone's strengths, even (especially) those who touch your hot buttons. This book's Color Q system outlines well-researched ways to stay engaged and make progress in work that is meaningful to you.

Here's how to use Color Q tools for fast results. Identify your Color Q personality type in Chapter 2. Then, familiarize yourself with the other color types listed in the self-assessment, paying particular attention to Introvert/Extrovert differences. Then, in your personality chapter, read about your own strengths and motivators. Study your individual blind spots and stressors. How many are operating against you right now? Eliminate what you can. Substitute your strengths and motivators.

the color Q personality system

its foundation and history

THIS CHAPTER WILL appeal primarily to Blues and Golds. Greens, read this material because it will help you when you are talking to Blues and Golds. Reds, skip this chapter altogether—go read your own Chapter 10 before you get too restless.

Even without formal study it's easy to categorize people into certain personality "types" like adventurous, artistic, practical, and intellectual. Although "personality typing" may be its trendy new name, the activity of grouping people into defined behavior patterns can be documented back to 400 B.C. At that time, intellects such as Aristotle, Hippocrates, and Galen identified four "humors"—sanguine (cheerful, confident), melancholic (pensive, gloomy), phlegmatic (hard to rouse to action, calm, cool), and choleric (quick-tempered).

The theme of four types continued into modern times. In the 1920s the pioneering psychologist Carl Gustav Jung, who had been a favorite student of Sigmund Freud's,[1] split away to develop his own theories. In his 1921 work *Psychological Types*, Jung theorized four "functions" by which humans engaged with reality—thinking, feeling, sensation, and intuition.

Jung's abstract work remained relatively unknown until 1942, when Katharine Cook Briggs and her daughter Isabel Myers began their work to develop an instrument for knowing one's Jungian personality type. Through quantified observations and scientific validation, the two American women created one of the most extensively tested personality typing systems ever developed, the Myers-Briggs Type Indicator. Nearly two million people take the Myers-Briggs Type Indicator personality inventory (MBTI assessment) each year.

In the 1950s, David Keirsey did work that overlaid the Greek humors onto the Jungian/Myers-Briggs types. In his 1978 book *Please Understand Me*, he outlined four temperament groups, which serve as the basis of the Color Q model in this book—the Blue, Gold, Green, and Red personality types.

The MBTI assessment has been in use for over fifty years. Today the work is continued by the next generation—Peter and Katharine D. Myers, co-owners of the MBTI copyrights. Katharine D. Myers, whose work with the instrument began in 1942, became the first president of APTi, the Association for Psychological Type International, the leading membership organization for the "type" community. Peter Myers—the former chairman of the Myers-Briggs Foundation—continues his mother Isabel Myers's work by promoting worldwide research. He believes "successful human endeavor results from the development of effective perception and decision making." The key is working with, instead of against, one's natural preferences.

"I view life through the Jungian framework—the same lens as Katharine Cook Briggs, Isabel's mother and the original theoretician of the indicator," says Katharine D. Myers. "I believe that Carl Jung, better than anyone else, explains human behavior, development, and the wholeness of wrestling with the conscious and the unconscious."

Typical of Greens, Katharine D. Myers has naturally fostered the growth of others, beginning her career as a counselor and school psychologist. "My passion for what I do is so great that I'm still working at [age] 86, which I never planned to do," she says. (Katharine D. Myers is profiled in Chapter 9, "Green/Backup Red Introverts.")

The advent of modern brain scanning has moved the MBTI out of the realm of theory into proven science. The behavioral impact of chemicals and stimulations to different parts of the brain have validated many of MBTI's theories, demonstrating that Jung was, indeed, correct. While each person is unique, it has been shown there is a core of preferences that remains solid and steady.

I developed Color Q as a quick introduction to personality "typing." For those who wish to investigate further, I would suggest taking the Myers-Briggs Type Indicator personality inventory and reading the works of Carl Jung and David Keirsey and other MBTI-related materials listed in the bibliography.

When running team-building and leadership seminars for corporate clients (the U.S. Treasury, Chemical Bank, Deloitte, Marine Corps Scholarship Foundation, Merrill Lynch, Nokia, Prudential, the Government of Pennsylvania Leadership Institute, UBS, USAID, and schools in Saudi Arabia, among others), I have seen firsthand how conflicts can instantly transform into productivity. I teach "style shifting," which involves recognizing and communicating with other personality types in ways that bring about the best response. With the cost of workplace conflict at $300 billion[2] annually and rising, addressing personality clashes is now paramount.

greens overall

GREENS REPRESENT approximately 17 percent of the world's population. If you are not a Green, but would like to learn how to identify and communicate with one, go to "How to Recognize a Green Colleague" at the end of this chapter.

News Personality Diane Sawyer

Diane Sawyer is one of the country's most-recognized Greens. As anchor of *ABC World News with Diane Sawyer*, she informs millions of Americans nightly.

Consider the news features she has handled at ABC since taking the anchor chair in December 2009: Chinese progress in education and green technologies; addressing misconceptions about Muslims; and the aftermath of Haiti's devastating earthquake all show a focus on world improvement. These subjects demonstrate typical Green traits of empathy and humanism. The impact on people is a driving force in her work: life in Camden, New Jersey, America's poorest city; the plight of Appalachian children; Russian orphanages; and abuse of the mentally handicapped.

Concern for others helped her earn the America's Junior Miss title in 1963. It also helped her survive a rocky entry into television journalism. Having been hired by Ron Ziegler to serve in the administration of President Richard Nixon (and subsequently on the Nixon-Ford transition team), she was shunned by CBS News colleagues in 1978 when she joined the network as a political correspondent. She overcame the taint of the Watergate scandal with two Green personality tools: natural charm and the ability to submerge ego for the sake of a story. Acceptance came slowly but grudgingly after she covered the Iranian hostage crisis by sleeping only one hour a night.

By 1981 viewers were responding to her Green warmth. Diane was promoted to anchor the *CBS Morning News*, then became the first female correspondent on the prestigious *60 Minutes* program in 1984. Here, her ability to surgically get under a subject's skin without drawing blood gained attention. (Greens listen intently and question diplomatically.)

In 1989 Diane jumped ship to ABC to coanchor the news magazine *Prime Time Live*, which ultimately became *20/20*. In 1999, she temporarily joined *Good Morning America*, later ascending to the anchor chair of *ABC World News* in December 2009.

Greens do very well in the television and film industries with their natural authenticity. Famous or not, you need creative opportunities to impact the lives of others. You excel at written and verbal communications and are heavily represented among writers, TV hosts, and biographers.

Television Personality Dr. Mehmet Oz

Dr. Mehmet Oz (estimated to be a Green) first appeared as a regular guest on *The Oprah Winfrey Show*, and in 2009 his own talk show debuted, focusing on personal health issues. In addition to hosting *The Dr. Oz Show*, he has authored six *New York Times* health-themed bestsellers—all while performing 250 heart surgeries annually! He practices Transcendental Meditation with a Green outlook: "When I meditate, I go to that place where truth lives. I can see what reality really is, and it is so much easier to form good relationships then."[1]

Outside the entertainment industry, Greens excel in sales, marketing, and public relations. Myers-Briggs Type Indicator co-owner Katharine Myers has put her Green skills to use in making the MBTI the world's most widely recognized personality typing system. (Color Q is based on the research of the Myers-Briggs community.) "Most important to me is to live consistently with my inner values," Myers, a Green/Red Introvert, says. "I constantly want to improve the world."

Her Highness Sheika Hessa Salem Al Salman Al Sabah

As a member of the royal family, Sheika Hessa is a Green and Color Q licensee who is using Color Q to help the people of her homeland, Kuwait. In addition to holding a position in the information systems department at the Central Bank of Kuwait for almost twenty years, she has supported numerous programs uplifting her country's young people.

When asked what she enjoys most, her Green personality is evident: "I listen to young people and enter into their depths to get to know their wishes and to guide them to achieve them," Sheika Hessa says. "I help people by providing information that helps them progress in life. Periodically I also arrange family meetings to enhance family ties." Her Highness devotes time as chairperson for the National Development Project, also known as ATAMANA, which prepares leaders to build the future. Previously she contributed her time to the National Kuwaiti Youth Society Association of Benefit and the 100% Kuwaiti Project, which fostered youth micro-projects. ATAMANA in English reads "I wish," and her work here enables Sheika Hessa "to assist young people to achieve their desires in life." The project is run by a group of academics, professionals, and ambitious young Kuwaitis. As she explains, it "aims to change the thinking of young people about their lives in the modern era and to live a balanced life which will bring them happiness and help them to build and develop their country."

Like all Greens, she finds it stressful when the needs of the youth she supports are delayed by bureaucratic red tape. When conflict arises in her work,

"I concentrate in some other activities which I like. I have learned from experience to replace the pain into hope and negative pessimism to optimism."

Her natural Green global orientation serves her well in her royal position. And, like most Greens, she has evolved a mission statement for herself: "To contribute my project in lighting young people's ways and to help them choose the path of life which contributes to the building and the development of their homeland, so it joins the ranks of developed nations. It is also my hope to publicize the project in the world for the interest of young people all over the world."

▸ ▸ ▸

Greens will gain special value from this book because of your natural fascination with people. You'll likely assess the colors of everyone close to you and test the supplied communications tips.

The other colors tend to (unfairly) consider your skills "soft." This book shows you how to leverage these skills to economic advantage and become stronger during conflict. Your exceptional marketing talents create lasting product brands and inspire customer loyalty. Your people skills calm turbulent teams/departments—a skill for which you should demand top compensation. Staff turnover plummets and productivity spikes under Green leaders.

Go now to your specific profile to discover your most natural path to winning in the workplace.

How to Recognize a Green Colleague

External Environment Clues

- Colorful/bohemian dress.
- Office adorned with art or sculpture; rich or warm colors; furniture arranged to maximize conversation.
- Hospitality on display—coffee, tea service, candy.
- Piles on desk (the Green easily finds what's needed).

‣ Plants and aquariums (where permitted).

‣ Many pictures of family and friends.

Personal Mannerisms—Body Language

‣ Welcoming, expressive gestures.

‣ Intent listener.

‣ Informal, warm, authentic demeanor.

Personal Mannerisms—Verbal

‣ Speaks fluently in generalizations, impressions, and/or metaphors.

‣ Self-deprecating humor.

‣ Global, "big picture" thinker; idealistic.

‣ Concerned, empathetic, diplomatic; draws the best out of people.

‣ Unusual ability to persuade.

‣ Bridge-builder; resolves conflicting views.

‣ Sensitive to criticism.

How to Communicate with a Green—"Style Shifting" Tips

‣ Pick a harmonious environment for meetings.

‣ Personalize the conversation—ask about family, hobbies, pets.

‣ Listen empathetically and give feedback diplomatically.

‣ Be idea-driven, creative, insightful.

‣ Expect nonsequential conversations, eventually returning to the main point.

‣ Stress all opportunities for personal growth and helping others.

‣ Suggest innovative, future-oriented solutions.

- Use positive, inspiring phrases.

- Limit mundane facts and details.

- Be collaborative; limit competitiveness (unless it's fun); avoid conflict.

The Green's Unique Conflict Style

Greens avoid conflict, giving priority to harmony and cooperation. However, if you challenge their inner values, they can be surprisingly aggressive. If you criticize, ignore the people factor, focus on facts/details, or engage in political backbiting, Greens become cold and uncooperative. They seek closure by listening to all sides and creating win-win situations.

green/backup gold extroverts

YOU'RE NOT ONLY a Green; you also have strong secondary characteristics of the Gold personality. And you have tested as a Color Q Extrovert, which means you recharge your batteries by being with others, rather than being alone. Green/Gold Extroverts are gifted communicators with an unusual ability to influence. A calming presence, you interact smoothly and easily deflect confrontation. Green/Golds thrive where inner values are affirmed and harmony prevails.

Top Motivators
As an Extrovert, you require supportive, inclusive interaction with others. You create win-win situations for coworkers and customers. Wise managers tap their Green/Gold Extroverts when damaged relations impede success.

Green/Golds like to help others succeed. You form 5 percent of the world's population, but have disproportionate impact for good in the world.

You may be tempted to skip the sections about your own personality type and dive into material about understanding your coworkers. But consider this—by understanding your own strengths first, you'll better understand others.

Corporate Culture—Finding the Optimal Fit

It is the responsibility of every personality to find or create their optimal work environment. Optimal cultures differ among Color Q personality types. Strengths in one company may be viewed as weaknesses elsewhere. The corporate culture itself may not be dysfunctional; for instance, Greens hate what Blues love. Conflict, sapped strength, resentment, and feelings of defeat are symptoms of poor cultural fit and can be avoided by understanding your preferences.

The Green/Gold Extrovert's **most preferred work environment** emphasizes:

- Working harmoniously with others
- Minimal competitiveness
- Rewards for loyalty
- Expressing oneself
- Giving positive, empathetic feedback
- Keeping surroundings orderly and attractive
- Balancing economic results with workers' needs

If you think these points are obvious, it means you've tested correctly. (Compare with a Blue/Red Introvert's ideal environment.)

The Green/Gold Extrovert's **least preferred environment** is defined by:

- Politics and competitiveness
- Management that ignores, challenges, or patronizes worker needs

> ▸ An indecisive corporate culture

> ▸ Frequent criticism, confrontation, backstabbing, and bullying

> ▸ Impersonal coworker relationships

> ▸ Lots of detail work

> ▸ Mandates to make tough, hurtful decisions

Leveraging Executive Presence and Building Personal Brand

Groups run by Green/Gold Extroverts tend to be stable, structured, and harmonious. As a leader, you're good at defining the corporate mission and employing the right people to implement it. You have strong ideals about how to treat workers. Instead of being authoritarian, you roll up your sleeves and assist the troops through tough times.

> *Build your personal brand on your unusual ability to influence through*
> *passion and positive expectations.*

Green/Gold Extrovert leaders excel at helping others to achieve their potential. Intrigued by new big-picture possibilities, you are very results-oriented. You easily defuse tension (often with humor). Your values inspire colleagues to nip high-level conflict in the bud.

- -

CASE STUDY 1: *Successful Green/Gold Extroverts*

Erik Detiger, Philanthropia, Inc.

Detiger is the founder and managing director of Philanthropia, Inc., in New York City. His clients are mostly prominent philanthropies (UNICEF, Women's Refugee Commission, Columbia University Institute for the Study on Human Rights). Detiger develops strategic partnerships, joint programming, and funding strategies for these deserving entities. His website, FundsforNGOs.org, provides a million visitors a month with free tools, resources, and training in fund-raising.

Since achieving his doctorate in political science from the Free University of Amsterdam, his career has been focused on human well-being issues. He has worked in the areas of human rights abuse, international health care, refugee assistance, and international child labor abuse. Detiger's Gold backup personality gives him the detail orientation needed to successfully raise funds and manage programs; his Extroverted talent for speaking and training has taken him to workshops in Asia, Africa, and the European Union.

"My long-term goal is not wealth or recognition," says this classic Green/Gold. "It is the satisfaction I get from helping people. I can help many more by using this web platform. My motivation is not money, but to do good."

Fiona Thompson, Urban Land Institute

Thompson shares similar values in her role as the director of human resources operations for the Urban Land Institute. She handles employee relations, professional development, retention, and morale building for the nonprofit research and education organization's U.S., London, German, and Hong Kong offices. "I like feeling that my job matters; that I have, in a small way, made the lives of our employees better, so they are more productive in advancing our company's mission." She has the innate Green/Gold talent for creating employee buy-in: "I have the relationships that encourage people to do it," she says.

Because handling conflict is part of the job, Fiona successfully tackles this Green/Gold weak spot frequently. "I have a hard time giving criticism. I dislike conflict, but I try to keep my patience—I alter my communication style to meet the personality of the other," she says. "I remind myself not to take it personally."

Participating In and Managing Productive Teams

Green/Gold Extroverts often are their team's leader or spokesperson, articulating team values and expressing what others only dare think. You enjoy idea exchanges where everyone is heard, drawing out quieter members. One of your strengths is building unlikely bridges between opposing teammates.

"I think most conflict is not worth the time and effort," says Detiger. "I defuse by using humor, showing respect and humility."

Naturally gifted at coordinating projects, processes, and resources, you rarely miss a deadline.

You work hard and make your own breaks. "I moved to New York without a job," says Detiger. "I landed a position at the United Nations, without contacts, on the strength of my resume."

Communications Style

Merely adjusting one's vocabulary to align with another color's style can elicit powerful positive responses. Empathetic vs. objective analysis, theoretical vs. practical, structured vs. adaptable—these clashes fuel most workplace conflicts. Being able to "style shift," like Fiona Thompson does, is your unique advantage in negotiations, managing, and interviewing; it is second nature to you.

Green/Gold Extroverts are talented conversationalists, responsive to nonverbal cues. You are so quick with replies that your less articulate coworkers may find it difficult to keep pace. Your preferred vocabulary features abstract concepts, metaphors, and analogies, emphasizing words like *values, relationship, feel,* and *friendly.* Conversely, Reds prefer to use words such as "stimulate," "enjoy," and "now." Blues prefer theoretical jargon, statistical data, and technical terms. Golds, with whom you share some personality traits, prefer "facts," "tradition," "respected," and "proven."

Green/Golds understand what other people want to hear. This capacity eases group tensions and facilitates business deals.

Blind Spots

These blind spots are prevalent in Green/Gold Extroverts overall (a few of them will apply to you):

- Using metaphors and analogies instead of concrete, practical words. (You can increase cooperation dramatically with Golds and Reds by "talking real.")

- Being unaware of how warmth and enthusiasm may seem unprofessional to other personalities, especially Blues.

- Being overcommitted.

- Placing secondary priority on learning or verifying facts.

- Idealizing others, then getting disappointed.

- Being overly critical of yourself; hearing constructive criticism as condemnation.

- Deflecting conflict prematurely without resolving core issues.

- Thinking problems are your fault when they're not.

- Irritating others by being moralistic.

Stressors That Produce Fatigue and Strife

Certain workplace conditions stress and fatigue Green/Gold Extroverts, including:

- Open-ended, nonstructured environments

- Lack of control

- Too much repetitive work

- Frequent last-minute changes

- Working alone for long periods

- Criticism, especially when it's mean-spirited

Green/Gold Extroverts under *extreme* stress often become bossy, obsessive, fault-finding, and snappy. You may (erroneously) think a disagreement means permanent relationship damage. Fatigued Green/Golds become cool, inflexible, and self-contained. In leisure hours there may be insomnia or avoidance of usually pleasurable activities.

Self-Coach Your Way to More Productive Work Relationships

The primary focus of the Green/Gold Extrovert who wants to self-coach for career advancement should be on how to handle personal challenges from a core of strength and confidence.

Problem Solving and Decision Making

The Green/Gold Extrovert has these strengths:

▸ Discerns other people's values quickly; keeps process on track

▸ Embraces ideas that have worked elsewhere

▸ Recognizes patterns, forms hypotheses, goes with hunches

▸ Has drive to decide quickly and tie up loose ends

▸ Frames all decisions by how they impact relevant parties

Strategies to Improve Effectiveness When Challenged

Interpersonal challenges detract from productivity. Here are self-coaching strategies for your biggest challenges:

▸ *Working with noncollaborative teammates.* Assess—through your pattern-recognition skills—their Color Q types and employ the suggestions for dealing with them (see the following "Political Savvy" section).

▸ *Coping with competitive, me-first attitudes.* Be the role model for a more collaborative approach; don't expect reciprocation, at least initially.

▸ *Handling debate that splinters harmony.* Propose a win-win solution, or excuse yourself until the situation cools down.

▸ *Getting overly involved with others and distracted from work objectives.* Create some distance—take a break or a vacation, or enforce a communications blackout—until objectivity can be reestablished.

▸ *Being easily offended by corrective feedback.* Practice objectivity. Focus on content, not tone. Role-play bothersome scenarios with a friend in a nonthreatening environment (what has worked for them?). Learn from Golds or Blues, who would perceive identical feedback as neutral.

> *Responding to chronic conflict with obsessive worrying about secondary details.* Sounds easy, but it's not—distance yourself from chronic conflict before it becomes a health issue.

> *Criticizing and confronting team members you think are violating values and standards.* Be sure to give criticism privately! State your concerns in a neutral tone; do not moralize or sidetrack into personal issues.

> *Pushing for closure too quickly.* Remember: Deflecting conflict is not the same as resolving and moving forward.

Your best coping mechanisms are rest, self-care (momentary or longer term), reflection, delegation, playing games with friends, and seeking objective opinions.

CASE STUDY 2: When a Career Isn't Working

It was graduation day for Jason's son. Now, Jason would finally be able to quit his job as an emergency room nurse. Although as a Green he loved the nursing profession, the emergency room was literally making him ill.

After fifteen years in pediatrics, Jason had transferred to the ER four years ago for the higher salary needed to pay his son's tuition. But he lacked a Red's appetite for the ever-changing demands of the doctors and endless crises. Emergencies don't respect rules, and Jason had become edgy, critical, and an obsessive worrier.

At the graduation party, Jason happened to sit with his niece Lisa. Intrigued by the Green aspects of her job as a public health educator, Jason was receptive to her stories about educating and helping others. With Lisa's assistance, Jason made the transition into an identical position with his county's health department. The collaborative environment (no emergencies!) made going to work a pleasure for Jason once again.

Political Savvy—Making Your Words Count

A valuable part of the Color Q system lies in learning how to harness the Red's spontaneous crisis-handling ability, the Gold's detailed concrete thinking and administrative talent, and the Blue's strategic thinking to your advantage. Engage irritating coworkers as powerful political allies.

Reds. *"I've rewritten this project's mission statement six times!"* Green/Gold Dirk complains that his Red colleague Andy keeps pointing out impracticalities that send Dirk back to the drawing board.

Your style can irritate a Red by emphasizing one preferred solution. The Red's strength is to expect, even welcome, midcourse corrections; Reds like to see how things play out in the real world. Your big picture may not seem realistic enough to a Red, who will challenge you with on-the-ground scenarios. To the Green/Gold Extrovert, the Red's style appears to be barely controlled chaos—flouting procedures frequently, respecting things over people. This is a setup for long-term conflict with a Green/Gold Extrovert. When these Red strengths become irritations but are ignored "for the sake of harmony," resentments boil over into conflicts that exhaust you but appear to energize and amuse the Red.

Negotiating Strategies

▸ Use these words with a Red and watch the response: "stimulate," "enjoy," "expedite," and "now."

▸ Forget the big picture. Using concrete, factual words, talk specifically about what needs to be done *now* to accomplish desired ends.

▸ Solicit their opinions. Reds can create contingency plans on the spot when needed.

▸ Do not micromanage; let them handle delays and unforeseen changes.

▸ Don't "give in" for harmony's sake. Stand your ground, preferably with some easy humor.

‣ Envision challenging Red coworkers as equals who can handle a firm "no," and practice holding firm until *your own* concerns are addressed.

Blues. *"My (Blue) colleague Amanda is driving me crazy,"* sighs Green/Gold Carol. *"I'm supposed to monitor her project's progress, but she just won't share what's happening until she's ready. All she does is critique* my *work!"*

The Blue is the least people-oriented of all the Color Q personality types. To a Green/Gold Extrovert, Blues appear to put all their formidable mental energy into creating strategies that ignore the impact on workers and customers. Your style can irritate a Blue by emphasizing the impact on people rather than overall strategy. The desire for harmony may strike a Blue as secondary to the task at hand, which in the Blue's mind must be challenged. The Blue will then pepper you with criticism and questions. This onslaught pressures the Green/Gold's ability to stand firm in the face of conflict. The Blue appears to judge the value of your concerns by your "inability" to fight and win. If overwhelmed with lots of questions by a Blue, *do not* take the challenge personally or as a threat. It's actually a compliment—this is how Blues show they're interested in your ideas.

Negotiating Strategies

‣ Be verbally short and concise.

‣ Use "if . . . then" sentences, which are very effective.

‣ Rehearse firmer, more effective responses: "I hear you; now here's my list of concerns." "Strategically, the problems I see are. . . ." "If you see customer relations as secondary, then how do you propose to deal with account cancellations?"

‣ Adjust your vocabulary and use theoretical jargon, statistical data, and technical terms. To prove a proposal's worth, point out several long-term benefits. Use ingenuity, logic, and wit to make your case.

‣ Don't react personally. Blues are hardwired for impersonal critical thinking.

▸ Display competence. Blues force you to be tough-minded and firm. They find your warmth and enthusiasm distracting; they need to see your competence on display.

Golds. *"Why is it always about money with her!"* Green/Gold John is complaining about his Gold coworker Patricia, who insists on including a detailed rather than general budget for their project, which will require all-nighters for the next two days.

You can deal with Gold/Greens. Gold/Blues are another matter. More authoritarian and less patient than you, they view your participative style as soft. Your style may irritate a Gold by being too abstract, without enough concrete evidence and linear thought to explain how to achieve desired ends. Greens listen to all sides; Golds see only right or wrong. Gold/Blues particularly value "doing" over "feeling" and may become irritatingly critical and bossy. Their communication style is much more challenging, impersonal, and verbally aggressive, which can erupt into confrontation. If a Gold/Blue challenges you, provide step-by-step plans. (Create these plans by envisioning how they'll help the people who will implement.)

Negotiating Strategies

▸ To ease tensions, pepper your sentences with words like "facts," "tradition," "respected," and "proven." Avoid metaphors and analogies.

▸ Use concrete words and concepts to create a comfort zone, so you can "talk the talk" with Golds (and Reds). They need grounded, practical words and tasks.

▸ Commit several low-pressure, self-directed minutes each day to understanding the vocabulary of investment, costs, time lines, and budgets.

Extrovert vs. Introvert

If the previous strategies are still missing the mark, you may be dealing with an Introvert. If so:

▸ Tone down your enthusiasm; listen more. It will be difficult for you to understand why Introverts shun interaction and prefer working alone. Respect, don't challenge, their need to recharge their batteries with privacy—it's not personal.

▸ Invite them to speak, but don't force them to speak until they've thought things through.

▸ *Do not* fill their pauses.

Recognize any of your coworkers in the preceding descriptions? Learn more about each personality type by reading each Color Q personality's overall chapter, then read Chapter 25, "Adjusting to the Workplace Styles of Others."

▸ ▸ ▸

In summary, with your Green/Gold Extrovert energy, warmth, and charm, you are an influential, charismatic leader. Tenacious, responsible, and opinionated, you usually work your magic by tactful persuasion but will do battle with the mean-spirited. You honor your commitments and expect the same of others. Well-defined teamwork, open communication, and appreciation describe groups you lead; but you need to have other colors look after impersonal details. Focus on standing firm when conflict first arises. It is critical to honor *your* desires and draw your lines in the sand.

----

green/backup gold introverts

YOU'RE NOT ONLY a Green, you also have strong secondary characteristics of the Gold personality. And you have tested as a Color Q Introvert, which means you recharge your batteries by being alone, rather than being with people. Green/Gold Introverts combine both warmth and reserve. Sharing warmly with those closest to you, you are reserved at work until trust is established. Your deep insights into people create win-win situations and help subordinates grow. You excel at organizing and follow-through.

Top Motivators
As an Introvert, you are less productive in open office settings, or when your privacy is not respected. Yet your interest in others is so strong that you run the risk of not having enough time alone to recharge.

Green/Gold Introverts form 4 percent of the world's population, and more of you are needed! Your work ethic is conscientious, goal-oriented, hardworking, and ambitious. An idealist with strong inner convictions, you'll go above and beyond when championing a cause. Decisive and frequently in a hurry, you are impatient with anyone who obstructs the to-do list.

Corporate Culture—Finding the Optimal Fit

It is the responsibility of every personality to find or create their optimal work environment. Optimal cultures differ among Color Q personality types. Strengths in one company may be viewed as weaknesses elsewhere. The corporate culture itself may not be dysfunctional; for instance, Greens hate what Blues love. Conflict, sapped strength, resentment, and feelings of defeat are symptoms of poor cultural fit and can be avoided by understanding your preferences.

The Green/Gold Introvert's **most preferred work environment** emphasizes:

- Predictable and orderly surroundings with well-communicated values
- Trustworthy coworkers in a harmonious, egalitarian atmosphere
- One-on-one interactions
- A focus on people-related issues
- A corporate culture that invests in staff development and societal well-being
- Private space, quiet time; ability to work independently
- Personal control over multiple projects

If these points seem obvious to you, it means you've tested correctly. (Compare with a Blue/Red Extrovert's ideal environment.)

The Green/Gold Introvert's **least preferred environment** has:

- Little privacy

- Too many details and repetitive routine
- No appreciation for creativity
- Superficial or rude coworkers
- Team members who are shortsighted, dismissive, or cannot stick to issues
- Tension and competition
- Tendency to exploit customers and staff

Leveraging Executive Presence and Building Personal Brand

Green/Gold Introverts are masters at turning visions into realities. You have an almost clairvoyant way of matching people with resources.

Your leadership style is one of future-oriented insights and loyalty to a cause. You see the big picture and believe it is attainable. Not one to bark orders or demand obedience, you quietly influence by persuasion rather than control; earned cooperation inspires subordinates' best efforts.

The Green/Gold Introvert's personal leadership brand should be built around your inner vision, which finds new meanings and possibilities around you. Tactful, complex, and articulate, you are that rare breed who can motivate staff with appreciation and support and also establish needed structure and organization.

- -

CASE STUDY 1: *The Successful Green/Gold Introvert*

Dr. Mobarak Abdulhadi Aldosari, Rowad Almaarefa Educational Consulting
Dr. Aldosari has been at the forefront of the career guidance and coun-seling field in Saudi Arabia for the past twenty-five years. He helped establish the first guidance center in the Kingdom's Eastern Province in 1998. His Ph.D. in guidance and counseling "matches my personality type," he says.

Dr. Aldosari's work with Color Q demonstrates the method's applica-bility across cultures. He owns the Rowad Almaarefa Educational

*Consulting firm in Saudi Arabia and is a Color Q licensee: "I have con-
ducted the Color Q personality system on more than 4,000 students [boys
and girls], teachers, and counselors in the Arab Gulf countries. This is
really what our people want," he says.*

*Dr. Aldosari is a highly intuitive Green/Gold who describes his profes-
sional strengths as wanting to help others, motivate them, and see them
succeed. He says that career guidance isn't available yet in many of his
kingdom's schools. "I was most frustrated when one day I asked a grade
twelve high school student about his dream. He answered, 'I am not
thinking about it yet.' That shocked me and led me to work and concentrate on the career guidance field." Today he focuses on helping students find their career paths.*

- -

Participating In and Managing Productive Teams

Green/Gold Introverts inspire their teammates with quiet enthusiasm and
can-do attitudes. You bring foresight, organization, and follow-through to
the table. Team leaders know you are dependable and will do more than is
required. You easily build bridges and defuse conflict with insight, tact,
and humor.

In practical terms you are results-oriented, focused, and keen on preventing resource waste. You manage complex interactions smoothly.
While conscientious about deadlines, you tackle problem solving with creative brainstorming.

Communications Style

Merely adjusting one's vocabulary to align with another color's style can
elicit powerful positive responses. Empathetic vs. objective analysis, theoretical vs. practical, structured vs. adaptable—these clashes fuel most workplace
conflicts. Being able to "style shift" brings a huge competitive advantage in
negotiations, managing, and interviewing.

Green/Gold Introverts are skillful listeners, responsive to nonverbal
cues. Personable yet quietly forceful, you enjoy discussing ideas, theories,
and models. Your energy and excitement often remain internal. Your preferred vocabulary features abstract concepts, metaphors, and feelings,

emphasizing words like *values, relationship, feel,* and *friendly.* Conversely, Reds prefer to use words such as "move," "stimulate," and "gusto." Blues prefer theoretical jargon, statistical data, and technical terms. Golds, with whom you share some personality traits, prefer "facts," "tradition," "respected," and "proven."

Green/Golds have an unusual capacity to understand the viewpoints of others. You are a natural at shifting styles. You like to think before replying, and prefer writing to talking, because thoughts come so quickly you may hesitate verbally.

Blind Spots

These blind spots are prevalent in Green/Gold Introverts (although only some of them will apply to you):

▸ Taking criticism too personally

▸ Avoiding giving constructive criticism

▸ Seeing temporary setbacks as insurmountable deal-killers

▸ Getting derailed by challenges to your inner beliefs

▸ Seeing the people issues of conflicts; making facts secondary

▸ Hanging on too long when a vision doesn't pan out

▸ Investing so much in others that there's not enough time for you to recharge alone

▸ Using metaphors and analogies when talking with Golds and Reds instead of the concrete, practical words they prefer

Stressors That Produce Fatigue and Strife

Certain workplace conditions produce stress and fatigue for Green/Gold Introverts. They include:

▸ Procedures and tasks that distract from the core mission

▸ Noisy, insensitive people

▸ Criticism, especially when it's mean-spirited

‣ Lack of control

‣ Too much repetitive work

‣ Frequent last-minute plan changes

Green/Gold Introverts under *extreme* stress often become uncooperative, withdrawn, fault-finding, and critical. Perfectionism and preoccupation with small details are common. Catherine Atwood, a leader of a 2011 Habitat for Humanity Bike & Build cross-country bicycle tour, noticed this about a Green/Gold Introvert coleader at mid-trip: "He would be focused on one particular thing that really was not top priority or as important as doing something else." (Catherine, a Green/Red knowledgeable of Color Q, was able to assess his color and help him refocus on the big picture.) Fatigued Green/Golds may stop cooperating, withhold information, or become impulsive decision makers. During leisure hours they may engage in excessive eating, drinking, or exercise.

Self-Coach Your Way to More Productive Work Relationships

The primary focus of the Green/Gold Introvert who wants to self-coach for career advancement should be on how to handle (rather than avoid) personality differences from a core of strength and confidence.

Problem Solving and Decision Making

The Green/Gold Introvert has these strengths:

‣ Excels at developing the vision

‣ Has faith in hunches and insights

‣ Finds change conceptually exciting but prefers advance warning

‣ Likes to solve problems in new ways; quickly grasps possibilities

‣ Sees both current and future implications, especially relating to people

‣ Feels comfortable dealing with complexity

Strategies to Improve Effectiveness When Challenged

Interpersonal challenges detract from productivity. Here are self-coaching strategies for your biggest challenges:

- *Lack of privacy.* Privacy is critical; you cannot be productive in a noisy, open environment. Make this a high priority in job negotiations. If you are too junior to have an office, explain these needs to your boss and ask if you can work occasionally in an empty conference room, so you have an opportunity to recharge.

- *Too much repetitive work.* Delegate! Or renegotiate your job description. If you don't, this situation will become a health issue.

- *Frequent last-minute changes of plans.* Volunteer to take charge of the next project and be a role model for focus and follow-through. Or focus on how the changes impact people, leaving details to others.

- *Being compassionate with problem performers.* Compassion doesn't get the work done. Balance personal issues against deadlines and make them equal; never let one take precedence over the other.

- *Discomfort when giving constructive criticism.* Criticism feels counterproductive, but a kind tone can deliver a tough message. Your greatest contribution is to appreciate and inspire others.

- *Ignoring conflict.* You prioritize harmony, but ignoring conflict doesn't make it go away. Air aggravations while they're still fresh and manageable—get used to it, and learn vital negotiating tactics along the way.

When dealing with challenges, your best coping mechanisms are learning to say no to people and demands, creating time to think things through, and delegating detail work. After 100 percent devotion to "the cause," prioritize yourself. Realize that other people don't automatically know what you have to offer. Don't always go it alone; ask for help occasionally. Review your accomplishments each day—you are making a difference in the world, but may need to remind yourself.

CASE STUDY 2: **When a Career Isn't Working**
The McKessons are a family with five generations in the finance field. Mildred and Frank were very gratified when their son John chose to become a stockbroker right out of college.

John's first week at his New York job was a blur of meeting people, training, and experiencing the excitement of the trading floor. Every night he e-mailed his progress to his family before collapsing into bed, hungry for the silence that Introverts need.

New stockbrokers have to make dozens of cold calls every day, all while keeping an eye on the computer screen tracking market movements. John couldn't think or analyze information over the din. His supervisor started to admonish him for working in the empty conference room rather than at his desk on the open floor.

John decided to confide in his uncle Bill, who worked at one of the big banks a few blocks away. Over lunch, Bill realized his nephew needed a position that would tap his obvious Green marketing abilities but in a less chaotic atmosphere. A position had opened up in the wealth management department of the bank, and with Bill's recommendation, John got the offer. Inherited clients, a private office, and a lot fewer cold calls were all John needed.

Today John looks forward to his days delving into the family issues and problems of his high net worth clients. Helping them is something this Green finds very rewarding; John is well on his way to becoming the lead producer in his department.

Political Savvy—Making Your Words Count
A valuable part of the Color Q system lies in learning how to harness the Red's spontaneous crisis-handling ability, the Gold's detailed, concrete thinking and administrative talent, and the Blue's strategic thinking to your advantage. Transform irritating coworkers into powerful political allies.

Reds. Your style can irritate a Red with its emphasis on the big picture. The Red's strength is to deal with the present; they like to see how things play out in the real world. Your big picture may not seem realistic enough to a Red, who will challenge you with on-the-ground scenarios. To the Green/Gold Introvert, the Red's style appears to be barely controlled chaos. Reds seem to flout the need for order every chance they get and to respect things over people. This is a setup for long-term conflict with a Green/Gold Introvert. When these Red strengths become irritations but are ignored "for the sake of harmony," resentments boil over into conflicts, which exhaust you but appear to energize and amuse the Red.

Negotiating Strategies

▸ Use these words with a Red and watch the response: "stimulate," "enjoy," "expedite," and "now."

▸ Downplay the big picture. Using concrete and factual words, discuss specifically what needs to be done *now*.

▸ Solicit their opinions. Reds can create contingency plans on the spot for all possible outcomes, not just the one targeted.

▸ Do not micromanage; let them handle delays, ambiguities, and unforeseen changes.

▸ Envision challenging Red coworkers as equals who can handle a firm "no," and practice holding firm until *your* concerns are addressed. Inject some easy humor.

Blues. The Blue is the least people-oriented of all the Color Q personality types. To a Green/Gold Introvert, Blues appear to put all their formidable mental energy into creating strategies that may ignore the impact on workers and customers. Your style can irritate a Blue by emphasizing the impact on people rather than overall strategy. A desire for harmony may strike a Blue as secondary to the task at hand, which in the Blue's mind must be challenged. The Blue will then pepper you with criticism and questions. This onslaught puts pressure on the Green/Gold to stand firm in the face of conflict. The Blue appears to judge the value of your concerns by your "inability" to fight and win. If overwhelmed with lots of questions from a Blue, *do not* take the challenge personally or as a threat. It's actually a compliment, because this is how Blues show interest and calm their inner insecurities.

Negotiating Strategies

▸ Be verbally short and concise.

▸ Use "if . . . then" sentences, which are very effective.

▸ Rehearse firmer, more factual responses: "I hear you; now here's my list of concerns." "Strategically, the problems I see are . . ." "If you see customer relations as secondary, then how do you propose to deal with account cancellations?"

▸ Adjust your vocabulary and begin using theoretical jargon, statistical data, and technical terms. To prove a proposal's worth, point out several long-term benefits. Use ingenuity, logic, and wit to make the case.

▸ Display competence. Blues force you to be tough-minded and firm; they need to see your competence on display.

▸ Don't react personally. Blues are hardwired for *impersonal* critical thinking.

Golds. You can deal with Gold/Greens. Gold/Blues are another matter. More authoritarian and less patient than you are, they view the people-first style as soft. The Green/Gold's style can irritate a Gold by being too abstract, without enough concrete evidence and linear processes to explain how to achieve the desired ends. Greens listen to all sides; Golds see right and wrong only one way. Gold/Blues particularly value "doing" over "feeling" and may become irritatingly critical and bossy. Their communication style is much more challenging, impersonal, and verbally aggressive. If a Gold/Blue challenges you, provide step-by-step plans. (Create these plans by envisioning how they'll help the people who will implement them.)

Negotiating Strategies

‣ To ease tensions, pepper sentences with words like "facts," "tradition," "respected," and "proven." Avoid metaphors and analogies.

‣ Make use of concrete words and concepts to create more of a comfort zone, so you can "talk the talk" with Golds (and Reds). They need grounded, practical words and tasks.

‣ Commit several low-pressure, self-directed minutes each day to focusing on the vocabulary of investment, costs, time lines, and budgets.

‣ Acknowledge and flatter their superior detail management capabilities, especially when they take on some of your detail work.

Extrovert vs. Introvert

If the aforementioned strategies are still missing the mark, your coworker may be an Extrovert. If so:

‣ It will be difficult to understand why they must be around people constantly, and how they can enjoy noisy environments. Respect, don't challenge, their need to recharge their batteries by interacting with others—they need this the way you need alone time.

‣ You're a good listener, but be sure to interject verbally often. Ask questions; share more of yourself.

‣ You can volunteer to handle tasks for them that require working alone. Benefit from their gratitude—and the time alone.

Recognize any coworkers in the preceding descriptions? Learn more about them by reading each Color Q personality's overall chapter and Chapter 25, "Adjusting to the Workplace Styles of Others."

‣ ‣ ‣

In summary, Green/Gold Introverts are deep and complex people who focus on their vision and inner world of ideas. Articulate, empathetic, and idealistic, you enjoy being of service to others. Once a goal is set, no argument based solely on practicality and reason will divert the mission. Do, however, engage other colors to look after details.

You have a special gift for understanding complicated issues and simplifying them for others. You listen deeply and help people see new ways of approaching their issues. Maintaining a harmonious team spirit is a top priority; but be tenacious about standing firm when conflict first arises. It is critical to honor your desires and draw your lines in the sand equally to others. Above all, schedule sufficient private time.

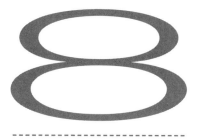

green/backup
red extroverts

YOU'RE NOT ONLY a Green, you also have strong secondary characteristics of the Red personality. And you have tested as a Color Q Extrovert, which means you recharge your batteries by being with people, rather than being alone. Green/Red Extroverts are keen observers, energized by new ideas. A free spirit intrigued by the unusual, this personality is often unconventional and admires other nonconformists. You shun routine, gleefully battle bureaucracy, and love challenges that highlight ingenuity. Gravitating to new goals and careers more frequently than most, your warmth, insight, and people skills open doors. A gift for discerning future trends fuels your ambitions.

Top Motivators

As an Extrovert, working alone for long periods makes you restless. Early in your career you likely were chided for roaming the halls when you should have been at your desk.

Green/Red Extroverts are most motivated by big-picture, people-oriented visions of the future. You believe in achievement through cooperation; liking others and being liked is the grease that makes your wheels turn. Green/Red Extroverts form only 4 percent of the world's population, but it would be boring without you!

Corporate Culture—Finding the Optimal Fit

It is the responsibility of every personality to find or create their optimal work environment. Optimal cultures differ among Color Q personality types. Strengths in one company may be viewed as weaknesses elsewhere. The corporate culture itself may not be dysfunctional; for instance, Greens hate what Blues love. Conflict, sapped strength, resentment, and feelings of defeat are symptoms of poor cultural fit and can be avoided by understanding your preferences.

The Green/Red Extrovert's **most preferred work environment** emphasizes:

- Freedom to express oneself in creative, humorous, and colorful ways
- Variety and change, with minimal rules and restrictions
- Being heard by peers and superiors
- People-related projects
- Placing high value on staff and clients
- Democratic, lively atmosphere

If you think these points are obvious, it means you've tested correctly. (Compare with a Blue/Gold Introvert's ideal environment.)

The Green/Red Extrovert's **least preferred environment** has:

- Little creativity, lots of bureaucracy

> ‣ Minimal social interaction (i.e., the sense of being ignored)
>
> ‣ Lots of rules, procedures, details, and repetitive routine
>
> ‣ Manipulative, controlling people and/or office politics

Leveraging Executive Presence and Building Personal Brand

Green/Red Extroverts are masterful at dealing with a broad range of events and people—simultaneously when necessary! Because of this ability, you see connections that others miss. Energized by new ideas and industries, you enjoy applying your skills in original and unique ways.

The Green/Red Extrovert's personal leadership brand should be built around your intuitive gifts for seeing the trends and pitfalls of the future. You have a strong sense of how to motivate and help others.

Your leadership style is one of dynamic initiation, especially valuable during start-up phases of projects or companies. You see a very big picture and believe it is attainable. An outside-the-box thinker, you know profitable ideas originate from new hires and twenty-year veterans. Persuasion, rather than control, of people creates buy-in that moves products quickly to market. Without trying, you build extensive networks of people.

- -

CASE STUDY 1: *The Successful Green/Red Extrovert*

Congresswoman Carolyn Maloney

Carolyn Maloney understands that leadership and success come from first mastering the issues and then mustering your forces. For nine terms she has represented the twelfth district of New York in the U.S. House of Representatives. She was the first woman to chair the Joint Economic Committee and is a nationally recognized leader in the fields of economic policy, financial services, national security, and women's issues. She was the powerhouse behind the landmark credit card reform legislation that the Pew Foundation says saves consumers $10 billion annually.

"I have managed to pass many important bills that people thought could never overcome the opposition of special interests," says Maloney, demonstrating the Green/Red's dynamic initiation and ability to persuade. In one session alone, she introduced more than seventy pieces of legislation, tying the record for the most bills from any legislator.

Her tireless efforts to secure badly needed health care for New York's ailing 9/11 heroes won her plaudits and admiration around the world. "If you really believe in and understand the importance of the goal," says Maloney, "it's not work. And no obstacle can withstand the unwavering determination of a united people committed to a just cause." She is also proud of helping draft the Anti-Terrorism Intelligence Reform Act, which changed the structure of the U.S. intelligence system.

Despite being a national leader, her deep concern for her constituents keeps her focus local. Maloney recently prevented the closing of a veteran's hospital on twenty-third Street in Manhattan. "Sometimes, it's not what you do, it's what you stop."[1] Her efforts to keep post offices open and fund the schools in her district have been decidedly Green endeavors.

She also has a feisty Red side, and her opponents know she is no easy target. A strong proponent of women's rights, she was a chief sponsor of the Equal Rights Amendment and author of the Debbie Smith Act, which funds the processing of DNA evidence in sexual assault cases. She has stood firm against right-wing opponents. When Representative Darrell Issa chaired a religious freedom and birth control panel with no female speakers, Maloney's question, "Where are the women?" resounded through the national media.

Her response to conflict is typical of a Green/Red Extrovert: "I deal with it in steps. A lot of it is educating people, and listening to all points of view, to see if there is a way to move forward together. It really works."

Participating In and Managing Productive Teams

Green/Red Extroverts inspire their teammates with warmth, insight, can-do attitudes, and passionate interest. Conflict provides information, and then is defused with humor. You establish rapport quickly and are a terrific collaborator.

By listening to everyone and everything, you make unusual connections and are often the first to offer creative solutions. Your many relationships ensure needed support.

Communications Style

Merely adjusting one's vocabulary to align with another color's style can elicit powerful positive responses. Empathetic vs. objective analysis, theoretical vs. practical, structured vs. adaptable—these clashes fuel most workplace conflicts. Being able to "style shift" gives you a personal competitive advantage in negotiations, managing, and interviewing.

Green/Red Extroverts are gifted at both verbal and written communications, often becoming writers and speakers. You like talking in person, rather than writing or texting. You favor abstract concepts, metaphors, feelings, and analogies, and your preferred vocabulary emphasizes words like "values," "relationship," "feel," and "friendly." Reds, with whom you share some personality traits, prefer words such as "move," "stimulate," and "gusto." Blues prefer theoretical jargon, statistical data, and technical terms. Golds, conversely, prefer "facts," "tradition," "respected," and "proven."

Green/Reds speak fluently, with liveliness. Style shifting for you means toning down, holding back, and disciplining yourself to talk sequentially rather than in a stream-of-consciousness manner. When needed, replace your usual exciting, vivid imagery, and personal stories with more concrete words and ideas. Put aside the charm and focus on here-and-now details and procedures. You're a good listener, keying in to your colleague's preferred style quickly.

Blind Spots

Certain blind spots are prevalent in Green/Red Extroverts (a few of them will apply to you):

- Starting too many projects, losing interest, or getting sidetracked.
- Overlooking important details, facts, analysis, and practicalities.
- Underestimating time and logistics.

> ‣ Keeping options open too long when decisions are needed.
>
> ‣ Taking criticism too personally.
>
> ‣ Using metaphors and analogies instead of practical, sequential words. (You'll dramatically increase cooperation with Golds by "talking real.")
>
> ‣ Not giving others time to evaluate or test ideas.

Stressors That Produce Fatigue and Strife

Certain workplace conditions produce stress and fatigue for Green/Red Extroverts. They include:

‣ Feeling manipulated or controlled

‣ Feeling cramped by structure and rules

‣ Lacking human connection, especially during difficult periods

‣ Being isolated from "the loop"

‣ Resenting those who disregard your values

‣ Being pressed for decisions before you're ready

Green/Red Extroverts under *extreme* stress often become distracted, rebellious, and gossipy. You may stir things up, create trouble, or obsess about health issues. Fatigued Green/Reds can become compulsive about details or make sudden, irrational changes.

Self-Coach Your Way to More Productive Work Relationships

The primary focus of the Green/Red Extrovert who wants to self-coach for career advancement should be on how to handle challenges to your inner values from a core of strength and confidence.

Problem Solving and Decision Making

The Green/Red Extrovert possesses these strengths:

▸ Brainstorms many possibilities and follows intuition

▸ Prioritizes people issues

▸ Listens to everyone and adopts what's important

▸ Focuses on areas of agreement; defuses conflict with fun and humor

▸ Improvises and confidently gets assistance when needed

▸ Makes keen, penetrating observations of multiple options

Strategies to Improve Effectiveness When Challenged

Interpersonal challenges detract from productivity. Here are self-coaching strategies for your biggest challenges:

▸ *Criticism that feels condemning and challenges your inner values.* Listen with dispassion. Then ask your criticizers if they respect your beliefs. Most likely, they do!

▸ *Ignoring conflict for as long as possible.* You prioritize harmony, but ignoring conflict destroys it. Force yourself to air aggravations while they're still fresh and manageable—you'll get stronger and acquire vital negotiating tactics.

▸ *Resistance to structure, rules, and bureaucracy.* You believe, rightly, in the value of brainstorming when problem solving. You chafe when structure overrides implementing ingenious solutions. Work within the system; develop allies who'll help you accomplish your goals.

▸ *Having to work alone.* Delegate such tasks to Introverts, who'll thank you for the alone time!

▸ *Making factual errors.* Other Color Q personality types need facts to allay anxieties. Facts seem to lead you astray, whereas gut feelings have always steered you right. Start intuitively, then back up your decisions with facts.

▸ *Leaving current projects incomplete when exciting new ones appear.* Put the new projects in a queue, and use your excited anticipation of the new to help complete the old projects.

When dealing with challenges, set and stick with daily priorities. You love to "wing it," so plan both organized and "wing it" times into schedules, presentations, and meetings. Learn from, rather than react to, critical feedback. Understand that deadlines are more important to other color personalities, who will manipulate and pressure you to meet them. Respect deadlines in order to enhance your credibility and stay "in the loop."

CASE STUDY 2: When a Career Isn't Working

Web designer Max Ogilvy was talking to himself, and it was scaring his family. A successful voice-over actor until the recession hit, Max had welcomed his lighter work schedule as an opportunity to transition into a more stable field.

Max used his knowledge of commercials and marketing, and his Green understanding of human desires, to create several well-received websites for prominent local businesses. He enjoyed interacting with business owners, his Red love of technology helping transform their corporate visions into digital realities.

Max hadn't counted on how many hours he would have to work at home alone in front of the computer. His Extroverted side revved up when his family came home, just when they wanted to relax.

Max badly needed to work with other people. To stay in touch with friends, he designed a website for fellow voice-over performers, complete with digital resumes and audio samples of their work. The site became so successful at connecting performers with work that Max opened an office—complete with coworkers and an audition room for new talent.

By the end of the day, he feels energized and fulfilled ... and the last thing on his mind is talking, especially to himself.

Political Savvy—Making Your Words Count

A valuable part of the Color Q system lies in learning how to harness the Red's spontaneous crisis-handling ability, the Gold's detailed and concrete thinking and administrative talent, and the Blue's strategic thinking to your advantage. Engage irritating coworkers as powerful political allies.

Reds. *"I'm trying to have a meeting of the minds with my (Red) committee member Samuel,"* says (Green/Red) philanthropist Muriel. *"I want our fundraiser to raise awareness of world hunger; he's excited because he got a deal on filet mignon! It sends the wrong message."*

Your style can irritate a Red with its emphasis on people-centered global visions. The Red's strength is to deal with the present; Reds like to see how things play out in the real world. Your global vision may not seem realistic enough to a Red, who will challenge with on-the-ground scenarios. To the Green/Red Extrovert, the Red's style appears to be amusing but barely controlled chaos. You may sympathize with their desire to flout order every chance they get, but it's irritating that Reds seem to respect things over people. This is a setup for long-term conflict. When these Red strengths become irritations but are ignored "for the sake of harmony," resentments boil over into conflicts, which exhaust you but appear to energize and excite the Red.

Negotiating Strategies

- Use these words with a Red and watch the response: "stimulate," "enjoy," "expedite," and "now."

- Downplay the global vision. Using factual, sequential words, discuss what needs to be done *now*.

- Solicit their opinions. Reds can create contingency plans on the spot when needed.

- Do not micromanage; let them handle delays, ambiguities, and unforeseen changes.

- Do not "give in" for harmony's sake. Stand your ground, preferably using a little easy humor.

- Envision challenging your Red coworkers as equals who can handle a firm "no," and practice holding firm until your concerns are addressed.

Blues. *"We've lost two clients to competitors. I say we train the reps in client retention techniques; he says fire the underperformers and hire fresh faces. He doesn't get how disruptive that would be to the department and existing clients."* Courtney, a (Green/Red) sales manager, is at loggerheads with the (Blue) vice president of operations, Adrian.

The Blue is the least people-oriented of all the Color Q personality types. To a Green/Red Extrovert, Blues appear to put all their formidable mental energy into creating strategies that may ignore the impact on workers and customers. Your style can irritate a Blue by emphasizing the impact on people rather than overall strategy. The desire for harmony may strike a Blue as secondary to the task at hand, which in the Blue's mind must be challenged. The Blue will then pepper you with criticism and questions. This onslaught pressures the Green/Red personality to stand firm in the face of conflict. The Blue appears to judge the value of your concerns by your "inability" to fight and win. If overwhelmed with lots of challenges by a Blue, *do not* take it personally or as a threat. It's actually a compliment—this is how Blues show interest.

Negotiating Strategies

- Be verbally short and concise.

- Use "if . . . then" sentences, which are very effective.

- Rehearse firmer, more effective responses: "Strategically, the problems I see are . . ." "If you see customer relations as secondary, then how do you propose to deal with account cancellations?"

- Speak in theoretical jargon, statistical data, and technical terms. To prove a proposal's worth, point out several long-term benefits. Use ingenuity, logic, and wit to make your case.

- Display competence. Blues force you to be tough-minded and firm; they need to see your competence on display.

- Don't react personally. Blues are hardwired for impersonal critical thinking.

Golds. *"He cuts me off when I describe how people will respond, and tells me I'm rambling. I'm trying to make him consider all sides of the equation."* (Green/Red) Assistant VP Will is frustrated with his (Gold/Blue) boss.

You can deal with Gold/Greens. Gold/Blues are another matter. More authoritarian and less patient than you, they view your people-first style as soft. The Green/Red's style can irritate a Gold by being too stream-of-consciousness and not offering enough concrete evidence and linear processes to show how to achieve the desired ends. Greens listen to all sides; Golds see right and wrong only one way.

Green/Red Extrovert Suzanne M. experienced this predicament with her Gold/Blue accounting colleague, explaining: "I had an invoice for health benefits for a Polish employee in the United States that needed to be paid right away, or the person would have been without coverage. The accountant did not like that I showed up in person and was too bubbly telling the story. He resisted, saying it was the end of the month; we do not have time to focus on one invoice; it was out of the ordinary. But I explained the fact that if it wasn't done the person would be without coverage, and he handled it. From then on, we had a relationship and I kept going to him."

Negotiating Strategies

▸ To ease tensions, pepper your sentences with words like "facts," "tradition," "respected," and "proven." Avoid metaphors and analogies.

▸ Make use of concrete words and concepts to create more of a comfort zone, so you can "talk the talk" with Golds (and Reds). They need grounded, practical, sequential communications.

▸ Commit several low-pressure, self-directed minutes each day to focusing on the vocabulary of investment, costs, time lines, and budgets.

▸ Acknowledge and flatter their superior detail management, especially when they take on some of your detail work.

Extrovert vs. Introvert

If the previous strategies are still missing the mark, you may be dealing with an Introvert. If so:

‣ Respect, don't challenge, their need to recharge their batteries with privacy—it's not personal, although it will be difficult for you to understand why they shun interaction and prefer working alone.

‣ Tone down your enthusiasm; listen more.

‣ Invite them to speak, but don't force them to speak until they've thought things through. Do not fill their pauses.

Recognize your coworkers in any of the preceding descriptions? Learn more about them by reading each Color Q personality's overall chapter and Chapter 25, "Adjusting to the Workplace Styles of Others."

‣   ‣   ‣

In summary, Green/Red Extroverts are open-minded and imaginative individuals who plunge enthusiastically into new possibilities. Typically multitalented, you often have several distinct careers as well as many creative endeavors. Charismatic and ingenious, you are less successful in jobs demanding routine and strict compliance to rules. Focusing on facts and details can be very stressful to Green/Reds, who typically have a short attention span and diverse interests. Overall, your key contribution is inspiring others to share your expansive approach to work and life. Maintaining harmonious team spirit is a top priority; but stand firm when conflict first arises. It is critical to honor your desires and draw *your* lines in the sand.

green/backup
red introverts

YOU'RE NOT ONLY a Green; you also have strong secondary characteristics of the Red personality. And you have tested as a Color Q Introvert, which means you recharge your batteries by being alone. Green/Red Introverts are most deeply motivated by their personal ideals. You often put money, fame, power, and even personal success secondary to inner values. In business, you need a mission that benefits others.

Top Motivators

As an Introvert, you're less productive working in open office settings that lack privacy. Yet interest in others is deep, so you may forfeit needed alone time.

Green/Red Introverts are motivated in workplaces that reward uniqueness and creativity. Working one-on-one or in small groups with empathetic coworkers is ideal. Green/Red Introverts form only 4 percent of the world's population; but we all benefit from your quiet, committed influence.

Corporate Culture—Finding the Optimal Fit

It is the responsibility of every personality to find or create their optimal work environment. Optimal cultures differ among Color Q personality types. Strengths in one company may be viewed as weaknesses elsewhere. The corporate culture itself may not be dysfunctional; for instance, Greens hate what Blues love. Conflict, sapped strength, resentment, and feelings of defeat are symptoms of poor cultural fit and can be avoided by understanding your preferences.

> The Green/Red Introvert's most **preferred work environment** emphasizes:
>
> - Empathetic coworkers and a democratic atmosphere
> - People-related missions promoting human understanding
> - Acknowledgments for creativity
> - Minimal rules/restrictions
> - Being heard by peers and superiors
> - Placing high value on the well-being of staff and clients
>
> If these points seem obvious, it means you've tested correctly. (Compare with a Blue/Gold Extrovert's ideal environment.)
>
> The Green/Red Introvert's **least preferred environment** has:
>
> - Lots of public speaking and mandatory socializing
> - Bureaucratic or highly political coworkers
> - Many rules, procedures, details, and repetitive routine
> - Pressure from tight deadlines, pushy superiors
> - Emphasis on discipline, with little creativity or brainstorming

Leveraging Executive Presence and Building Personal Brand

Green/Red Introverts masterfully deal with multiple events and people—simultaneously when necessary. You are especially energized during start-ups, and keep the team moving forward with clear, steadfast focus. Big visions seem quite attainable when you're around. You know valuable ideas come from unusual sources and can spot connections other people miss. Persuasion, rather than control, creates buy-in that speeds products through the pipeline.

> *The Green/Red Introvert's personal leadership brand should highlight your ability to build consensus, getting troubled teams or organizations back on track.*

You're great at inspiring people; they do their jobs well because you believe in them. With strong personal values, you quietly assert influence. You are, however, stubborn about achieving set goals, pitching in wherever necessary. You inspire deep loyalty that keeps turnover minimal and clients in place during tough times.

Catherine Atwood has used Color Q since 2008. She applied it during the 2011 Bike & Build cross-country bicycle trip with thirty-four riders working for Habitat for Humanity and other affordable housing organizations. "Color Q became one of the tools that helped me reach out to people with whom I'd previously felt there was some kind of barrier. I felt good about that."

CASE STUDY 1: The Successful Green/Red Introvert

Katharine Myers, Co-Owner, Myers-Briggs Type Indicator®
MBTI is the personality system that helped inspire Color Q. As the co-owner of the MBTI copyrights, Katharine Myers was a founding board member of the Center for the Application of Psychological Type, Inc. (CAPT), which is the MBTI's research laboratory and resource center. She was also the first president of the Association for Psychological Type International (APTi), the MBTI's leading membership organization.

First exposed to the MBTI in eleventh grade, when creator Isabel Myers tested the entire grade in which her son Peter was enrolled, Katharine had a revelation. "I learned I preferred introversion, and it was a perfectly okay way to be. This insight freed me to go comfortably into any situation anywhere in the world...." Isabel continued to expose Katharine to MBTI concepts throughout her college years at Vassar; in 1973, Katharine married Isabel's son Peter.

Katharine remained affiliated with the MBTI from then on. "I motivate and inspire people to develop themselves; our culture is too willing to tell people what is wrong with them. So I focus on telling people what is right."

Katharine describes herself as a typical Green/Red Introvert: "I like starting things, then moving on. I present provocative ideas with an emphasis on the big picture."

Her intensity and passion for what she believes in are keys to her success. "I constantly want to improve the world," she says. "I want to pass on to the next generation an organization that is effective and ethical." She engages in conflict "when I see something that is unfair or dishonest."

Says Katharine: "Outside of having been in the crowd when Martin Luther King gave his 'I Have a Dream' speech, my proudest accomplishment is the care I have taken to protect Isabel Myers's work."

- -

Participating In and Managing Productive Teams

Green/Red Introverts work doggedly on important tasks. Team harmony is necessary for personal productivity. Often the conscience of the group, you listen closely, hear what is really being said, then focus on areas of agreement. Committed to your team, you are patient with complexity and conflicting values.

You make startling connections and then offer creative solutions. Loyal relationships ensure needed support. Says Catherine Atwood of her Bike & Build team, "Eventually you find a common ground with everybody on the trip. I would consider every single one of them my friend."

Communications Style

Merely adjusting one's vocabulary to align with another color's style can elicit powerful positive responses. Empathetic vs. objective analysis, theoretical vs. practical, structured vs. adaptable—these clashes fuel most workplace conflicts. Being able to "style shift" brings greater response during negotiations, managing, and interviewing.

Green/Red Introverts are gifted communicators, writers, and visual artists. You need time to think before talking and dislike small talk and confrontation. Your preferred vocabulary features abstract concepts, metaphors, values, and analogies, emphasizing words such as "relationship," "feel," and "friendly." Reds, with whom you share some personality traits, prefer words like "move," "stimulate," and "expedite." Blues prefer theoretical jargon, statistical data, and technical terms. Golds respond to "facts," "tradition," "respected," and "proven."

Green/Red Introverts are calm, quiet speakers. Your inner intensity is seldom seen except by those you know well. Style shifting for you means speaking concretely and assertively; sequentially rather than metaphorically. Trade your global thoughts for present-centered details and technical strategy. You're an excellent listener, easily discerning colleagues' preferred styles.

Blind Spots

Certain blind spots are prevalent in Green/Red Introverts (only some of them will apply to you). They include:

- Spending more time reflecting than acting
- Stalling a decision while gathering feelings/opinions
- Prioritizing ideals and appearing impractical
- Using intuition instead of facts and analysis
- Underestimating time logistics
- Taking criticism personally
- Using metaphors and analogies instead of practical, concrete words
- Being overly demanding of self

Stressors That Produce Fatigue and Strife

Certain workplace conditions can stress and fatigue Green/Red Introverts, including:

- Too much social interaction

- Being the unexpected center of attention

- Pervasive office politics and misinterpretation of words/actions

- Having to compromise inner values

- Too much repetitive work or details

- Lack of privacy and time to think

Green/Red Introverts under extreme stress often become self-critical, sensitive, and defensive. Cutting remarks and outbursts over minor issues are common. You will tend to withdraw when forced to let go of important people or projects. Fatigued Green/Reds may become unyielding, unfocused, or disorganized. You'll ignore physical symptoms and during leisure hours might engage in eating, drinking, or exercising to excess.

Self-Coach Your Way to More Productive Work Relationships

The primary focus of the Green/Red Introvert who wants to self-coach for career advancement should be on how to handle (rather than avoid) challenges to inner values with strength and confidence. You also need increased focus on money as a tool for helping others.

Problem Solving and Decision Making

A Green/Red Introvert has the following strengths:

- Evaluates impacts on people and takes challenges in stride

- Gathers lots of input; offers broad, innovative, original solutions

- Perceives where and how to get help

- Knows conflict provides information about genuine needs

- Finds newness in the mundane

Strategies to Improve Effectiveness When Challenged

Interpersonal challenges detract from productivity. Here are self-coaching strategies for your biggest challenges:

- *Resistance to structure, rules, and bureaucracy.* You believe, rightly, in the value of brainstorming and chafe when rules hinder implementation of ingenious solutions. Work within the system; develop supportive allies who will help you accomplish your goals.

- *Seeing money as secondary to the mission.* They're equal—one cannot advance without the other. Apply this tool to the vision and you'll be unstoppable.

- *Having to work in large teams or open offices.* Ask to work primarily on smaller subcommittees. Negotiate a private work space . . . you'll be stressed without one.

- *Criticism that feels like personal condemnation.* Listen with dispassion. Ask if those criticizing respect your values. Most likely, they do.

- *Making factual errors.* Other colors require facts to allay anxieties. For you, factual analysis usually proves your intuitions correct . . . later. Start intuitively, then prove yourself right.

- *Ignoring conflict indefinitely.* Harmony is the priority, but ignoring conflict breeds resentment. Air aggravations while they are fresh . . . you'll master some vital negotiating tactics in the process.

When dealing with challenges, set daily priorities. Find a nonjudgmental mentor whose strengths are finance and logic. Role-play confrontations to build strength; put an iron fist in a velvet glove. Decide beforehand how well a job needs to be done so that perfectionism doesn't blow deadlines. Above all, honor your real needs for rest and privacy.

CASE STUDY 2: **When a Career Isn't Working**

The big-picture, people-oriented nature of political science attracted Green/Red Introvert Candace Fox; it was her college major. Long hours alone in the library researching the impact of policy on populations energized her; her grades were top tier and her future in the Democratic Party looked bright indeed.

In the summer before her senior year, she won a key volunteer role in the local political campaign for Barack Obama. Her team's mission was to coordinate local fund-raising through social media.

Developing the website and building Twitter accounts was fulfilling, but for Candace, the experience was marred by having to sit in an open gymnasium-size room full of ringing phones, telemarketers, and frequent public arguing. Green Introverts have trouble focusing through noise and disharmony. Her supervisor's feedback was increasingly critical; this demotivated Candace and destroyed her productivity.

Candace used her senior year to rethink her political ambitions and redirect her career goals. With her parents' support, she decided to go for a Ph.D. in political science and become a college professor. Unlike those who are pressured by a "publish or perish" tenure track, Introverted Candace relished long hours of research and writing. She began designing a blog on the political perspective of the younger voter.

Political Savvy—Making Your Words Count

A valuable part of the Color Q system lies in learning how to harness the Red's spontaneous crisis-handling ability, the Gold's detailed thinking and administrative talent, and the Blue's strategic planning to your advantage. Engage irritating coworkers as powerful political allies.

Reds. Green/Red Pauline, a customer service manager, always finds Red Jake annoying when he comes to upgrade their computers. *"When he shuts down our computer system, our whole department goes into chaos—but he thinks it's amusing."*

Your style can irritate a Red with its emphasis on global vision and being able to "read between the lines." These qualities may not seem realistic enough to a Red, who will challenge with on-the-ground scenarios. The Red's strength is dealing with the present; Red personalities like to see how things play out in the real world. Your reserved manner and ability to hear what's unspoken confuses them. To the Green/Red Introvert, the Red's style appears to be a barely controlled chaos. You support when Reds flout bureaucracy, but their respect for things over people is annoying. This creates long-term conflict with a Green/Red Introvert. When these Red strengths become irritations but are ignored "for the sake of harmony," resentments boil over into conflicts that exhaust you but appear to energize and excite the Red. The collegial Red enjoys seeing beneath your reserved veneer.

Negotiating Strategies

▸ Use these words with a Red and watch the response: "stimulate," "enjoy," "expedite," and "now."

▸ Downplay global visions and future trends. Discuss, factually and sequentially, what needs to be done *now*.

▸ Solicit their opinions. Reds can create contingency plans on the spot when needed.

▸ Do not micromanage; let them handle delays, ambiguities, and unforeseen changes.

▸ Curb tendencies to "give in" for harmony's sake. Stand your ground, preferably with some easy humor.

▸ Envision challenging your Red coworkers as equals who can handle a firm "no," and practice holding firm until your concerns are addressed.

Blues. Green/Red Jeremy owns a commercial design studio. He's thinking of buying out his Blue partner Ed. *"His strategies helped build the business. His abruptness with people drives customers away."*

The Blue is the least people-oriented of all the Color Q personality types. To a Green/Red Introvert, Blues appear to put all their formidable mental energy into creating strategies that may ignore the effect on workers and customers. Your style can irritate a Blue by focusing on people and ideals rather than overall strategy. Big pictures lacking strategic details in the Blue's mind must be challenged. Blues then pepper you with criticism and questions. This onslaught pressures the Green/Red to stand firm in the face of conflict. The Blue appears to judge the value of your concerns by your "inability" to fight and win; you withdraw because of the apparent contempt. If overwhelmed by a Blue's challenges, do not take it personally or as a threat. It's actually a compliment; this is how Blues show interest.

Negotiating Strategies

▸ Be verbally short and concise.

▸ Use "if . . . then" sentences, which are very effective.

▸ Rehearse firm, effective responses: "Strategically, the problems I see are . . ." "If you see customer relations as secondary, then how do you propose to deal with account cancellations?"

▸ Adjust your vocabulary and start using theoretical jargon, statistical data, and technical terms. To prove a proposal's worth, point out long-term benefits. Make the case with ingenuity, logic, and wit.

▸ Display competence. Blues force you to be tough-minded and firm; they need to see your competence on display. Follow through at all costs.

▸ Don't react personally, or feel intimidated by their logic. Blues are hardwired for impersonal critical thinking.

Golds. Jane, a Green/Red, usually has an excellent relationship with clients. One of them, Rich (a Gold/Blue), is abrupt and challenging. He peppers Jane with questions and argues with her answers. He seems annoyed when she tries to personalize the relationship and inquire about his hobbies.

Always balance a team with a Gold; you need the Gold's skills in financial and detail management. You'll prefer Gold/Greens. Gold/Blues are another matter. More authoritarian and less patient, they view any people-first style as soft. The Green/Red's style can irritate all Golds by being too idealistic, lacking concrete evidence and linear processes for showing how to achieve desired ends.

If a Gold/Blue such as Rich challenges you, be ready to provide step-by-step plans. (Create them in order to help the people who will implement them.)

Negotiating Strategies

‣ To ease tensions, sprinkle sentences with words like "facts," "tradition," "respected," and "proven." Avoid metaphors and analogies.

‣ Make use of concrete words to create a comfort zone, so you can "talk the talk" with Golds. Respect their need for structure and grounded, practical, sequential words.

‣ Commit several low-pressure, self-directed minutes each day to focusing on the financial concepts behind business plans, investment, costs, time lines, and budgets.

‣ Acknowledge and flatter their superior detail management capabilities, especially when they take on some of your detail work. Show respect for their position and title (even if such things seem superficial to you).

Extrovert vs. Introvert

If the aforementioned strategies are still missing the mark, the colleague may be an Extrovert. If so:

‣ Respect, don't challenge, their need to recharge their batteries by interacting with others—they need this the way you need alone time (even though it will be difficult for you to understand why they must constantly be around people and how they can enjoy noisy environments).

‣ Ask questions; share more of yourself.

‣ Exploit your skills at being a good listener—but interject verbally often.

‣ Volunteer to handle tasks for them that require working alone. Benefit from their gratitude . . . and the solitude.

Recognize any coworkers in the preceding descriptions? Learn more about them by reading each Color Q personality's overall chapter and then Chapter 25, "Adjusting to the Workplace Styles of Others."

▸   ▸   ▸

In summary, Green/Red Introverts are creative, sensitive people who support the development of others. One of the least likely colors to aspire to top management, you prefer the (very powerful) role of key adviser to decision makers. If it will help people you'll accept, but dislike, the number one role. You'll also quickly groom successors with managerial aptitude.

Green/Red Introverts have a deep commitment to causes and individuals they respect. Guided by strong inner values, you may appear too idealistic to some other Color Q personalities. If someone challenges those values, though, you'll surprise yourself (and them) with an aggressive defense. Otherwise, conflict is routinely avoided.

Green/Red Introverts must, however, continuously balance their idealism with realism, and honor their deep need for privacy and solitude.

10

---

reds overall

REDS REPRESENT approximately 27 percent of the world population. If you are not a Red, but would like to learn how to identify and communicate with one, go to the section on "How to Recognize a Red Colleague" at the end of this chapter.

Countess Editha Nemes

Former New York real estate broker Countess Editha Nemes may not be as well known a Red as her colleague Donald Trump, but she is a very pure example of this personality. Ditha, as she is called, enjoyed the ever-changing nature of real estate, handling it with ease and experience from a life with many bizarre twists of fate.

At age 19, Ditha married one of Hungary's wealthiest aristocrats. But the communist invasion forced the couple and their child to flee to Switzerland with the clothes on their backs and their jewelry concealed in a piece of cloth worn as a belt. At the border, Ditha dropped the belt on the table and, with a Red's innate crisis-handling skill, injected some easy collegiality while submitting to a search. The distraction complete, she nonchalantly put the belt back on. The jewelry would fund their trek to a refugee camp and ultimately to North Africa.

Funds dwindled; the family was granted political asylum at the court of King Farouk of Egypt. Neither adult possessed work skills. When their hostess, Princess Zeinab, admired their infant daughter's dresses, Red Ditha recognized her first money-making opportunity. She rented a space, hired a cutter and seamstresses, and began designing Parisian-style children's fashions. (Reds have an innate appreciation for haute couture and finer things.) When the king's three daughters appeared in her creations, the "designing countess" became an overnight Cairo sensation.

Crises bring out the best in Reds. For almost a decade, Ditha's business supported her family. The Egyptian aristocracy frequented her showrooms; their children modeled at her annual fashion shows. Each prince and princess had pieces designed seasonally; clients clamored for exclusive designs. Typical of the Red personality, Ditha kept minimal records and details in a small black book.

Political turmoil in 1952 displaced the family yet again. On "Black Saturday," militants, religious fundamentalists, communists, and radical students inspired by Egyptian Army Colonel Gamal Abdel Nasser burned down much that had given Cairo its glamour.[1] When Nasser became Egypt's president, King Farouk was forced into exile and Europeans took flight. Well advanced into pregnancy with her second child, Ditha again rose to the challenge. Using incoming cash from seasonal orders, Ditha financed her family's exit to the United States. Determined to give birth to an American citizen, Ditha set foot in Los Angeles one hour before her child was born. These are vivid memories that will remain with me forever. Ditha Nemes is my mother, and this is my story as well.

The challenge of starting over in the United States again demanded Ditha's Red capabilities. With the aid of the Folger family of San Francisco,

Ditha held a fashion show in the coffee magnate's living room, using eleven-year-old Abigail Folger and her friends as models. A buyer from I. Magnin was encouraging; five years later "the designing countess" was serving 300 stores around the United States.

But Reds prefer the excitement of a start-up and the flexibility of a small concern. For the next thirty years, Ditha focused her Red negotiating talents in real estate. What to others is high stress is pure stimulation and joy to freewheeling Reds. "Do what you like to do," Ditha advises. "When you are on your own, you have to push. So you become successful."

Like all Reds, "I never plan into the future," she says. "I don't worry about tomorrow."

"Anything can change without warning, and that's why I try not to take any of what's happened too seriously. The real excitement is playing the game. Money is not the main motivation. I don't spend a lot of time worrying about what I should have done differently, or what's going to happen next."[2] No, this is not Ditha Nemes describing her work style; it's Donald Trump, describing his.

Donald Trump, the Trump Organization
Estimated by the MBTI community to be one of America's best-known Reds, "The Donald," as he is called, is chairman and president of the Trump Organization and had a net worth in excess of $2.9 billion as of 2012 (as reported by *Forbes*).

"My style of deal making is quite simple and straightforward," Trump says. "I aim very high, and then I keep pushing and pushing and pushing to get what I'm after. . . . More than anything else I think deal making is an ability you're born with. . . . It's not about being brilliant. It does take a certain intelligence, but mostly it's about instincts."[3]

Edward Koch, Former Mayor, City of New York
Another famous New Yorker and Red is Ed Koch. (Koch has been assessed in person by author Shoya Zichy.) In his post–City College of New York days, he earned two battle stars and the Combat Infantry Badge during World War II military duty. Upon his return, he earned a law degree, then served for two years on the New York City Council and nine years as a

congressman before serving three terms as New York's mayor from 1978 to 1989.

Today, at the ripe young age of 87, this energetic Red is a partner in the law firm of Bryan Cave LLP, hosts a call-in radio talk show on Bloomberg Radio AM 1130, appears on NY1 television with former Senator Alfonse D'Amato, lectures nationwide, and writes a weekly commentary.

His Red crisis management acumen saved New York City from bankruptcy, restored fiscal responsibility by instituting a Generally Accepted Accounting Principles (GAAP) balanced budget, and created a merit judicial selection system. "I took the politics out of the appointment of judges," says Koch, noting that this is one of the accomplishments of which he is most proud. "I was always willing to stand alone, even with no one behind me."

Thus it was a major stressor when two officials in his administration were found to be engaged in corruption. Koch recalls, "I was clinically depressed over this, afraid it would be a smear on me. But John Cardinal O'Connor called and said, 'Ed, I know you're depressed but you should not be; everyone knows you are an honest man.'"

In an organization as large as the City of New York's government, conflict is inevitable. Koch's Red response kept him in office for three terms. "I have a good sense of humor and lead by convincing people to follow me. If you follow me I will lead you across the desert. I inspire people to work together," Koch says.

Randolph A. Hogan, Former Editor, *New York Times Book Review*

It isn't only business and politics in which Reds excel. Randolph A. Hogan is a semiretired freelance writer and editor who worked for sixteen years on a number of sections for the *New York Times*. His core discipline, however, was editing. Inspired by his father's reverence for the newspaper, "when I was about ten, I started reading the *New York Times Book Review*. It was serendipitous that I eventually became an editor of the *Book Review* for so many years," Randy says.

With a Red's keen aesthetic appreciation, Randy made assigning his reviewers an art unto itself. "It's like walking through a minefield, if you're responsible," he recalls. "I was looking at the reviewer's style and intellectual approach, the conception and execution of the writing."

His present-centered Red orientation fit perfectly into the newspaper culture. "I never did strategize for the future," Randy recalls. "When you work at a newspaper, everything becomes irrelevant after a day."

▶   ▶   ▶

With superb negotiation and troubleshooting skills, Reds excel in careers such as real estate, government, and newspaper publishing in which no two days are alike. They trust what they can see, touch, taste, smell, or hear for themselves. Physically restless, Reds need independence and they hate to feel trapped, either in work or relationships. Although loyal to friends and family, guilt, obligation, and duty rarely motivate them. The pursuit of excitement drives many Reds. Their motto might be: *He who dies having worn out the most toys wins.*

Impatient with reading books like this, you are to be congratulated for getting this far. The person who encouraged you to read this material will be pleased; even more pleased if you skim the part of your specific chapter on how best to communicate with that person's own personality style. That's the most practical part. Reward yourself now—go do something!

How to Recognize a Red Colleague

External Environment Clues

- Desk with many piles
- Collection of gadgets, sports memorabilia, and exotic vacation souvenirs
- Clocks that run late to create small, stimulating "crises"
- Handsome, well-built furnishings

Personal Mannerisms—Personal Behaviors

- Casual
- Restless, physically expressive

- Often late
- Given to technical, mechanical tinkering
- Richly colored, high-quality clothes; expensive watches
- Taste for artisanal or haute cuisine, liquors

Personal Mannerisms—Verbal

- Prefers activity to conversation; seeks excitement and adventure
- Uses short, crisp sentences
- Displays a great sense of humor
- Promotes camaraderie
- Reacts spontaneously
- Shows superlative negotiating talents, yet able to inject fun into work

How to Communicate with a Red—"Style Shifting" Tips

- Avoid meetings, or schedule them in fun places; make presentations brief; tell humorous stories.
- Use action verbs like *attack, challenge, expedite, stimulate,* or *enjoy.*
- Avoid theories and get to the point; use here-and-now, bottom-line language.
- Explain with hands-on demonstrations.
- Offer options in conversation and plans.
- Stress immediacy—"this will help right now."
- Allow them to follow their instincts.
- Be candid about risk levels (Reds find risk-taking exciting).
- Acknowledge and appreciate their crisis-coping skills.

11

red/backup
blue extroverts

YOU'RE NOT ONLY a Red; you also have strong secondary characteristics of the Blue personality. And you have tested as a Color Q Extrovert,
which means you recharge your batteries by being with people, rather than
being alone. You form 6 percent of the world's population. Red/Blue
Extroverts are likely reading this book only to please someone else. You
should find that most of this chapter confirms who you are (if not, retest). It
also gives you activities, tools, and experiments to try with your coworkers.

Top Motivators
To an Extrovert, working alone for long periods is frustrating. You'll create
variety and action, even if disruptive. Working in open environments is
most productive for you.

If you are a Red/Blue Extrovert, negotiate during hiring or review for these workplace motivators:

- Chance to make on-the-spot decisions about real problems

- Frequent new experiences

- Access to the latest technology/gadgets

- Action/crisis management (which energizes you)

- Work balanced with fun

Corporate Culture—Finding the Optimal Fit

It is the responsibility of every personality to find or create their optimal work environment. Optimal cultures differ among personality types. Strengths in one company may be unneeded elsewhere. The corporate culture itself may not be dysfunctional; it's just that Reds hate what Golds love, for instance. Conflict, sapped strength, resentment, and feelings of defeat are symptoms of poor cultural fit and can be avoided by understanding your preferences.

The Red/Blue Extrovert's **most preferred work environment** emphasizes:

- Stimulating variety of responsibilities and tasks

- Small teams of collegial, results-oriented coworkers

- Short-term, nonrepetitive projects

- Tangible products

- Comfortable, attractive surroundings

- Physical freedom to work and socialize

- Entrepreneurial spirit, competition, and direct problem solving

If these points seem obvious to you, it means you've tested correctly. (Compare with a Gold/Green Introvert's ideal environment.)

The Red/Blue Extrovert's **least preferred environment** is fueled by:

- Long-term projects and abstract concepts or strategies

- Bossy people who impose their "right way"

- Hierarchy, with meetings and memos bogging down action

- Lots of details and repetition

- Tight schedules under a micromanager who discourages humor and play

- Forced respect for status and position

Leveraging Executive Presence and Building Personal Brand

One of the critical tasks of a Red/Blue Extrovert manager is to build one's executive reputation or "brand." There are concrete reasons for having a personal brand. You'll achieve tangible results internally and be able to market yourself externally when necessary.

> *The Red/Blue Extrovert's leadership brand should be built around your strength for quickly sizing up situations, trusting your instinct, negotiating effectively, and achieving goals during times of crisis and change.*

You are a hands-off, "down in the trenches" manager who even now wants to stop reading this book and get out and do! This is brand-building in action.

Here are other concrete actions that build your brand:

- Troubleshooting (and getting credit for it)

- Identifying and utilizing the abilities of subordinates and senior staff

- "Bottom-line-savvy" risk-taking (using your talent for making mid-course corrections)

- Keeping things moving with tension-breaking humor

This said, you are not keen to manage a large organization. When your department reaches a certain size you may want to consider moving to a smaller unit.

- -

CASE STUDY 1: Successful Red/Blue Extroverts

Sheila L. Birnbaum, Skadden Arps

What does it take for a grocer's daughter to become the leading product liability lawyer in the world? The innate abilities of the Red/Blue Extrovert—including a need for action and variety; competitiveness; negotiating strength; crisis management capability; and a direct problem-solving approach. Red/Blue Extrovert Sheila L. Birnbaum has leveraged her personality style with so much success that she has been dubbed "Queen of Torts." Today, she is cohead of Skadden Arp's Mass Torts and Insurance Litigation Group, which she helped to create.

One common thread runs through her extensive career in public service—fairness. Reds are uniquely sensitive to fairness, which Birnbaum illustrates in her positions as a member of the New York State Judicial Commission on Minorities and executive director for the U.S. Court of Appeals for the Second Circuit's Task Force for Racial, Ethnic, and Gender Fairness. In May 2011, Birnbaum, a lifelong New Yorker, was appointed by U.S. Attorney General Eric Holder to head the September 11th Victim Compensation Fund. Formerly a fourth grade teacher, she gained recognition for mediating a settlement of $500 million for ninety-two families of victims of the September 11, 2001, terrorist attack on the World Trade Center.[1] (Reds are superb mediators.)

Reds everywhere will nod in agreement with this Birnbaum statement: "The worst thing that can happen," she says, "is that the telephone doesn't ring all day. The more that is going on, the calmer I am," she adds, "and the more I can handle."

Michael Naso, FBN Securities, Inc.

"I work well under pressure," concedes Michael Naso, a partner at the New York institutional broker dealer FBN Securities. "I am flexible and adaptable, and change directions quickly."

Typical of Red personalities, Naso enjoys "managing my own team without too many rules and hierarchies." This keeps his company nimble while providing clients with research, trading strategies, capital introductions, and corporate access. "I enjoy creating strategic partnerships to make new opportunities and revenue streams," he says. Naso's Red adaptability has allowed his team to exceed sales targets.

Part of his success is the way he handles conflict within his team. "First, I address the problem directly—then I sit down, listen to all points of view, and come to a logical solution." In that statement, his Blue component comes through.

Naso strategizes for the future as Red personalities do—very here and now. "I continue to add value creating new products for clients in a constantly changing environment," he says.

Participating In and Managing Productive Teams

On a team, you're the troubleshooter, clear thinker, technical expert, negotiator, and inspirer of fun. You contribute by:

▸ Applying common sense

▸ Focusing on practicalities and enjoyment

▸ Working through a diversity of people

▸ Getting conflicting teammates to agree

▸ Helping to keep meetings to the point

Communications Style

Adjusting vocabulary to align with another color's style creates powerful positive responses. Empathetic vs. objective analysis, theoretical vs. practical, structured vs. adaptable—these clashes fuel most workplace conflicts. Being able to "style shift" brings great competitive advantages in negotiations, managing, and interviewing.

Bottom line: You are direct and blunt. You prefer talking in person, can read body language well, and are socially at ease. Your preferred vocabulary is active, favoring words like "move," "stimulate," and "expedite." Greens prefer abstract concepts and metaphors, emphasizing words like "values," "relationship," "feel," and "friendly." Blues, with whom you share some personality traits, prefer theoretical jargon, statistical data, and technical terms. Golds prefer "facts," "tradition," "respected," and "proven."

Red/Blues want action, not talk. You make points with enthusiasm and personal stories. Style shifting for you means accommodating the emotions, strategies, and rules of others. Understand the anxieties of those who impose rules; address them with win-win solutions.

Blind Spots

These blind spots are prevalent in Red/Blue Extroverts (although only some of them will apply to you):

- Acting on impulse without enough data or long-term thinking
- Beginning too many projects and missing deadlines
- Staying unaware of others' emotions/responses
- Being too casual about commitments or "illogical" rules and procedures
- Going into meetings unprepared
- "Winging it" instead of managing time

Stressors That Produce Fatigue and Strife

The following workplace conditions can stress and fatigue Red/Blue Extroverts:

- Having to develop detailed plans before acting
- Having little physical, social, or problem-solving freedom
- Inflexible or slow-moving people/situations
- Unsettling emotions and challenges to principles
- Being forced to defend your ability or trustworthiness
- Demands that prevent workers from having fun and time for recharging

If you are under *extreme* stress, take action to curtail your tendency toward defiance, withdrawal, pessimism, or feeling unappreciated and bored. Talk to your superior and explain that you have more to offer! Make suggestions that fulfill your need to move and socialize.

Self-Coach Your Way to More Productive Work Relationships

The primary focus of the Red/Blue Extrovert who wants to self-coach for career advancement should be on how to handle other people's emotional issues, rules, and abstract thinking.

Problem Solving and Decision Making

The Red/Blue Extrovert has these strengths:

- Makes penetrating observations and identifies logical actions

- Processes large amounts of information; makes difficult decisions

- Reacts quickly under pressure

- Finds needed resources

- Circumvents rules and procedures that hamper solutions

- Trusts own instincts

Strategies to Improve Effectiveness When Challenged

Interpersonal challenges detract from productivity. Here are self-coaching activities to help solve your biggest challenges:

- *Resistance to structure, rules, and bureaucracy.* You believe, rightly, in the value of sizing up a problem and acting on it. You chafe when structure overrides implementing logical solutions. Curry favor with Golds who run the system; develop allies who'll help you accomplish your goals.

- *Having to work alone.* Delegate these tasks to Introverts; they'll thank you for giving them assignments that bring alone time! Request a populated environment to increase your productivity.

▸ *Loss of freedom—being tied down.* Defying those who inhibit you is tempting. But minimal work or subtle sabotage ultimately affect career advancement. Instead, go to the gym at lunch for a hard workout. Maneuver politically for more freedom. Use this book to convince the company it will benefit by giving you freer range.

▸ *Working long and hard for little result.* When fatigue and gloom settle in, recharge with activities that bring you pleasure. Mountain climbing, racing, skydiving, deep-sea diving, surfing, traveling, listening to music, dancing, whatever sounds good to you—do it.

▸ *Not having control over decisions.* Role-playing, preferably with a strategy-oriented Blue, works well. Talk with others who've faced similar dilemmas; swap real-life solutions.

▸ *Others' emotional reactions that cloud logic.* Find a Green to mentor you through emotional logic. View emotions as "if … then" equations that can produce more well-rounded decisions (e.g., "if he feels this, then he'll likely do that").

When dealing with challenges, exploit your talent for sizing up situations, implementing, and managing crises. Avoid jobs requiring long-term strategy and routine. Young Red/Blue Extroverts often change projects or jobs frequently until they find the right mix of freedom and crisis-handling responsibility.

- -

CASE STUDY 2: When a Career Isn't Working

Chef Philippe Monte knew it was time to move on. His body hurt everywhere. His restaurant had just been sold to a micromanaging owner. His marriage to Jenella was rocky. And the highly successful chef with a sterling reputation in three major cities wanted to own his own place.

An inn had become available in upscale Newport, Rhode Island, for which the couple could pay cash. His wife was thrilled about spending more time with her husband; Philippe looked forward to working fewer hours, healing his body, and serving fewer guests more innovative cuisine.

It didn't work out that way. After buying the inn money was tight, and Philippe had to take over housekeeping and front desk management. The days became a grind of routine—clean the rooms, prep for new guests, handle credit card submissions. A Gold would not have minded; but Red Philippe preferred handling the frequent (and exciting) repair crises. Unfortunately, he had little time to plan his dinner specials or source seasonal ingredients.

After their first year, Jenella gave him an ultimatum. "Hire a front desk manager or sell the place." Cash flow revealed it was possible if they hired carefully. Within a month, Philippe hired Debbie, a local thrilled to have the job. Having someone else manage the front desk allowed Philippe to devote his Red strengths to the hands-on repair crises and the haute cuisine. The inn has since blossomed into a profitable four-star destination.

Political Savvy—Making Your Words Count

A valuable part of the Color Q system lies in learning how to harness the Green's marketing and people skills, the Gold's detail thinking and administrative talent, and the Blue's strategic thinking to your advantage. Make irritating coworkers powerful political allies.

Greens. *"We're upgrading our manufacturing process. When I need facts, all James brings me is how management and line workers are likely to respond."* Juan (a Red/Blue) doesn't know how to deal with his coworker James (a Green).

Green is the most people-oriented of the four primary Color Q personalities. The Green's abstract visions and long-term orientation may seem, to you, eccentric. Your style can irritate a Green by focusing on logic, gadgetry, and the present moment without concern for long-term or interpersonal consequences. You both like to keep your options open as long as possible before making decisions, but Greens gather emotional feedback whereas you just want the facts. You dislike hand-holding when a crisis is afoot! As a result, your style may seem blunt or dismissive of Greens' concerns. Greens won't confront you, but they'll become cold and unsupportive.

Negotiating Strategies

▸ Be patient with the Green's abstract visions and long-term thinking. These qualities prevent future problems, allowing you to concentrate on needed midcourse corrections and real crises.

▸ Ask them how you're perceived. Their feedback will be gentle and tactful.

▸ Give them step-by-step directions when you want them to do something here and now. Otherwise, Greens will only visit the present moment occasionally.

▸ Factor in their values when making decisions, to ensure their political buy-in.

▸ Keep it real. Remember that while you are comfortable "trying out" behaviors to see how people respond, this approach perplexes Greens and makes them withdraw.

Blues. *Rob (a Red/Blue) complains that "Peter (a Blue) sits in his office all day coming up with strategies for the next 100 years. If he'd come chat in the bullpen with us, we could save him hours of time and get him working on something immediate."*

To a Red/Blue Extrovert, Blues seem to have little collegiality and appear to formulate strategies that may ignore immediate implementation. Your style can irritate your Blue coworkers by challenging their strategy with real-world scenarios. Slow down; explain why your plans will work. If you come to a meeting unprepared, the Blue will challenge your credibility with criticism and questions. This onslaught pressures the Red/Blue to respond with long-term considerations. The Blue appears to judge the value of your concerns by your "inability" to factor in these considerations. If overwhelmed with lots of criticisms by a Blue, *do not* take it personally or as a threat. It's actually a compliment, because it is how Blues show interest.

Negotiating Strategies

‣ Be verbally short and concise.

‣ Use "if . . . then" sentences, which are very effective.

‣ Rehearse responses that show a longer-term focus: "If I do this today, then in six months XYZ will occur." "Strategically, the problems I see are . . ."

‣ Adjust your vocabulary and use theoretical jargon, statistical data, and technical terms. To prove a proposal's worth, point out long-term benefits. Use ingenuity, logic, and witty humor to make your case.

‣ Display competence. Blues force you to be tough-minded and prepared; they need to see your competence on display.

‣ Don't react personally. Blues are hardwired for *impersonal* critical thinking.

Golds. *"I'm going to quit!" exclaims Muriel, a Red/Blue. "I make some fast, on-the-ground decisions in order to retain an important client. Then Constance (a Gold) undermines me by insisting I leave the original discount percentage in place."*

Golds are your nemesis. The rule makers and procedure setters of the world, their administrative demands just seem to slow everything down. But in order to be efficient and effective, Golds need structure. You hate when Golds drag their feet procedurally, or plan and schedule everything in advance, because it makes you feel hemmed in and controlled. When you're tardy or ill-prepared for meetings, Golds will be the first to chide you. However, they become paralyzed in a crisis and need your talents. In exchange they will organize your office, project, or company to peak efficiency.

Negotiating Strategies

‣ To ease tensions, pepper your sentences with words like "facts," "tradition," "respected," and "proven." Downplay changes, midcourse corrections, or crises.

‣ Bond over your mutual preference for concrete words and practical tasks.

‣ Commit several low-pressure, self-directed minutes each day to understanding the vocabulary of investment, costs, time lines, and budgets.

‣ Acknowledge and flatter their superior detail management; impress them with your keen observation of detail.

‣ Make a consistent effort to meet deadlines and commitments. Never change appointments or schedules if it can be helped.

Extrovert vs. Introvert

If the strategies described so far are still missing the mark, your coworker may be an Introvert. If so:

‣ Respect, don't challenge, their need to recharge their batteries with privacy. Although it will be difficult for you to understand why they prefer working alone, it's not personal.

‣ Tone down your enthusiasm; listen more.

‣ Invite them to speak, but don't force them until they've thought things through.

‣ Do not fill their pauses.

Recognize any of your coworkers in the preceding descriptions? Find more experiments in each Color Q personality's overall chapter and in Chapter 25, "Adjusting to the Workplace Styles of Others."

‣   ‣   ‣

In summary, Red/Blue Extroverts are outgoing and pragmatic, functioning best when free of tradition, emotion, and theory. You thrive on action, which is why Red/Blue Extroverts make dynamic entrepreneurs and engaging negotiators.

Spontaneous and competitive, work becomes play at every opportunity. You enjoy work teams that function like sports teams. You prefer action to conversation and dealing with short-term problems. Your endless supply of jokes and stories helps ease tense situations and gets conflicting parties to agree.

Now take these negotiating strategies and experiment on the next coworker you see!

red/backup
blue introverts

YOU'RE NOT ONLY a Red; you also have strong secondary character-istics of the Blue personality. And you have tested as a Color Q Introvert, which means you recharge your batteries by being alone rather than with people. Red/Blue Introverts reading this chapter should know that the underpinning scientific system has been researched and tested worldwide for over half a century.

Top Motivators

Cutting to the chase, you fulfill obligations, link people with resources, and inject fun into the workplace. Simplifying, saving time, and solving real problems—these are your strengths. Inwardly, you operate after reflection and analysis; outwardly, it's action and living on the edge. As an Introvert, you can work for many hours without interruption.

You are most motivated when developing special skills and expertise. Red/Blue Introverts form only 5 percent of the world's population; but, especially for unusual problems, your logical reasoning proves superior to others' approaches.

Corporate Culture—Finding the Optimal Fit

It is the responsibility of every personality to find or create their optimal work environment. Optimal cultures differ among Color Q personality types. Strengths in one company may be weaknesses elsewhere. The corporate culture itself may not be dysfunctional; for instance, Reds hate what Golds love. Conflict, sapped strength, resentment, and feelings of defeat are symptoms of poor cultural fit and can be avoided by understanding your preferences.

The Red/Blue Introvert's **most preferred work environment** emphasizes:

- Autonomy on action-oriented, practical tasks
- Informality, with minimal rules, paperwork, and supervision
- Small teams of do-it-now coworkers and little hierarchy
- Tolerance for unorthodox approaches
- Minimal social politics with objective job evaluation

If these points seem obvious to you, it means you've tested correctly. (Compare with a Gold/Green Extrovert's ideal environment.)

The Red/Blue Introvert's **least preferred environment** is characterized by:

- Lots of rules, procedures, meetings, and memos
- Micromanagement and having to wait around for things to happen
- Little appreciation for logical analysis
- Rejection for being "too critical"
- Narrow-minded, emotional, or illogical coworkers
- Little opportunity to work uninterrupted

Leveraging Executive Presence and Building Personal Brand

Red/Blue Introverts most often become leaders during crises. A gifted nego-tiator, you can make logical and difficult decisions, all critical skills during challenging times. Your leadership ambitions are more accomplishment-than status-oriented; you prefer immediate projects to long-term manage-ment. Coordinating people and tasks for maximum efficiency is your strength. Your motto: Get to the point!

> *The Red/Blue Introvert's personal leadership brand should be built around trusting your own instincts, sizing up problems, and moving in for the solution.*

A freethinking risk taker who likes to keep things simple, you will do all that is necessary to achieve results. Your fair-minded, even-tempered lead-ership empowers subordinates.

CASE STUDY 1: *The Successful Red/Blue Introvert*

Margaret Davis, Marine Corps Scholarship Foundation

Since 2009, Margaret Davis has served as president and CEO of the Marine Corps Scholarship Foundation, the nation's oldest and largest need-based scholarship organization for military children. It honors service men and women by educating their children, providing scholar-ships for post–high school education/training to sons and daughters of marines and navy corpsmen (especially those whose parents were killed or wounded in combat). Under Davis's leadership, the fund has grown rapidly and also received four stars from Charity Navigator. Her thirty-year career in nonprofit management, communications, and resource development has included positions with Washington National Cathedral, the Center for Public Leadership at Harvard's Kennedy School of Government, Ravinia Festival, and Northwestern University. In 2008, she was awarded the Department of the Navy Superior Public Service Medal.

Both her Red and Blue components are called into play at the scholar-ship foundation: "We've built a great national team of capable volunteers and staff professionals. We enjoy making an immediate difference while also benefiting those in future decades," Davis says. "Providing $6 million of scholarships each year, while also planning for today's fourth graders tomorrow, is a distinct honor."

Typical of Red/Blues, Davis makes complicated things happen: "I try to distill complex projects and recognize the resources needed while marshaling them from a variety of sources," she explains. "We work to optimize deployment of human, financial, and social capital while staying focused on achieving goals."

Davis says that "representing a critical national mission, in-person across the country, while also leading six major departments and keep-ing up with daily communication," is a continuous productivity juggling act, and "the best solution is to delegate and trust the excellent team we have to do the great job they do every day."

In using the Color Q system, Davis has learned the benefits of sur-rounding herself "with people who are different from me—especially in planning," she says. "I often need the discipline of an outside planner, someone with the ability to balance my passion and eagerness with structure and a realistic timetable."

Participating In and Managing Productive Teams

Red/Blue Introverts mediate well, energize others, and ease tensions with gentle humor. A strong self-starter who can work quickly and indepen-dently on assignments, you have much to offer small, collegial teams. A warehouse of facts and figures, you contribute efficiency and logic and quickly locate resources that keep projects on track.

You tolerate diverse work styles, except for those of overly emotional types. (See Greens under this chapter's "Political Savvy" section and follow the simple negotiating techniques.) Bottom line: You have realistic expecta-tions of others. If given enough data, processing time, and respect for your analyses, you are of great value to your team.

Communications Style

Merely adjusting one's vocabulary to align with another color's style can elicit more concise responses. Empathetic vs. objective analysis, theoretical vs. practical, structured vs. adaptable—these clashes fuel most workplace conflicts. Being able to "style shift" provides competitive advantage in negotiating, leading, and interviewing.

Red/Blue Introverts are succinct and no-nonsense. Your preferred vocabulary features words like "move," "stimulate," and "expedite." Intuitive Greens, conversely, favor abstract concepts and metaphors, emphasizing words like "values," "relationship," "feel," and "friendly." Blues, with whom you share some personality traits, prefer theoretical jargon, statistical data, and technical terms. Administrative-minded Golds respond to "facts," "tradition," "respected," and "proven." (Test and observe.)

Red/Blue Introverts are very observant and listen more than speak. You meet conflict head-on by analyzing what's wrong, viewing disagreement as constructive. You are concrete and realistic when focused on the present, and can accurately analyze many inputs when focused on the future. Style shifting occurs most easily when you are communicating with Blues and Golds; Greens will require patience.

Blind Spots

Certain blind spots are prevalent in Red/Blue Introverts; some of them will apply to you:

- Focusing on short-term rather than long-term goals

- Prolonging internal analysis

- Missing deadlines; being casual about rules or procedures valued by others

- Putting off or abandoning unpopular tasks

- Being impatient with discussions of abstract ideas

- Critiquing too quickly

Stressors That Produce Fatigue and Strife

Certain workplace conditions can stress and fatigue Red/blue Introverts. They include:

- Being micromanaged

- Colleagues who get too personal

- Lack of privacy and time to process

- Too much routine, repetitive work, or too many details

- Little control over time or decisions and tight schedules/deadlines

- Situations that defy logic

Red/Blue Introverts under *extreme* stress often overreact. The world, usually governed by logic, may suddenly seem "illogical." Digging in your heels or working harder helps you stay in control. During leisure hours you may withdraw socially to avoid the effort of managing your deep feelings.

Self-Coach Your Way to More Productive Work Relationships

Red/Blue Introverts who want to self-coach for career advancement should focus on how to logically analyze and factor in other people's feelings and procedures.

Problem Solving and Decision Making

As a Red/Blue Introvert, you should leverage your strengths, which include the ability to:

- Size up problems better than other Color Q personalities and make tough decisions.

- Build detailed models and blueprints in your head.

- Identify pragmatic solutions, eliminating waste.

- Base important decisions on facts, inner reasoning, and observation.

- Bring people and tasks together in a way that overcomes obstacles and inspires action.

Strategies to Improve Effectiveness When Challenged

Interpersonal challenges detract from productivity. Here are self-coaching strategies for your biggest challenges:

▸ *Resistance to rules and bureaucracy.* You believe, rightly, in the value of brainstorming when problem solving. You chafe when structure overrides implementing ingenious solutions. Work within the system; develop supportive allies.

▸ *Abandoning tasks that bore you.* When it seems logical to abandon a task, have you factored in how it will impact coworkers or the company's mission? If not, you haven't sized up the whole problem; your decision will be faulty.

▸ *Going to important meetings and expecting to "wing it."* Midcourse corrections are your forte, but being unprepared in front of colleagues and superiors can have career-altering consequences.

▸ *Emotion-based challenges to your commonsense solutions.* "It makes so much sense," you think. "Why can't they just get with the program and drop the irrelevant emotions?" A Green can help you decipher the additional input and wisdom that emotion-focused coworkers contribute.

▸ *Mandatory networking, social occasions, and small talk.* You itch to leave and do something real. So, set numerical goals—talk to ten people, distribute eight business cards. Then indulge your need for freedom and action . . . perhaps extending an invitation to someone you've just met. Build business relationships around your fun-loving side, despite your preference for solitary activities.

When challenged, plan each day; prioritize a few weekly goals. Find a nonjudgmental mentor whose strengths are people skills and long-term thinking. Exciting, hands-on activities (mountain climbing, deep-sea diving, surfing, tinkering mechanically, whatever sounds good to you) will help you blow off steam. Also relaxing are watching action movies, reading how-to books, fixing things, landscaping, renovating, model-building, fine dining, playing chess, or listening to good music. You need action, but also rest and privacy.

- -

CASE STUDY 2: When a Career Isn't Working

Operations vice president Toby Sanchez eased his BMW into his reserved spot at Montgomery Manufacturing and broke into his usual Monday morning sweat. Although he had been with the firm for only a year, he immediately recognized that it faced significant challenges from technologically advanced competitors.

"Toby, we've reviewed your memorandum," said the CEO in their weekly prep meeting that morning. "Your facts and figures make a good case . . . but you can't redirect a ship this big that fast. We've always done things this way. We'll keep an eye on the marketplace, but we don't feel the need to institute your recommendations this year. . . ." Toby stopped listening at this point; Reds chafe under management that resists change.

"Didn't go for it, did they?" his secretary said when he stormed into his office. "'Stability is efficiency,' my old boss in sales used to say."

Toby was desperately in need of his first vacation in a year. "Did you book that flight to San Francisco next week?" His secretary handed him the tickets.

At a Napa Valley wine tasting, Toby met a young man named Philip Norton, who was trying to get a tech start-up off the ground—one that focused on computer-driven prosthetic devices. "We really need someone who is good at both the hands-on and solving theoretical problems," Norton said. It was just what Red/Blue Toby craved!

"I'll send you a resume," Toby promised. Within a month, he joined them as VP of operations, relishing the hands-on, the problem solving . . . and the responsiveness. Five years later when the firm was acquired, Toby sold his stock options and is set for life at age 38.

- -

Political Savvy—Making Your Words Count

A valuable part of the Color Q system lies in learning how to harness the Green's intuitive, people-focused strengths, the Gold's detailed concrete thinking and administrative talent, and the Blue's strategic abstract thinking to your advantage. Here's how to engage irritating coworkers as powerful political allies.

Greens. *"My coworker Jennifer (a Green) thinks we can double company revenues in three years by merging customer service with sales and being tops in customer satisfaction," says Wayne (a Red/Blue). "But she has no ideas for addressing the current price disparities between us and our competition."*

The Green is the most people-oriented of the four primary Color Q personalities. As a Red/Blue Introvert, your style can irritate a Green by being too focused on logic, objects, and the present moment, with little focus on vision or long-term consequences. You both keep your options open as long as possible before deciding, but Greens gather emotional feedback whereas you just want the facts. You are irritated by their hand-holding and nurturing when a crisis is afoot. As a result, your style may seem blunt or dismissive of the Green's concerns. Greens won't confront you, but they'll grow cold and unsupportive.

Negotiating Strategies

▸ Take time to establish rapport with a Green. Because you prefer to share experiences rather than emotions and social niceties sometimes seem unnecessary to you, Greens help you navigate the occasional negative consequences of your detachment.

▸ Factor in their values when making decisions, to ensure their political buy-in.

▸ Check in with them about how you're perceived. Their feedback will be gentle and tactful.

▸ Collaborate with at least one Green in your office, and let this coworker interface with the team. Whereas you dislike collaboration, Greens adore it.

▸ Be patient with the Green's abstract, long-term thinking. This prevents future problems, allowing you to concentrate on needed mid-course corrections and real crises.

Blues. *"My boss, Mr. Taylor (a Blue/Gold), called an urgent meeting with fifteen minutes notice. Then he's all over me for 'winging it,'" says Shirley (a Red/Blue).*

To a Red/Blue Introvert, Blues appear to put all their formidable mental energy into creating strategies that may ignore immediate implementation concerns. Your style can irritate Blues because you challenge their overall strategy with real-world scenarios. Slow down, explain why your plans will work, and expect to be challenged in return. If you come to a meeting unprepared, the Blue will challenge your credibility with critiques and questions. This onslaught pressures the Red/Blue's preference to focus on current problems rather than long-term strategies. The Blue appears to judge the value of your concerns by your "inability" to factor in long-term consequences. If overwhelmed with criticisms by a Blue, *do not* take the challenge personally or as a threat. It's actually a compliment, because this is how they show interest.

Negotiating Strategies

▸ Be verbally short and concise.

▸ Use "if ... then" sentences, which are very effective.

▸ Rehearse responses that have a longer-term focus: "Strategically, the problems I see are ..." "If I do this now, in six months we'll also have to do XYZ."

▸ Adjust your vocabulary and use theoretical jargon, statistical data, and technical terms. To prove a proposal's worth, point out long-term benefits. Use ingenuity, logic, and witty humor to make your case.

▸ Display competence. Blues force you to be tough-minded and prepared; they need to see your competence on display.

▸ Don't react personally. Blues are hardwired for impersonal critical thinking.

Golds. *"Honore (a Gold) drives me nuts," says Hector (a Red/Blue). "I finished my project and she made me totally redo it so her paperwork would be perfect. Three extra hours of work, and it'll just sit in the files gathering dust!"*

Golds are your nemesis. The rule makers and procedure setters of the world, their administrative demands seem perpetually at odds with getting things done. You hate when Golds impose procedures, plan and schedule everything in advance, or push a single way of doing something. This makes you feel hemmed in and controlled. When you skirt procedures or "wing it" at meetings, Golds will be the first to chide you. But in order to be effective, Golds need structure and guidelines. When paralyzed by crisis, they need you; in exchange, they will organize your office, project, or company to peak efficiency.

Negotiating Strategies

- To ease tensions, sprinkle your sentences with words like "facts," "tradition," "respected," and "proven." Downplay changes, mid-course corrections, or crises.

- Bond over your mutual preference for concrete words, practical/sequential tasks, and keen observation of detail.

- Commit several low-pressure, self-directed minutes each day to fulfilling procedures. Practice the vocabulary of investment, costs, time lines, and budgets.

- Acknowledge and flatter their superior detail management.

- Make a consistent effort to meet deadlines and commitments, and *never* change appointments or schedules if it can be helped.

Extrovert vs. Introvert

If the previous strategies are still missing the mark, you may be dealing with an Extrovert. If so:

- Recognize that it will be difficult for you to understand why they must constantly be around people and how they can enjoy noisy environments. But respect, don't challenge, their need to recharge their batteries by interacting with others—they need this the way you need alone time.

‣ Ask questions; share experiences.

‣ Listen closely, but interject verbally often.

‣ Volunteer to handle tasks for them that require working alone. You'll benefit from their gratitude—and the solitude.

Recognize any of your coworkers in the preceding descriptions? Learn more about them by reading each Color Q personality type's overall chapter and then Chapter 25, "Adjusting to the Workplace Styles of Others."

‣　　‣　　‣

In summary, Red/Blue Introverts are reserved and independent, more interested in action than talk. You operate out of curiosity and impulse, supported by your keen and detailed powers of observation. Red/Blue Introverts prefer working with real things and tangible products. In business and finance, you will rise high by combining a no-nonsense approach to facts and figures with a "let's give it a try" openness to new strategies.

In a nutshell, Red/Blue Introverts must continuously balance their logic with empathy and honor their needs for privacy and solitude.

13

red/backup green extroverts

YOU'RE NOT ONLY a Red; you also have strong secondary characteristics of the Green personality. And you have tested as a Color Q Extrovert, which means you recharge your batteries by being with people, rather than being alone. Red/Green Extroverts form 8 percent of the world population.

As an Extrovert, working alone for long periods is frustrating. You'll generate variety or action, even if disruptive. Discuss with your boss your needs for physical movement and people contact to be productive.

You are likely reading this book to please someone. This chapter should credibly confirm who you are (if not, retest). It also will give you activities, tools, and experiments to try out with challenging coworkers.

Top Motivators

During hiring or review, negotiate for assignments or responsibilities that really motivate you. These motivators include:

▸ The chance to tackle real-world problems where you see results

▸ Variety and action

▸ Crisis-handling (which you do brilliantly) or troubleshooting responsibility

▸ Meeting new people and sharing experiences

▸ Work that's balanced with humor and celebration

Corporate Culture—Finding the Optimal Fit

Want a more optimal workplace environment? Conflict, sapped strength, resentment, and feelings of defeat are symptoms of poor cultural fit. Optimal cultures differ among Color Q personality types. Strengths in one company may be unneeded elsewhere. The corporate culture itself may not be dysfunctional; for instance, Reds hate what Golds love. Years of frustration can be avoided by understanding your preferences.

The Red/Green Extrovert's **most preferred work environment** emphasizes:

▸ Occasional, stimulating crises and change

▸ Adaptable, friendly, fun coworkers and cooperative teams

▸ Concurrent short-term projects and rewards for fast-paced work

▸ Use of expertise to help in real ways

▸ Comfortable, attractive surroundings

▸ Physical freedom with minimal paperwork or supervision

▸ Independence to act on what you observe (i.e., rule-bending tolerated)

If these points seem obvious, it means you've tested correctly. (Compare with a Gold/Blue Introvert's ideal environment.)

The Red/Green Extrovert's **least preferred environment** is defined by:

- Long-term projects, with lots of planning for potential rather than real problems

- Bossy people who insist on having their way

- Hierarchy, with meetings and memos that bog down action

- Lots of details, repetitive tasks, rules, and procedures

- Tight schedules, with no control over decisions (being forbidden to take action)

- Humorless coworkers and an overly serious atmosphere

Leveraging Executive Presence and Building Personal Brand

One of the critical tasks of a Red/Green Extrovert manager is to build one's executive reputation or "brand." While abstract, brand building requires concrete actions. These actions empower you to achieve tangible goals by increasing your internal influence and also to market yourself externally when necessary.

> *The Red/Green Extrovert's leadership brand should be built around your superior ability to size up situations, inspire staff, and achieve results now (especially during project or business start-ups).*

Astute and independent, you are a hands-off manager who even now wants to stop reading this book and get out and do! You'll build your brand by doing just that. Here are some concrete brand-building actions for Red/Green Extroverts:

- Troubleshooting (high-profile)

- Mobilizing others' skills, especially during a crisis, project start-ups, or change initiatives

▸ Making a difference in the world through negotiation, mediation, and risk-taking

▸ Keeping things moving with humor and offering hands-on assistance

Overall, you are not keen to manage a large organization. When your department reaches a certain size, you may want to consider moving to a smaller unit.

CASE STUDY 1: Two Successful Red/Green Extroverts

Consider first the example of Steve, an investment banker who enjoys the fast pace and exhilaration of his work. As a Red/Green, however, he has a strong artistic side. With four children in college, leaving his job was not an option. Once he discovered a talent for making jewelry, however, he found a way to express it. He creates pieces on weekends, showcases them on the Web, and supplies a small store in his Long Island community. With typical adaptability, he can now satisfy his major financial and creative needs.

Hugh Heisler, Heisler, Feldman, McCormick & Garrow

Heisler is a Red/Green Extrovert lawyer whose Green side has led him to cases that inspire social change and whose Red side gives him the skills needed to win cases. Those skills are critical, because Heisler does not charge his clients. "We provide free representation to low-income clients in civil legal matters in Massachusetts," explains Heisler. This is not just his pro bono work; it's all he does. He and his five associates at the sixteen-year-old firm of Heisler, Feldman, McCormick & Garrow handle what are known as "fee shifting provisions" cases. They make money when the other side pays their fees . . . if they win. In recognition of their contributions, the firm has been the recipient of several awards including the John Quincy Adams Pro Bono Publico Award from the Supreme Judicial Court of Massachusetts.

Reds work well under pressure, but Heisler almost didn't become a lawyer because of it. As only a Red can pull off, he graduated from law

school one day before getting his college degree! "I had completed all my college course work, but not my thesis. As I was finishing with my law studies, I saw I'd better hustle. I contacted my old professor, who said get the thesis in and I will do the paperwork. And I did," Heisler explains.

"I like the give-and-take that occurs in negotiating," he says, typical of a Red. "Most results are achieved through negotiations and mediation. But we also are active trial lawyers; I enjoy being in front of a judge making legal arguments."

Heisler brings his Red mediation abilities to his office as well as the courtroom. "I have tended to be the person to whom others look to resolve conflict," he says. "I try to find common ground, bring fun to the office and everything I do. I keep things light and positive."

Participating In and Managing Productive Teams

On a team, you are fun-loving, fast-paced, cooperative, realistic, and a skilled negotiator, troubleshooter, and excellent resource manager. The Red/Green's special talents include:

▸ Getting conflicting parties to agree

▸ Keeping meetings to the point

▸ Revealing new opportunities

▸ Bringing excitement to the team

Communications Style

Adjusting your words to align with another color's style elicits powerful positive responses. Empathetic vs. objective analysis, theoretical vs. practical, structured vs. adaptable—these clashes fuel most workplace conflicts. Being able to "style shift" brings exciting competitive advantages in negotiations, managing, and interviewing.

Focused on the "now," you think on your feet and speak without hidden agendas. You get to the point, then act. You have a preferred vocabulary of action words: *move, stimulate,* and *expedite.* Conversely, Greens (with whom you share some personality traits) like abstract concepts, metaphors, and analogies, emphasizing words like "values," "relationship," "feel," and "friendly." Blues prefer theoretical jargon, statistical data, and technical terms. Golds respond to "facts," "tradition," "respected," and "proven."

Red/Greens are noted for tact, exuberance, and humor. You persuade others by developing rapport and sharing personal stories. Style shifting for you means paying more attention to the emotions, strategies, and the rules of others. You key in to your colleagues' preferred style and then make them laugh. When you are stymied by rules or abstract thinking, understand the anxieties of those who impose them and seek solutions.

Blind Spots

These blind spots are prevalent in Red/Green Extroverts (only some of them will apply to you):

- Difficulty seeing the "big picture"

- Emphasizing short-term vs. long-term

- Going for the quick fix

- Being too literal and missing the subtext

- Being casual about rules, authority, commitments, and deadlines

- Chafing when following procedures and/or being held accountable

Stressors That Produce Fatigue and Strife

Certain workplace conditions stress and fatigue Red/Green Extroverts. They include:

- Working alone

- Inactivity and spinning wheels

- Too much speculative, long-range thinking

- Loss of professional or personal relationships

- Having too few options

‣ Coworkers who are inflexible, critical, unrealistic, and/or indecisive

‣ Financial constraints

Under *extreme* stress, Red/Green Extroverts experience pessimism about the future, diminished adaptability, and/or indecisiveness. Negotiate responsibilities that allow movement and socializing.

Self-Coach Your Way to More Productive Work Relationships

Red/Green Extroverts benefit by becoming more adept at handling the demands of rules, long-term strategy, and other people's emotions.

Problem Solving and Decision Making

The Red/Green Extrovert has these strengths:

‣ Reacts quickly under pressure

‣ Makes keen observations and realistically sizes up situations

‣ Trusts own instincts; goes with gut feel

‣ Negotiates skillfully, sometimes beyond rules

‣ Uses humor to ease tensions

Strategies to Improve Effectiveness When Challenged

Interpersonal challenges detract from productivity. Here are self-coaching activities to help solve your biggest challenges:

‣ *Resistance to rules and bureaucracy.* You believe, rightly, in the value of sizing up a problem and applying realistic solutions. You chafe when structure overrides practicality. Curry favor with the Golds who implement procedures; develop allies who'll help you accomplish your goals.

‣ *Having to work alone.* Delegate these tasks to Introverts (who'll thank you for the alone time). Negotiate working in open environments.

- *Loss of freedom—being tied down or controlled.* You're tempted to do something to undermine those who inhibit you. Minimal work or subtle sabotage may feel satisfying but ultimately will boomerang. Instead, hit the gym at lunch hour for an invigorating workout. Negotiate for more freedom (using this book to prove the company will benefit).

- *Having to develop long-term strategies or budgets.* Do these tasks in small steps over time, then reward yourself by doing something enjoyable. Mountain climbing, racing, skydiving, motorcycling, deep-sea diving, surfing, hunting, traveling, playing music, dancing . . . if it sounds good, do it!

- *Not having control over decisions.* Realistic role-playing, preferably with a strategy-oriented Blue, works well. Talk with others who've faced similar dilemmas; swap real-life solutions.

- *Emotional reactions that cloud logic.* Find a Green mentor. View emotions as "if . . . then" equations (e.g., "if I do this, then he'll feel this and respond like that.")

When dealing with challenges, convert pessimism to realism by exploring facts. Avoid jobs that emphasize long-term strategy and routine. Young Red/Green Extroverts often change jobs every few years until they find the right mix of freedom and crisis-handling responsibility.

- -

CASE STUDY 2: When a Career Isn't Working

Bruce Gregory's career as a six-figure risk manager for a prominent insurance company looked great—from the outside.

Inside his well-appointed office, Bruce (a crisis-loving Red) was bored. He'd done his job too well. Instead of being a dynamic crisis manager, Bruce felt like a babysitter watching a well-behaved charge.

It was time for a change. But the golden handcuffs were hard to shake off. Restoring his 1960s era Porsche 356 evenings and weekends was his only hands-on outlet for stress.

One morning, Bruce saw a big red For Sale sign in the showroom of the antique car garage where he had purchased his Porsche. Coming to a screeching halt, Bruce felt a needed surge of adrenaline. Reds thrive on excitement, and he hurried in to talk to the owner.

Two months later, Bruce had leased (with an option to buy) the garage. He shares management responsibilities with the head mechanic while keeping his day job. The stimulation of this new venture, vital to Reds, is enough to keep Bruce at his risk management job until retirement in six years.

Political Savvy—Making Your Words Count

A valuable part of the Color Q system lies in learning how to harness the Green's marketing and people skills, the Gold's administrative talent, and the Blue's strategic and theoretical thinking to your advantage. Engage irritating coworkers as powerful political allies.

Greens. *"If talking could solve this new challenge from our competition, Harry (a Green) would have had it licked by last month!"* says Ruby (a Red/Green). *"He keeps asking how customers are going to react. I say, float a pilot project to get our new beta design out there. Then you'll find out!"*

The Green is the most people-oriented of the four primary Color Q personalities. Their abstract visions and long-term orientation make them seem, to you, eccentric and out of touch with reality. Reds can irritate a Green by being too focused on the present without considering long-term consequences. Greens find it exasperating that you have a hard time verbalizing your feelings; they'll recognize them before you do! But you dislike hand-holding when a crisis is afoot, which may seem blunt or dismissive of the Green's concerns. While Greens won't confront you, they'll become cold and unsupportive. Ask a Green to help you navigate the things below the surface that influence responses.

Negotiating Strategies

‣ Be patient with the Green's abstract visions and long-term thinking. They'll prevent a lot of problems, allowing you to concentrate on true surprises, midcourse corrections, and crises.

- Check in with them about how you're perceived. Their feedback will be gentle and tactful.

- Give them step-by-step directions when you want them to do something here and now. That's because Greens are future-oriented, only visiting the present moment occasionally.

- Factor in their feelings (with "if . . . then" equations) when making decisions, to ensure their political buy-in.

- Assert yourself. Because of your desire to please, you sometimes won't assert yourself. Greens are most pleased when you share what you're really feeling, good or bad. Take a risk; they'll reward you.

Blues. *"Jason (a Blue) and I make a good team—usually. He's the thinker; I'm the doer. But he hates it when I improvise midcourse solutions," says Nick (a Red/Green).*

To a Red/Green Extrovert, Blues appear to put all their formidable mental energy into creating strategies that may ignore immediate implementation. Reds can irritate a Blue by challenging the overall strategy with real-world scenarios. Slow down; explain why your plans will work. Blues can show you how to avoid mistakes others have made. If you come to a meeting unprepared, Blue will question, criticize, and challenge your credibility. This onslaught pressures the Red/Green to respond with long-term thinking. The Blue appears to judge the value of your concerns by your "inability" to factor in long-term consequences. If overwhelmed by Blue's criticisms, do not take the challenge personally or as a threat. It's actually a compliment; this is how they show interest.

Negotiating Strategies

- Be verbally short and concise.

- Use "if . . . then" sentences, which are very effective.

- Rehearse responses that show a longer-term focus: "Strategically, the problems I see are. . . ." "If our budget is only $100,000 for the year, which additional funds cover crises?"

- Adjust your vocabulary to use theoretical jargon, statistical data, and technical terms. To prove a proposal's worth, point out several long-term benefits. Use ingenuity, logic, and witty humor (easy for you) to make your case.

- Display competence. Blues force you to be tough-minded and pre-pared; they need to see your competence on display.

- Don't react personally or bluntly. Blues are hardwired for imper-sonal critical thinking.

Golds. *"I worked for hours on the script for our sales presentation," says Christina (a Red/Green). "I worked in five-minute segments of free time for responding to client questions; sometimes you have to go off-book and wing it to keep them on the hook. Then in our planning meeting, Stu (a Gold) ignored my hard work and criticized the free-time segments! I'm really frustrated."*

Golds are your nemesis. The rule makers and procedure setters of the world, their administrative demands seem perpetually at odds with getting things done. But in order to be effective, Golds need more structure than you. You hate when Golds drag their feet procedurally or plan everything in advance. It makes you feel hemmed in and controlled. When you're tardy or ill-prepared for meetings, Golds will be the first to chide you. However, they become paralyzed in a crisis and need your talents; in exchange they'll organize your office, project, or company to peak efficiency.

Negotiating Strategies

- To ease tensions, use words like "facts," "tradition," "respected," and "proven." Downplay changes, midcourse corrections, or crises.

- Bond over your mutual preference for concrete words and practical tasks.

- Commit several low-pressure, self-directed minutes each day to the vocabulary of investment, costs, time lines, and budgets.

- Acknowledge and flatter their superior detail management; impress them with your keen observational skills.

▶ Make a consistent effort to meet deadlines and commitments; never change appointments or schedules if it can be helped.

Extrovert vs. Introvert

If the aforementioned strategies are still missing the mark, you may be dealing with an Introvert. If so:

▶ It will be difficult for you to understand why they shun interaction and prefer working alone. Respect, don't challenge, their need to recharge their batteries with privacy—it's not personal.

▶ Tone down your enthusiasm; listen more.

▶ Invite them to speak, but don't force them to speak until they've thought things through.

▶ Do not fill their pauses.

Recognize any coworkers in the preceding descriptions? Explore further tools by skimming each Color Q personality's overall chapter and then reading Chapter 25, "Adjusting to the Workplace Styles of Others."

▶   ▶   ▶

In summary, Red/Green Extroverts are fun, vivacious, cheerful people who are always ready to see the brighter side of life. You're at your best when around people and juggling several activities at once.

Realistic and pragmatic, you trust what you experience directly and accept things as they are. You try to understand people rather than control them. As a result, you are often the best at getting conflicting parties to agree.

Take some of these negotiating strategies and go experiment on the next coworker you see!

14

red/backup green introverts

YOU'RE NOT ONLY a Red; you also have strong secondary character-istics of the Green personality. And you have tested as a Color Q Introvert, which means you recharge your batteries by being alone rather than with people. Red/Green Introverts likely are reading this book only under orders or to please someone else. But this chapter provides step-by-step activities, tools, and fun experiments to try with coworkers.

Top Motivators
Here are your greatest motivators:

- Acting from inner values

- Physical and decision-making freedom

- Working behind the scenes to improve efficiency and produce positive impact

- Variety, flexibility, exploration

- Harmony

As an Introvert, you're less productive in open offices; small, collegial teams work best for you. You focus on the well-being of other people, often forfeiting time alone to recharge. Red/Green Introverts form only 8 percent of the world's population, but your strong inner values have shaped entire cultures.

Corporate Culture—Finding the Optimal Fit

It is the responsibility of every personality to find or create their optimal work environment. Optimal cultures differ among Color Q personality types. Strengths in one company are unneeded elsewhere. The corporate culture itself may not be dysfunctional; it's just that, for instance, Reds hate what Golds love. Conflict, sapped strength, resentment, and feelings of defeat are symptoms of poor cultural fit and can be avoided by understanding your preferences.

The Red/Green Introvert's **most preferred work environment** emphasizes:

- Minimal paperwork or supervision

- Attractive private work space

- Supportive, courteous coworkers

- Work on tangible products with immediate results

- Rapport with a hands-off boss who provides flexibility and security

- Immediate responses to occasional crises

If these points seem obvious, it means you've tested correctly. (Compare with a Gold/Blue Extrovert's ideal environment.)

The Red/Green Introvert's **least preferred environment** is characterized by:

- Challenges to inner values

- Emphasis on strategic long-term thinking

- Micromanagement (so worker has no control over time, decisions, or privacy)

- Noisy, critical, or aggressive coworkers and ongoing conflicts

- Overly serious atmosphere that discourages humor and emphasizes details

Leveraging Executive Presence and Building Personal Brand

One of the critical tasks of a Red/Green Introvert manager is to build one's executive reputation or "brand." Your brand empowers you to achieve tangible goals and increase influence, as well as the ability to market yourself externally when necessary. Brand building requires concrete actions.

> *To build your leadership brand, lead by example and excite people about their mission. You shine during times of change or crisis, trusting instinct, sizing up problems, and implementing solutions.*

While sensitive to people, you are especially good at keeping meetings short and to the point. Go with your preference to participate in a management team or to coordinate rather than lead.

- -
CASE STUDY 1: *Successful Red/Green Introverts*

Christopher L. Dutton, Vermont Electric Power Company
Chris Dutton is a Red/Green Introvert who holds the title of president and chief executive officer of a major utility—Vermont Electric Power Company (VELCO). Previously, he held the same position at Green Mountain Power and was a practicing attorney in Canton, Ohio.

*Chris has achieved his position through his creative thinking and con-
cern for how business decisions in the utility industry impact on people.
VELCO's board chairman, Robert Clarke, says Dutton is "recognized
across the state as an innovative and thoughtful leader."*

*Chris started his career as a trial lawyer. He liked the work, he says,
"because each case is different." Red/Green Introverts crave challenge
and nonrepetitious work, especially if they can be involved on a personal
level. He further makes a positive impact on people through his volunteer
work, which is substantial. He has served as director of the Chittenden
County United Way as well as the Flynn Center for the Performing Arts.
He is chair of the Vermont Telecommunications Authority and has served
on the board of the Vermont Electric Power Company since 1997.*

John Sawyer, Chon Resources

*Red/Greens love tools, mastering them quickly and well. In the 1970s
John Sawyer found that he was immediately able to use his company's
first computer and explain it to others. When their programmer disappeared in the middle of a project, John finished the job. Two years later
he joined a software vendor. Today he provides full-time technical support for users of enterprise applications; on weekends, he is a web
developer for his company, Chon Resources, specializing in WordPress,
a content management system.*

*"I am good at troubleshooting computer problems and software
issues," says John. "I'm good at explaining technical information to non-
technical users [and] also at simplifying complex information."*

*Very typical of a Red, John finds rigid deadlines stressful, which he
handles by working with a local animal shelter and "interacting with my
own three rescued dogs." (Reds have deep affinity for animals.)*

*As to the future? "I don't strategize much," says John, again a classic
Red response. "I just take it day by day."*

Participating In and Managing Productive Teams

Red/Green Introverts are productive team members—fulfilling obligations,
linking people with resources, and injecting fun into the workplace. You
value harmony, mediate well, energize others, and ease tension with gentle

humor. You want to simplify, save time, and solve real problems, not indulge in power plays. When conflict arises, you are often the team conscience.

Communications Style

Merely adjusting one's vocabulary to align with another Color Q personality's style can elicit powerful positive responses. Empathetic vs. objective analysis, theoretical vs. practical, structured vs. adaptable—these clashes fuel most workplace conflicts. Being able to "style shift" brings tangible advantages in negotiations, managing, and interviewing.

Red/Green Introverts want to hear all perspectives, ask questions, and get to the point. Developing rapport is important, but you'd rather act than talk. Your preferred vocabulary features action verbs like "move," "motivate," and "expedite." Greens (with whom you share some personality traits) like abstract concepts, metaphors, and analogies, emphasizing words like "values," "relationship," "feel," and "friendly." Blues prefer theoretical jargon, statistical data, and technical terms. Golds respond to "facts," "tradition," "respected," and "proven."

Red/Green Introverts are calm, quiet listeners who focus on the present and remember details. You convince others by being straightforward and sharing personal stories. Style shifting for you means paying attention to the emotions, strategies, and rules of others. You assess your colleague's preferred style and then emphasize similarities. When frustrated, attempt to understand the other person's motivating anxieties and address them directly.

Blind Spots

Certain blind spots are prevalent in Red/Green Introverts (although only some of them will apply to you):

- Taking on too much, then losing interest
- Investigating too many perspectives before acting
- Finding logical argument difficult
- Being too trusting and unwilling to challenge others
- Being casual about rules, procedures, and deadlines
- Finding it difficult to envision long-term consequences

Stressors That Produce Fatigue and Strife

The following workplace conditions can stress and fatigue Red/Green Introverts:

- Bossy people who override your inner values

- Pressures to make decisions while considering only long-range objectives

- Too much interaction with others

- Lots of routine, repetitive work, or details

- Lack of privacy

Red/Green Introverts under *extreme* stress can become hypersensitive, confused, or unable to focus. Sometimes you'll be self-critical; other times, blunt or moralistic. In leisure hours you may fear the worst or go into isolation because of emotional exhaustion.

Self-Coach Your Way to More Productive Work Relationships

The primary focus of the self-coaching Red/Green Introvert should be on how to handle challenges to inner values from a core of strength and confidence.

Problem Solving and Decision Making

The Red/Green Introvert has these strengths:

- Prefers immediate problems over long-term challenges

- Sizes up problems and seeks pragmatic solutions

- Tempers values with practicality

- Operates outside procedures and can be adaptable

- Decides quickly once all inputs are evaluated

Strategies to Improve Effectiveness When Challenged

Interpersonal challenges detract from productivity. Here are self-coaching strategies for your biggest challenges:

- *Resistance to structure, rules, and bureaucracy.* You believe, rightly, in the value of pragmatic solutions and chafe when procedures override your ability to implement. Work within the system; develop allies who'll help you accomplish your goals.

- *Standing tough, then backing down.* When others barrage you with logic, it causes you to doubt your gut instincts. If your gut says stay put, argue with pros and cons.

- *Having to work in large teams or open offices.* Ask to work on smaller subcommittees. Negotiate a private work space . . . you'll never feel comfortable without one.

- *Rebelling against corrective feedback.* Ask the challenger to be more positive; redirect your anger into some physical activity, for example, a gym workout.

- *Being the center of attention.* Attention may make you freeze or downplay your strengths. But careers are made or broken at these moments. Role-play confident responses to avoid lost opportunities.

- *Having to make long-range plans or decisions.* (You'll need practice here because long-range thinking is not a Red/Green's natural talent. Start with "if . . . then" statements; think one day, one week, one month, one year into the future. Get a Blue mentor.

When dealing with challenges, stay physically active or create new experiences to keep your batteries charged. Use long swims or marathon runs to refocus on your values. You may need to temporarily downplay helping others in order to satisfy your own needs. Prioritize your need for privacy and thought-processing time.

CASE STUDY 2: When a Career Isn't Working

Timothy R. is a Renaissance man who dropped out of engineering school because he "preferred to do hard physical work at that age" and ultimately worked his way up to overseeing close to 600 workers on $80 million construction projects. A typical Red, he was energized by the pressures, crises, and hands-on work. "I loved bringing in projects on time and on cost," he says. When a motorcycle accident laid him up for a few months, "I hated it," he says.

Reds are driven by deeply held core values, anchoring them even as their lives seem outwardly chaotic. Tim felt very strongly that corners should not be cut just to meet deadlines and that workers should be treated fairly. Typically he would hold his tongue about offending practices until, he says, "I would just unload on my boss, making my position therefore untenable." A classic Red/Green Introvert, Tim was often the team conscience.

But Tim's skills were recognized, and he made good money in a series of projects. One opportunity led him to an old master carpenter, who recognized in Tim the architectural appreciation needed to work on England's oldest buildings. "Forget construction. You should be a carpenter," he told Tim. It didn't pay much, but it was deeply rewarding work. Tim sourced materials in nearby forests and "basically lived in the eighteenth century doing specialized tasks with hand tools." Performing skilled labor mostly on one's own with a respected boss is especially fulfilling for Red/Green Introverts.

A turning point came when Tim was diagnosed with cancer and told that he might have only two years to live. "That started me thinking about what I really wanted to do with my life," he recalls. He sold his house and started traveling. Always intrigued with making parts for vintage motorcycles, he took some machinist courses. "But there was no work in England," so he traveled to America, where he purchased an old Indian motorcycle. Fixing it took him to the doorstep of one of the country's premiere Indian restorers. Tim gladly apprenticed himself to another respected boss "who is good at constructive criticism."

A typical Red/Green Introvert whose inner values have always guided him, Tim currently enjoys the ability to work mostly on his own for long periods, doing skilled physical labor. He knows he will have to move on and worries he "might have to take on a real job." Always focused on his passions, he seems unaware that he is the envy of many office-bound peers.

Political Savvy—Making Your Words Count

A valuable part of the Color Q system lies in learning how to negotiate the Green's marketing and people skills, the Gold's administrative talent, and the Blue's strategic, theoretical thinking to your advantage. Engage irritating coworkers as powerful political allies.

Greens. *"My boss (a Green) tells me I have to start thinking before I act. I do think about how to achieve my goal by doing X now. But he says I have to think about future impact. That's impossible; things change daily," says a puzzled Roy (a Red/Green).*

Greens are the most people-oriented of the four primary Color Q personalities. Their abstract, long-term visions make them seem, to you, eccentric and out of touch with reality. Reds can irritate a Green by being too focused on the present moment without concern for long-term consequences. Greens find it exasperating when you can't verbalize your feelings, and will often do it for you. But you dismiss the nurturing stuff when a crisis is afoot. As a result, your style may seem blunt or disrespectful of the Green's concerns. Greens won't directly confront you, but they'll become cold and unsupportive. Ask a Green to help you navigate the subtext that influences outcomes.

Negotiating Strategies

▸ Be patient with the Green's long-term thinking. Greens can help prevent a lot of problems, allowing you to concentrate on midcourse corrections and real crises.

▸ Ask them how you're perceived. Their feedback will be gentle and tactful.

- Give them step-by-step directions when you need immediate action, because Greens are future-oriented, visiting the present moment only occasionally.

- Factor in their values (with "if . . . then" equations) before making decisions, to ensure their political buy-in.

- Assert yourself. Greens are most pleased when you share your feelings, good or bad. You may avoid asserting yourself out of concern for showing thoughtfulness. Take a risk; Greens will reward you.

Blues. *"Is it not logical to stick with a strategy that took a month to develop?" says Eliza (a Blue) critically, to which Sam (a Red/Green) replies: "Is it not necessary to change course when your biggest client's needs change?"*

To a Red/Green Introvert, Blues appear to put all their formidable mental energy into creating strategies that may ignore the impact on workers and customers. Your style can irritate a Blue by focusing on people and crises rather than overall strategy. "I rough out a schedule, then adapt," says Tim R. "I'm better at panic management." Lack of strategy, in the Blue's mind, must be challenged with criticism and questions. This onslaught pressures the Red/Green to argue logically. The Blue appears to judge the value of your concerns by your "inability" to apply detached logic. If overwhelmed by challenges from a Blue, do not take it personally or as a threat. It's actually a compliment; this is how they show interest.

Negotiating Strategies

- Be verbally short and concise.

- Use "if . . . then" sentences, which are very effective.

- Rehearse firm, effective responses: "Strategically, the problems I see are . . ." or "If you see customer relations as secondary, then how should we deal with account cancellations?"

- Adjust your vocabulary and use theoretical jargon, statistical data, and technical terms. To prove a proposal's worth, emphasize long-term benefits. Make the case with ingenuity, logic, and wit.

▶ Display competence. Blues force you to be tough-minded and firm; they need to see your competence and follow-through on display.

▶ Don't react personally or feel intimidated by their logic. Blues are hardwired for impersonal critical thinking.

Golds. *"You're spending too much time and money at the pub with clients,"* *says sales manager Alex (a Gold). "I rarely close a deal anywhere else, sir. My* *prospects are relaxed and receptive there," replies (Red/Green) sales rep Dirk.*

Always balance your team with a Gold; you need their detail management skills. You'll prefer Gold/Greens. Gold/Blues are another matter. More authoritarian and less patient, they view people-first styles as soft. Red/Greens can irritate all Golds by being too focused on people impact, treating accountability or budgeting as secondary. This makes Golds critical and bossy. Their communication style is much more impersonal, which can erupt into confrontation. If a Gold/Blue challenges you, provide step-by-step plans. (Create them in order to help the people who will implement them.)

Negotiating Strategies

▶ To ease tensions, use words like "facts," "tradition," "respected," and "proven."

▶ Make procedures a comfort zone so that you can "talk the talk" with Golds. Respect their need for structure and rules.

▶ Commit several low-pressure, self-directed minutes each day to focusing on the vocabulary of business plans, investment, costs, time lines, and budgets.

▶ Acknowledge and flatter their superior detail management capabilities, especially when they perform your detail work.

Extrovert vs. Introvert

If the previously listed strategies are still missing the mark, the colleague may be an Extrovert. If so:

▶ Respect, don't challenge, their need to recharge their batteries by interacting with others—they need this the way you need alone time (even though it will be difficult for you to understand why they must constantly be around people and how they can enjoy noisy environments).

▸ Ask questions; share more of yourself.

▸ Apply your skills as a good listener—but interject verbally often.

▸ Volunteer to handle tasks for them that require working alone. Benefit from their gratitude—and the solitude.

Recognize any coworkers in the preceding descriptions? Learn more about them by reading each Color Q personality's overall chapter and Chapter 25, "Adjusting to the Workplace Styles of Others."

▸　▸　▸

In summary, Red/Green Introverts are quiet, spontaneous, and practical. You gravitate to fields where your sensitivity and keen powers of observation can help others. Patient, flexible, and easygoing, you have little need for control. You live in the moment and do not plan more than necessary. When problems arise, you are confident of your ability to handle them.

You can get so involved with others that you neglect your own needs. You have now pleased the person who asked you to read this book, so go reward yourself by doing something fun! Be sure to toot your own horn and let that person know you read (even though we know you just skimmed) the whole thing!

15

blues overall

BLUES ARE THE rarest of the four Color Q types, representing just 10 percent of the overall world population. If you are not a Blue but want to read about how to identify or improve communications with one, go to "How to Recognize a Blue Colleague" at the end of the chapter.

Hillary Rodham Clinton, United States Secretary of State

Hillary Clinton is not only one of the best-known Blues in the country; she is also a strong example of the Blue's strategic career planning and consistent high achievement. (Although not directly tested, it is the consensus of the Myers-Briggs community that she is a Blue. Author Shoya Zichy has met Clinton personally several times and concurs.)

Growing up in Park Ridge, Illinois, Hillary was characterized as assertive, purposeful, and determined (all inborn Blue characteristics). A tireless worker and consistent overachiever, she was a National Merit Scholar in high school. Her teachers noted her exceptional ability to take in information, debate thoroughly, but change her mind when new input demanded it (core Blue abilities).

In her senior year, she was voted most likely to succeed. She went on to become a high achiever in both college (Wellesley student body president and first student commencement speaker) and at Yale Law School. Her first career position was an assignment to the impeachment inquiry staff investigating Richard Nixon, where she worked often from dawn to midnight seven days a week. (Blues work relentlessly on problems of interest, functioning without significant stress in solemn or tense environments.)

That summer she worked on Bill Clinton's campaign for an Arkansas congressional seat, already emotionally involved with the young up-and-comer. The campaign manager, Paul Fray, struggled with the hard-nosed young woman over strategies he deemed his turf, but later admitted, "She was an organizational genius."[1]

Bill Clinton knew a good thing when he saw it; they married in 1975. She continued her law career until becoming First Lady of Arkansas in 1979. Interest in the issues facing women and children began at this time; Hillary cofounded Arkansas Advocates for Children and Families and served as chairwoman of the Arkansas Education Standards Committee.[2]

In 1993 Bill Clinton began his term as President of the United States. In her role as First Lady, Hillary helped strategize the creation of a national health care plan, which failed congressional passage. Her ongoing interest in women and children's issues resurfaced, and she led bipartisan efforts to create the Children's Health Insurance Program, improve adoption and foster care, and reduce teen pregnancy.[3]

In 2000 she was elected as the first female senator representing the state of New York. This was the first time a former First Lady of the United States had ever been elected to the United States Senate. With a strategic eye on a long-term bid to become the nation's first female President, Hillary dove into building her credibility by serving on the Senate Armed Services Committee; the Health, Education, Labor, and Pensions Committee; the

Environment and Public Works Committee; the Budget Committee; and the Select Committee on Aging.

These assignments served her well in her presidential bid. But when Barack Obama ultimately won the election, her support was rewarded with an appointment to become secretary of state. Hillary thus became the only former First Lady to serve in a President's cabinet. In typical Blue fashion, she has instituted changes to maximize departmental effectiveness; created the concept of "smart power" to define the country's global leadership; and has made effective use of social media for global communication.

As secretary of state, Hillary operates in a highly strategic environment to which she brings both natural and well-learned skills. She has established specific objectives for the State Department's missions abroad and instituted the Quadrennial Diplomacy and Development Review to ensure achievement. In September 2010, she unveiled a hunger initiative that proactively focuses on providing food as a strategic part of U.S. foreign policy.

When Hillary retires as secretary of state, it is almost certain that she will remain a force on the national political scene for some time to come.

Phyllis Haberman, Egret Capital Partners and Golden Seeds LLC

Not all Blues are as high-profile as Hillary Rodham Clinton, but the drive to achieve runs deep. Phyllis Haberman earned a B.S. in mathematics from Simmons College and an MBA in finance from Columbia University. (Blues often have advanced degrees.) Phyllis was the first and only female MBA in each of the departments where she worked for Celanese Corporation. She then worked for twenty years with Charterhouse Group, a middle-market private equity firm. She was a member of Charterhouse's investment committee and served on the board of directors and audit committees for a number of portfolio companies. Then she became a founding partner of Egret Capital Partners, a private equity firm, and managing director at Golden Seeds, LLC, a network of angel investors dedicated to investing in early stage companies founded and/or led by women. (It is interesting to note that both Clinton and Haberman take a long-term strategic view about empowering women.)

▶ ▶ ▶

You as a Blue will critique every point made in a book like this, preferring a more intellectual focus. Therefore, this book contains strategies for learning how to interact more effectively and efficiently with even the most sensitive people in your life. It offers strategies that work when other efforts have failed.

The most logical way to proceed with this book is to first read about your own specific personality (Blue with its backup and Introvert/Extrovert dimension), where you'll find strategies for dealing with all the other Color Q personalities. If you currently own or plan to start a company, harnessing the strengths of the four primary personalities will be essential to your success. Chapters 5, 10, and 20 provide an "overall" description and an end-of-chapter section on how to recognize other Color Q personalities. As you become more skilled at assessing others, read Chapter 25, "Adjusting to the Workplace Styles of Others," for finely tuned interpersonal strategies.

How to Recognize a Blue Colleague

External Environment Clues

- ▶ Professional, conservative, quietly high-quality dress (sleeves often rolled up).
- ▶ Frequently have advanced degree(s).
- ▶ Trophies or plaques for achievement on display.
- ▶ Lots of high-tech tools and technical reference materials.

Personal Mannerisms—Personal Behavior

- ▶ Voracious readers.
- ▶ Insatiably curious.
- ▶ Competitive.

Personal Mannerisms—Verbal

- ▶ Prefer talking about strategies or future-oriented topics.
- ▶ Speak in compound sentences.
- ▶ Use precise vocabulary and abstract words.

‣ Express clear, direct ideas.

‣ Display jousting wit, which can be intimidating.

‣ Disregard opposition and what others think of them.

How to Communicate with a Blue—"Style Shifting" Tips

‣ Keep relationship professional, limit chitchat, be brief and concise.

‣ Acknowledge their intellect.

‣ Using sophisticated vocabulary, demonstrate your own competence.

‣ Talk "big picture."

‣ Outline the theoretical framework, expertise of product designers.

‣ Bring up comparative studies and innovative advances.

‣ Limit facts and details; present essentials in executive summary; list pros and cons and testimonials by experts.

‣ Communicate long-term potentials for improving system efficiencies.

‣ Use ingenuity and logic; be consistent.

‣ Allow the Blue to challenge, critique, and question; be aware these are signs of interest and respond accordingly. (Blues expect their ideas to be critiqued by you.)

‣ Engage with jousting wit.

‣ Avoid emotional appeals and words like "feel" or "believe;" instead, ask what they *think* or *deduce*. Appeal to their sense of fairness and logic rather than diplomacy; don't exaggerate or flatter.

‣ Compose strategies *with* the Blue, not *for* the Blue.

16

blue/backup gold extroverts

YOU'RE NOT ONLY a Blue, you also have strong secondary characteristics of the Gold personality. And you have tested as a Color Q Extrovert, which means you recharge your batteries by being with people rather than alone. Blue/Gold Extroverts are logical, competent individuals who form just 3 percent of the population. Combining expertise and innovation, you're a high achiever who can solve the world's most complex problems given enough intellectual freedom and strategizing time.

Top Motivators

As an Extrovert, working alone for long periods is frustrating. Negotiate working in open environments. You need to be around people (as long as they're as competent and dedicated as you). Debate and critique are necessary; otherwise, your effectiveness is curtailed.

During hiring or review, negotiate for these Blue/Gold Extrovert motivators:

- Intellectual freedom

- Ongoing development of competence and expertise

- Ability to debate and critique new concepts, theories, processes, and decisions

- Opportunities to solve complex problems and/or do strategic planning

- Rewards for logic, competence, and innovation

- Fair, equitable work environment

Corporate Culture—Finding the Optimal Fit

It's the responsibility of every personality to find or create their optimal work environment. Optimal cultures differ among Color Q personality types. The corporate culture itself may not be dysfunctional; for instance, Blues hate what Reds love. Conflict, sapped strength, resentment, and feelings of defeat are symptoms of poor cultural fit and can be avoided by understanding your preferences.

The Blue/Gold Extrovert's **most preferred work environment** is defined by:

- Competent, tough-minded, decisive coworkers who relish competition

- Logical and lively debate about analyses, models, theories, solutions, and improvements

- Long-range strategic master plans

- Respected superiors who impose minimal procedures, bureaucracy, and paperwork

- ▸ Rewards for being a decisive, autonomous, results-oriented multitasker

- ▸ Technical, financial, and human resources available as needed

If these points seem obvious, it means you've tested correctly. (Compare with a Red/Green Introvert's ideal environment.)

The Blue/Gold Extrovert's **least preferred environment** has:

- ▸ Entrenched bureaucracy, with an emphasis on details and practicalities

- ▸ Unclear goals and a lack of organization

- ▸ Closed-door policies, where information is withheld and input into decisions is rejected

- ▸ Sensitive, emotional, or myopic coworkers

- ▸ Lots of discussion about feelings

- ▸ Being required to work alone

Leveraging Executive Presence and Building Personal Brand

One of the critical tasks of a Blue/Gold Extrovert manager is to build executive reputation or "brand." You'll excel at this because of your strategic capabilities. It helps to build power internally and market yourself externally when necessary.

> *The Blue/Gold Extrovert's leadership brand should highlight your strength for creating visions, devising strategies, establishing plans, and taking charge to make it all happen.*

You are a forceful implementer who presumes leadership is yours through competence and expertise. Frank, direct, and intuitive, you understand power and its uses; immediately grasp inner organizational workings; and can act quickly, even when making tough decisions. These abilities quickly push you up the ladder. Because you think in whole systems and big pictures, you are most effective at the top of any group. You enjoy solving complex problems and mobilizing resources. Inefficiency, bureaucracy, and losses are eliminated. Your subordinates learn to do their jobs extremely well or leave. For those who stay, you become a role model of confidence, fairness, and consistency.

---

*CASE STUDY 1: **The Successful Blue/Gold Extrovert***

Mark W. Smith, Smith Valliere, PLLC

Mark W. Smith is proud of what he has accomplished before the age of forty. He is a high-stakes, high-profile Wall Street litigator who handles large, complex business and other disputes among people over money, business, and power at a law firm he founded, Smith Valliere, PLLC. He is a New York Times *bestselling author of four books on politics, economics, and law and regularly appears on CNN and Fox News. Smith has typical Blue/Gold strengths: strategic planning, goal-focus, and hard work with high standards. Those high standards occasionally trigger a Blue/Gold weakness: "I can be blunt and demanding with people with whom I work—I have high standards, and when they are not met, I can become frustrated." Smith advises, "Always be rational and logical while trying to appear sensitive to the needs and concerns of others. We try to balance collegiality required for a small close-knit group while working to ensure that heavy client demands are met in the high-pressured environment of major lawsuits and conflicts." Smith, like most Blues, operates with a long-term focus. "I have a three-year outlook for the law firm while holding a multi-decade view for myself," he says. He also embraces competition: "I am an intellectual mercenary who hates to lose. Lots of lawyers were good students who went to law school. I was a talented athlete who went to law school. This is my competitive advantage over other lawyers."*

Participating In and Managing Productive Teams

On a team, you push others to achieve goals, especially if you've been involved in designing them. If your team faces complex problems, you're likely the first to have a breakthrough (given enough autonomous thinking time). You enjoy the process of change. Outgoing and eager to debate solutions, you may run into resistance if you don't factor in people's feelings or values.

Any team is fortunate to have you because you are eager, determined, great at multitasking, and frugal with time and resources.

Communications Style

Adjusting vocabulary to align with another Color Q personality's style elicits powerful positive responses. Empathetic vs. objective analysis, theoretical vs. practical, structured vs. adaptable—these clashes fuel most workplace conflicts. Being able to "style shift" brings superior competitive advantages in negotiations, managing, and interviewing.

You are outspoken and enthusiastic, bonding with others through witty wordplay. You enjoy respectful and well-informed debate, and prefer talking over texting or writing. Your preferred vocabulary is theoretical jargon, statistical data, and technical terms. Golds, with whom you share some personality traits, respond to words like "facts," "tradition," "respected," and "proven." Reds use active words: "move," "stimulate," and "expedite." You are uncomfortable around Greens, who prefer metaphors, feelings, and analogies, emphasizing words like "values," "relationship," "feel," and "friendly." Blue/Golds ask why and what if, seeking cause-and-effect data to assemble systems and strategic plans. Style shifting for you means accommodating the emotions, practical considerations, and rules of others. Work with Reds by analyzing real-time crises, or Greens by allowing the honest wisdom of emotions to support logic. Address the anxieties of Golds who impose rules and strategize win-win solutions. Your cool-headedness keeps everyone balanced.

Blind Spots

Certain blind spots are prevalent in Blue/Gold Extroverts (although only some of them will apply to you):

- Being overconfident of your own competence, logic, or strategy
- Believing everything must be rational and oversimplifying "messy" scenarios
- Overlooking implementation realities or midcourse corrections

> ‣ Being unaware of, or dismissing, other people's emotions/responses
>
> ‣ Steamrolling others to achieve goals; being abrupt, dogmatic, challenging
>
> ‣ Assuming leadership is due you because of your accumulated expertise or achievements

Stressors That Produce Fatigue and Strife

Certain workplace conditions stress and fatigue Blue/Gold Extroverts, including:

- ‣ Powerlessness, loss of autonomy, lack of influence in critical decisions

- ‣ Negative or emotional coworkers

- ‣ Unclear guidelines and indecisiveness

- ‣ Illogical procedures that masquerade as "efficiency"

- ‣ Having to deal with the incompetence of others or, worse, your own

- ‣ Being accused of treating people like objects

If you are under extreme stress, your competence will be compromised. You may experience self-pity, illogical emotions, inflexibility, fear of losing control, or you can withdraw when angered. In leisure hours you can experience self-doubt, insomnia, even illness. (For coping mechanisms, see the section on "Strategies to Improve Effectiveness When Challenged.")

Self-Coach Your Way to More Productive Work Relationships

The primary focus of the Blue/Gold Extrovert who wants to self-coach for career advancement should be on how to handle others' emotional issues, rules, and immediate practicalities.

Problem Solving and Decision Making

The Blue/Gold Extrovert has these strengths:

▸ Contributes significant expertise during initial phase; analyzes untried solutions

▸ Achieves goals by long-term, strategic planning

▸ Likes complex challenges

▸ Conceptualizes and theorizes better than most people

▸ Assesses flaws in ideas and processes; makes tough decisions fast and cuts losses

Strategies to Improve Effectiveness When Challenged

Interpersonal challenges detract from productivity. Here are self-coaching activities to help solve your biggest challenges:

▸ *Fear of negative outcomes.* You doubt your competence until you see successful results. Review your track record of successes. Ask a Red colleague for help making midcourse corrections to keep projects on track.

▸ *Having to work alone.* Delegate these tasks to Introverts (who'll thank you for the alone time!). Or negotiate working near peers to increase productivity.

▸ *Emotional reactions that cloud reality and logic.* Acknowledge the different types of intelligences. Feelings can be valuable, make-or-break inputs. Find a Green to mentor you. View emotions as " if . . . then" equations (e.g., "if he feels this, then he'll likely do that").

▸ *People rejecting your contributions because you haven't factored in their needs.* When presenting your complex ideas, explain them either step-by-step (for Reds and Golds) or explain how the idea will benefit people (for Greens). Acknowledge, with appreciation, other people's contributions before proposing your own.

▸ *Pushing through obstacles by dismissing others' opinions.* Your logical analysis has identified the "right" direction; you've no use for those who go "with the gut" or "the way it's always been done." In a low-risk situation, step back and let other people do it their way. Carefully analyze outcomes.

When dealing with challenges, rely on your innate cool-headedness and drive for closure. Avoid jobs dealing primarily with crisis or routine. Blue/Gold Extroverts are tough-minded and strategically brilliant, but they fold like a napkin in the face of strong emotion. Find a Green ally to help with these situations.

CASE STUDY 2: When a Career Isn't Working

Blue/Gold Extrovert Joey Bates was the scion of a theatrical family—his father was a director, his mother an actress, his grandfather a prominent vaudevillian. Unfortunately, Joey showed hardly any performing talent as a child. He felt this disappointment keenly until at age 15 he found a niche—stage management. While other kids vied for starring roles, Joey developed his Blue ability to solve complicated staging, prop, and scene support problems. At age 25, Joey got his stage manager's union card. He had earned his stripes . . . so why was he feeling angry and stressed? It made no sense, which bothered him even more. One day, a particularly demanding star unfairly challenged Joey's competence. It came out of the blue, and so did Joey's reaction—an angry outburst of an unfairly treated Blue. The star fled to her dressing room, and Joey finally realized he could no longer deal with emotional actors. He retreated to the local pub, where he exchanged a few professional complaints with a security analyst. Blues love strategic thinking; what would have been a two-minute chat turned into a fascinating two-hour conversation . . . and ultimately, a career change. Now Joey analyzes securities on Wall Street, where his Blue strategic thinking, complex problem solving, and tough decision making have captured the attention of senior partners. His career trajectory has been described as "meteoric."

Political Savvy—Making Your Words Count

A valuable part of the Color Q system lies in learning how to harness the Green's marketing and people skills, the Gold's detail thinking and administrative talent, and the Red's crisis management capabilities to your advantage. Transform irritating coworkers into powerful political allies.

Greens. *"You're a fool if you think we can cut fewer than 1,500 people from the payroll and still meet projections," says Max (a Blue/Gold). "You're blind if you think you can decimate the incomes of that many local families and still increase sales enough to meet those projections," retorts Chris (a Green).*

The Green is the most people-oriented of the four primary Color Q personalities. Their people smarts may appear to be a soft and secondary focus, but it's a vital balance to your logical, strategic orientation. Your style can irritate a Green by emphasizing competence and expertise and downplaying emotions. You prefer to be competent in relationships; Greens need to feel emotionally open and honest. That's why they avoid conflict, debate, and challenges. But challenge their values and you'll find Greens surprisingly assertive! You both are highly intuitive, but Greens gather emotional feedback while you base your intuitions on facts and logic. To them, your style seems cold and detached. Greens won't confront you, but they'll become distant and unsupportive. Explain to them that you find it difficult to discuss emotions, which might be overwhelming to you, and a Green will instantly support you.

Negotiating Strategies

▸ Find common ground with Greens and their abstract, long-term visions. Use their people skills to increase buy-in for your strategies and ideas.

▸ Ask them how you're perceived. Their feedback will be gentle and tactful.

▸ Show appreciation for their people skills and substantial marketing abilities.

▸ To ensure their political buy-in, factor in their values and intuitions when formulating strategies and making decisions.

▸ Explain that your love of debating and critiquing is just your process and should not be taken personally. They'll have a hard time understanding this about your personality, so reiterate often.

Golds. *Tom, a Blue/Gold sales manager, was beaming because he had some impressive news for Aldo, the (Gold) senior vice president of finance: "After eight months of calling, writing, and cutting off the competition, I've landed the Boeing account; I've just kept the company afloat for another year!" Aldo looked up impassively. "Great, Tom, but I'll bet you don't have your expense account done yet."*

Golds are the rule makers and procedure setters of the world. They may irk you by focusing too much on "irrelevant" details, but in order to be effective, Golds need structure. Find common ground with Golds over preferring logic to emotion. To make a Gold an ally, explain step-by-step how your ideas will work. This is especially true when formulating business plans because you need the Gold's input on administrative details.

Negotiating Strategies

▸ To ease tensions, use words like "facts," "tradition," "respected," and "proven."

▸ Bond over your mutual preference for logic.

▸ Explain that your critiques and debates are not personal, just ways to find the "right" answer.

▸ Acknowledge and flatter their superior detail management.

▸ Include them when formulating strategic plans or product innovations. Golds can point out deal-breaking implementation issues.

Reds. *"The Forest grant came in, but it's only half what we requested. We'll have to cut the Swan Lake ballet dates by six weeks," said Lottie, a (Red) grants manager. Alicia, the (Blue/Gold) executive director, replied: "No, we won't. We're building our corps around the classics and establishing our long-term endowment strategy based on this plan. We can't backpedal. Find us more money."*

Your style can irritate a Red with its emphasis on just one "right" direction. The Red's strength is to expect, even welcome, midcourse corrections.

Reds like to see how things actually play out. Your long-term strategy may not seem realistic to a Red, who will challenge with on-the-ground scenarios. To the Blue/Gold Extrovert, the Red's style appears to be barely controlled chaos. This is a setup for chronic conflict with an achievement-oriented Blue/Gold Extrovert. But when crisis looms, send in the Red, who'll be enthused and energized.

Negotiating Strategies

- Use action words and expressions with a Red, *move, stimulate, expedite, "let's get some real work done,"* and evaluate the response.

- Forget talking strategically. Using concrete words, discuss specifically what needs to be done *now* to accomplish desired ends.

- Do not micromanage. Let them handle delays, ambiguities, and unforeseen changes.

- Curb tendencies to argue semantics and abstract points.

- Find common ground with your mutual focus on the issues and the ability not to take others' actions personally.

- Invite input from Reds into a business plan. They'll minimize your intellectual complexities and contribute concrete steps and contingency plans that can make or break a venture.

Extrovert vs. Introvert

If the strategies outlined so far are still missing the mark, your coworker may be an Introvert. If so:

- Respect, don't challenge, their need to recharge their batteries with privacy—it's not personal, although it will be difficult for you to understand why they shun interaction and prefer working alone.

- Tone down your enthusiasm; listen more.

- Invite them to speak, but don't force them until they've thought things through.

‣ Do not fill their pauses.

Recognize any coworkers in the preceding descriptions? Find more negotiating strategies in each Color Q personality's overall chapter and in Chapter 25, "Adjusting to the Workplace Styles of Others."

‣   ‣   ‣

In summary, Blue/Gold Extroverts are natural leaders who respect logic, unvarnished truth, and efficient planning. Their intuition drives their vision and defines their goals.

You strategically assign the right people to each task. But those people better be up to the challenge. Blues have little sympathy for ineffective or inefficient work, and you hate confusion. Being structured, you may misunderstand the value of more flexible personalities like Greens and Reds. That may be a serious mistake. They're the ones who most often contribute creative solutions and solve crises. Fascinated by the very concept of intelligence, all Blue/Golds share an inner drive to perform. Your self-critical nature continually strives for self-improvement. More than other people, you must balance your creative spontaneity with a need for order.

17

blue/backup gold introverts

YOU'RE NOT ONLY a Blue; you also have strong secondary character-istics of the Gold personality. And you have tested as a Color Q Introvert, which means you recharge your batteries by being alone. Blue/Gold Introverts will read this chapter skeptically and critically. We're prepared. The Color Q system is based on the work of the Myers-Briggs community, incorporating more than seventy years of worldwide research (read in-depth background in Chapter 4, "The Color Q Personality System: Its Foundation and History"). Strategically speaking, this chapter provides tools designed to give you social and political advantages over other person-ality types in your organization.

Top Motivators

Let's test whether these claims are true. Are these your greatest motivators?

- Strategic thinking; intuition backed by logic

- Competence; achievement; pursuit of excellence

- Freedom to debate and critique in search of truth

- Strategizing large-scale improvements that make a genuine difference

- Creating new systems and ideas

Sound true? Then continue.

As an Introvert, you're less productive in open office settings. It is critical to work where your complex mental modeling is uninterrupted. Blue/Gold Introverts account for only 2 percent of the world's population, but your problem-solving capabilities have molded today's world.

Corporate Culture—Finding the Optimal Fit

It is the responsibility of every personality to find or create their optimal work environment. Optimal cultures differ among Color Q personality types. Strengths in one company may be unneeded elsewhere. The corporate culture itself may not be dysfunctional; for instance, Blues hate what Reds love. Conflict, sapped strength, resentment, and feelings of defeat are symptoms of poor cultural fit and can be avoided by understanding your preferences.

The Blue/Gold Introvert's **most preferred work environment** emphasizes:

- Opportunities to increase knowledge and competence
- Thinking outside the box
- Decision-making power
- Coworkers who are smart, independent, and motivated by competition
- Complex projects

> In-depth, uninterrupted mental modeling

If these points seem obvious, it means you've tested correctly. (Compare with a Red/Green Extrovert's ideal environment.)

The Blue/Gold Introvert's **least preferred environment** is characterized by:

> Bureaucracy ("This is the way we've always done it")

> Excessive paperwork, procedures, details, and rules

> "Incompetent" coworkers who are too sensitive, resist change, miss deadlines, and squabble

> Patronizing superiors or clients

> Mandatory teamwork

Leveraging Executive Presence and Building Personal Brand

One of the critical tasks of a Blue/Gold Introvert manager is to build one's executive reputation or "brand." This brand building empowers you to implement strategies by increasing your internal influence (while also allowing you to market yourself externally when necessary). Here is the Blue/Gold Introvert's leadership brand, in executive summary form:

> *A born strategist, you are the first to see the big picture. You create compelling visions, devise strategies, and establish both primary plans and contingencies.*

You set extremely high standards but give your people autonomy. They find your clear thinking and thoughtful debate inspiring. You'd rather work on your own than lead, but attract upper-echelon remuneration and prestige because of your intellectual depth, superior expertise, and competence. Your long-term strategic thinking, marketplace trend-spotting ability, and tough decision making make you a strong executive. Though you dislike politics, your intuitive understanding of an organization's inner workings brings job security.

CASE STUDY 1: Successful Blue/Gold Introverts

Mark Taylor, Vistage International

Mark Taylor isn't a doctor or a lawyer, but he is an Indian chief. He's actually the senior tribal leadership trainer for CultureSync,™ a management consulting organization that teaches teams to produce superior results by synchronizing culture and strategy. An accomplished CEO with thirty-five years of experience, he runs "think tanks" for Manhattan CEOs. He founded Taylor Systems Engineering Corporation—TSE (which, until he sold it in 2005, was number 58 on the list of fastest-growing companies in the state of Michigan) and also RedRoller, an Internet start-up shopping service that compared rates of multiple shippers (and went public in 2007). He is chair for Vistage International, billed as "the world's leading chief executive organization."

"My core values are service, care, and learning in support of a noble cause to transform the workplace," Mark says. He accomplishes this goal through Blue strategic means. With a bachelor of science in management and computers in addition to his MBA, Mark applies strategy to corporate cultures to optimize their success rates. He held the very Blue position of chief logistics officer for RedRoller.

His Vistage work is perfect for a Blue/Gold. "I am innovative and adept at creating new visionary solutions," Mark says. "I get to test ideas by working with fifty CEOs, and translate them into real-world results." His greatest joy is giving others a new way of thinking.

Vanessa A. McDermott, MWH, Inc.

Blue/Gold Introvert Vanessa McDermott knew at age 4 that she wanted to attend the United States Military Academy at West Point. At age 18, she did. In active duty, she rose to the rank of army captain in three years. Her Blue long-term strategic thinking served her well as a maintenance and logistics officer in the United States, Korea, and Iraq, where she was responsible for operation planning, execution, and resource allocation for more than 1,000 international personnel. Today she leverages her ability to understand complex issues as a management consultant for MWH, Inc., a global hydro-engineering firm. She focuses on risk man-

agement, reporting across four major capital projects totaling $3 billion Canadian in accordance with ISO 31000 and PMI standards.

Having to soften her interactions with teammates is at times stressful. "I am not guided by emotions, but by logic," says McDermott. "I can be too blunt and impatient, so I have worked to take the time for social niceties in order to ensure buy-in and team building."

Participating In and Managing Productive Teams

Blue/Gold Introverts work best independently. You are most valuable during the initial design/strategy phase of a business or project, where you can shape the vision, debate options, and set direction. Watch the tendency to push "logical" options while excluding emotional input. This tendency of yours generates conflict that may not be solved logically or rationally.

You are recognized for your deep concentration, logic, and sharp and resourceful analysis of complex problems, as well as your ability to reliably meet deadlines and help teammates understand "the system."

Communications Style

Adjusting one's vocabulary to align with another Color Q personality's style can elicit powerful positive responses. Empathetic vs. objective analysis, theoretical vs. practical, structured vs. adaptable—these clashes fuel most workplace conflicts. Being able to "style shift" brings strategic, competitive advantages in negotiations, managing, and interviewing.

Blue/Gold Introverts are among the most mentally exact of personalities. You prefer writing to talking (preferably with experts), using brief, precise, objective language. Stating "the obvious" is an irritant to you, and you will move on if conversation isn't sufficiently stimulating. You keep interactions professional and succinct. Debate and critique are expected; it surprises you when they hurt other people's feelings.

Technical jargon and statistical data engage you. Conversely, Reds prefer concrete words and action verbs like "move," "stimulate," and "expedite." Golds, with whom you share some personality traits, respond to "facts," "tradition," "respected," and "proven." Greens (with whom you are least comfortable) prefer abstract concepts and symbols, emphasizing words like "values," "relationship," "feel," and "friendly." (The "Political Savvy" section suggests methods you can adopt for style shifting.)

Blind Spots

Certain blind spots are prevalent in Blue/Gold Introverts (although only some of them will apply to you). You may:

- Exclude others until the end of project, then refuse their input
- Critique too quickly and not hear another person's whole idea
- Become impatient and dogmatic with the less intellectual
- Define emotion as secondary, and become frustrated when emotion is the focus
- Dislike having to share responsibility (i.e., "If you want something done right, do it yourself")
- Decide matters logically and ignore "gut" instincts and traditions

Stressors That Produce Fatigue and Strife

Here are specific workplace conditions that stress and fatigue Blue/Gold Introverts:

- Lack of privacy and micromanagement
- Implementing arbitrary, illogical decisions
- Having to constantly justify one's actions
- Not having enough time to evaluate situations; needing answers that require more than logic
- Making midcourse corrections to "the plan"
- Coworkers who are incompetent, stubborn, or resist change
- Other people's emotional outbursts and squabbling

Blue/Gold Introverts under extreme stress are prone to be snappy and sarcastic, then stubborn, blunt, and hostile. You may shut out all emotions as "irrelevant." You'll obsess over secondary details or avoid social situations until you reestablish a sense of competence.

Self-Coach Your Way to More Productive Work Relationships

The primary focus of the Blue/Gold Introvert who wants to self-coach for career advancement should be on how to incorporate emotional components into decision making.

Problem Solving and Decision Making

The Blue/Gold Introvert has these strengths:

- Identifies a problem's origin, then extrapolates future possibilities and new systems

- Fits intuitive understanding into logical framework

- Creates visions, devises strategies, builds complex models, and accurately predicts final outcomes

- Seeks strategic advantage by addressing flaws and analyzing added-value

- Makes tough decisions by compartmentalizing emotion

Strategies to Improve Effectiveness When Challenged

Interpersonal challenges detract from productivity. Here are self-coaching strategies for your biggest challenges:

- *Resistance to structure, rules, and bureaucracy.* You believe, rightly, in the value of applying strategic and logical solutions to long-range problems and become impatient with bureaucratic obstacles. Work within the system; develop both peer and upper-echelon support.

- *Having to work in large teams or open offices.* Ask to work primarily on smaller subcommittees. Negotiate a private work space, then deliver increased productivity.

‣ *Obsessive searches for truth.* If your competence is challenged, you'll work until it's reestablished. You may ignore your physical needs for so long that you become ill. True competence requires stamina, so provide yourself nutritious food, adequate sleep, and exercise.

‣ *Defeating buy-in by ignoring emotional components.* Humans are illogical; feelings get hurt for bewildering reasons. Find a Green mentor to help you master "emotional intelligence" with "if . . . then" equations. Journaling, which you enjoy, can help.

‣ *Difficulty focusing on details and practicalities.* Details are the strength of Golds, practicalities of the Reds. Form alliances through mutual respect for ability. If you dislike asking for help, barter.

‣ *Lack of competence in self and others.* You dismiss competencies that are not intellectual. But can you smooth over a stalled negotiation like a Green? Handle a crisis like a Red? Administer as smoothly as a Gold? When you sense a lack of competence in yourself, you withdraw; this habit just feeds the problem. Keep yourself in the game—respect and harness other people's competencies.

When dealing with challenges, pursue leisure activities that combine business and pleasure. This warms up coworkers. Relinquish the need to control everything. If your sense of competence is low, make a physical improvement—paint a room, reorganize your office. Prioritize your real needs for privacy and thought-processing time.

- -
CASE STUDY 2: When a Career Isn't Working

Father William Ferguson performed the funeral rites over his mother's and his older brother's coffins, changed out of his vestments, and escaped to his office. Of all the illogical, nonsensical emotions, why would he be feeling . . . relieved? Was this normal?

His mother had groomed him for the ministry and his older brother to lead the family's business consulting empire. Never much of a people person, Father William had still made a name for himself using his Blue/Gold strategizing to help formulate diocesan policy. He treated the counseling demands of his profession like a chess game; what was the next move?

When Father William visited the consulting business for the first time after the terrible auto accident that claimed his family's lives, he felt more at home than he ever had at the church. Remembering he had counseled his parishioners to accept all feelings during the grief process as vital in the eyes of God, he noted it and moved forward. Blues are at ease strategically evaluating a business and projecting its future direction. In one month, he totally overhauled weaker systems and put the company on firm footing for his brother's successor.

Naturally, the board of directors offered him the position. As he started to decline, he stopped in midsentence. Instead of disloyalty to his mother, he felt . . . energized.

After asking the board for a few days to think (and make sure grief wasn't making him irrational), William accepted. He realized the choice was to be an adequate priest or a really good CEO; he made the only rational decision.

Political Savvy—Making Your Words Count

A valuable part of the Color Q system lies in learning how to harness the Green's marketing and people skills, the Gold's administrative talent, and the Red's crisis and midcourse correction abilities to your advantage. Engage irritating coworkers as powerful political allies.

Greens. The Green is the most people-oriented of the four primary Color Q personalities. Their understanding of people's internal desires may seem soft and secondary; but it's a vital balance to your logical, strategic orientation. Your style can irritate a Green by emphasizing competence and expertise and downplaying emotions. You prefer competence when in relationships; Greens operate through emotional openness and honesty. They dislike conflict and will avoid your debate and challenges. But challenge their values and they'll hand you your head on a platter! You both are highly intuitive, but Greens gather emotional feedback; you base your intuitions on facts and logic. To them, your style seems cold and detached. Greens won't confront you, but they'll become distant and unsupportive. Explain to them that you find it difficult to discuss emotions because they are deep and might be overwhelming, and a Green will instantly support you.

Negotiating Strategies

▸ Find common ground with Greens and their abstract vision, long-term thinking, and intuition.

▸ Engage their people skills to increase buy-in for your ideas.

▸ Ask them how to increase emotional competencies. Their feedback will be gentle and tactful.

▸ Show patience, respect, and appreciation (even if it's irritating) for their people skills and marketing acumen.

▸ To ensure their political buy-in, factor in their values when making decisions.

▸ Explain that your love of debating and critiquing is just your process and should not be taken personally. They'll have a hard time understanding this about your personality, so reiterate often.

Golds. Golds are the rule makers and procedure setters of the world. Their administrative talents may irk you by focusing on "unnecessary" details, but in order to be effective, Golds need structure. Find common ground with Golds over a shared desire never to bend the rules and through jointly developing schedules and time lines. To make Gold coworkers your allies, take time to detail how your ideas and strategies will work. Keep at it until they've achieved a comfort level. This is especially true when formulating business plans; you'll need their procedural input.

Negotiating Strategies

▸ To ease tensions, use words like "facts," "tradition," "respected," and "proven."

▸ Bond with a Gold/Blue over your mutual preference for facts and logic.

‣ Explain that your critiques and debates are not personal, just attempts to find the "right" answer. They will resist when you try to "improve" their structures.

‣ Acknowledge and flatter their superior detail management when they perform these tasks for you.

‣ Include them from the start when initially formulating strategic plans or proposing product innovations, rather than at the end. They'll identify implementation issues that might otherwise sideline a project.

Reds. Your style can irritate a Red with its emphasis on just one "right" direction and sticking to "the plan." The Red's strength is to handle crises that can derail the plan. You need a Red on your team to create rapport with others and handle practicalities. To the Blue/Gold Introvert, the Red's style appears chaotic—it's mostly play, some work, with frequent rule-bending. This is a setup for chronic conflict with an achievement-oriented Blue/Gold. But if a crisis threatens your well-laid plans, send in a Red who'll be energized by it.

Negotiating Strategies

‣ Use these words and phrases with a Red—*move, stimulate, expedite, "let's get some real work done"*—and evaluate the response.

‣ Forget about talking strategically. Simplify. Using concrete factual words, discuss specifically what needs to be done *now* to accomplish desired ends.

‣ Solicit their opinions during initial strategy sessions. Reds can create contingency plans on the spot when needed. They'll simplify your intellectual complexities and point out practicalities that can derail a venture.

‣ Do not micromanage. Let them handle delays, ambiguities, and unforeseen changes.

‣ Resist arguing semantics and abstract points.

▶ Find common ground with your mutual openness to untried solutions.

Extrovert vs. Introvert

If the aforementioned strategies are still missing the mark, the colleague may be an Extrovert. If so:

▶ Respect, don't challenge, their need to recharge their batteries by interacting with others—they need this the way you need private time. Accept that it will be difficult for you to understand why they must constantly be around people and prefer noisy environments.

▶ Engage in thoughtful debate; be neutral, not challenging.

▶ Interject verbally often; help keep them on point.

▶ Volunteer to handle tasks that require working alone. Benefit from their gratitude—and the solitude.

Recognize any coworkers in the preceding descriptions? Learn more by reading each Color Q personality's overall chapter and Chapter 25, "Adjusting to the Workplace Styles of Others."

▶　▶　▶

In summary, Blue/Gold Introverts are creative and independent. You demand a great deal of yourself and others. Introspective and reserved, you trust intuition backed by logical analysis to guide your thoughts and decisions. With your theoretical and strategic focus you can succeed in many industries, from those relying on math and science to more philosophical disciplines. You frequently ascend to high levels of business management. Blue/Gold Introverts do especially well in senior positions of companies undergoing change.

blue/backup red extroverts

YOU'RE NOT ONLY a Blue; you also have strong secondary character-istics of the Red personality. And you have tested as a Color Q Extrovert, which means you recharge your batteries by being with people, rather than being alone. Your personality comprises 3 percent of the world population; you're a rare breed. Blue/Red Extroverts are driven by desire for competence and recognition in their chosen field. Your eye is trained on the big picture, spotting competitive and strategic advantages.

Top Motivators
As an Extrovert, however, working alone for long periods is draining and is always difficult; you need a populated environment. Exploration and

competition are necessary; without competent, dedicated, and independent coworkers, your effectiveness is curtailed.

During hiring or review, negotiate for these Blue/Red Extrovert motivators:

- Entrepreneurial freedom; collaboration with expert coworkers

- Ability to originate new products/solutions through nonstructured exploration

- Opportunity to unearth competitive and strategic advantages

- Diversity of projects

- Ongoing development of expertise

- Encouragement of on-the-job fun and excitement

Corporate Culture—Finding the Optimal Fit

It's the responsibility of every personality to find or create their optimal work environment. Optimal cultures differ among Color Q personality types. Strengths in one company may be unneeded elsewhere. The corporate culture itself may not be dysfunctional; for instance, Blues hate what Greens love. Conflict, sapped strength, resentment, and feelings of defeat are symptoms of poor cultural fit and can be avoided by understanding your preferences.

> The Blue/Red Extrovert's **most preferred work environment** emphasizes:
>
> - Work on intriguingly complex problems
> - Fun, challenging competition
> - Opportunities to increase mastery, influence, and respect
> - Working for a high-status company that provides interaction with powerful, influential people
> - Freedom, spontaneity, and improvisation
> - Minimal hierarchy, rules, and procedures

If these points seem obvious, it means you've tested correctly. (Compare with a Green/Gold Introvert's ideal environment.)

The Blue/Red Extrovert's **least preferred environment** has:

- Emphasis on details and practicalities
- Unclear goals; little emphasis on long-range planning and innovation
- Entrenched bureaucracy
- Coworkers who are emotional, myopic, or lack initiative
- Micromanagement
- Limited collaboration (i.e., people working alone for long stretches)

Leveraging Executive Presence and Building Personal Brand

One of the critical tasks of a Blue/Red Extrovert manager is to build one's executive reputation or "brand." Use your intrinsic strategic abilities to leverage power internally and market yourself externally when necessary.

> *The Blue/Red Extrovert's leadership brand should be built around your high intellectual energy and creativity, insightfulness, and contagious enthusiasm. Inquisitive and clever, you are alert to new opportunities and persuade through the power of ideas.*

Autonomy is allowed, provided your staff has demonstrated high levels of competence. Taking risks is encouraged as long as the cost-benefit analysis works. Staff is pushed to exceed targets with accurate, supportive, tough yet fair feedback.

You theorize systems, then act as a catalyst for their adoption. You already will have analyzed patterns and relationships behind key issues. Those who object are usually outclassed by your superior grasp of the big picture.

CASE STUDY 1: **The Successful Blue/Red Extrovert**

Matthew B. Alsted, Calvert Investments

Alsted "likes to balance creativity and pragmatic business solutions." That's good, because his work as vice president, channel marketing and brand strategy for Calvert Investments in Washington, D.C., is complex. "My primary responsibility is for setting marketing strategy within our core distribution channels . . . the other is championing brand development and leadership initiatives including market research, positioning, and execution work [putting strategy into action]."

Alsted has accomplished much in his sixteen years in the financial industry. He started as a product analyst at BayBank in Boston, where he was responsible for competitive analysis and financial reporting and moved up to product manager. Next, he joined T. Rowe Price as assistant vice president in product marketing and customer development. In 2002 he moved on to Riggs Bank in Washington, D.C., where, as vice president, he led marketing communications and e-business strategies and contributed to the restructuring and repositioning of numerous business lines.

A typical Blue/Red Extrovert, Alsted lists his top strengths as an ability to keep focus, tap the ideas and approaches of others, and network (which he does several nights a week). When asked what's stressful about working with him, he says, "I'm a little impatient [and] take on too many things. I am more interested to start projects."

Even as a boy, Alsted thought strategically. "A lightbulb went off that I was at risk of not doing well financially. I went home and said I wanted to go to boarding school, get into a good college. The family was making a big investment, so I knew I had to work hard; it was a great confidence booster." It paid off. Today he collaborates closely with Calvert's distribution company president, key account managers, and fifteen field wholesale managers, and supervises a team of five channel marketing managers.

Participating In and Managing Productive Teams

Cream rises, and you are often nominated to lead your team. Collaboration with a broad range of people increases your productivity. On a team, you take initiative, energize others, provide objective analysis of issues, and generate unique solutions. Your can-do attitude is best applied during a project's initial phase; you'll need other personalities to handle implementation details.

Reducing tensions with humor, you are versatile, ingenious, and great at multitasking. Remember that outcomes are just as important as processes and systems.

Communications Style

Adjusting vocabulary to align with the style of another Color Q personality elicits powerful positive responses. Empathetic vs. objective analysis, theoretical vs. practical, structured vs. adaptable—these clashes fuel most workplace conflicts. Being able to "style shift" brings superior strategic advantages in negotiations, managing, and interviewing.

In business dealings, you are confident, assertive, and articulate; you summarize complexities and persuade others with enthusiasm. Quick on your feet socially, your wit, wordplay, and banter both delight and intimidate. Your preferred vocabulary is theoretical jargon, statistical data, and technical terms. Reds, with whom you share some personality traits, use active words—"move," "stimulate," and "expedite." Golds respond more to words like "facts," "tradition," "respected," and "proven." You are uncomfortable with Greens, who emphasize feelings and prefer words like "values," "relationship," "feel," and "friendly."

Blue/Red Extroverts want to be businesslike first and favor talking rather than writing. You approach conflict with frankness and logic. Style shifting for you means accommodating the emotions, practical considerations, and rules of others (finding the loopholes doesn't count!). Strategize your way through practical demands; understand that logic-clouding emotions can provide unusual but effective problem-solving insights. Analyze the anxieties of those who impose rules; address them with win-win solutions.

Blind Spots

These blind spots are prevalent in Blue/Red Extroverts; some of them will apply to you:

- Initiating many projects, then abandoning some
- Too quickly dismissing "incompetents" and remaining unaware of their strengths
- Becoming too focused on "the model"
- Unintentionally offending those who prioritize harmony
- Seeing deadlines and commitments as secondary to formulating strategies and systems
- Setting high expectations and engaging in self-criticism, leading to burnout

Stressors That Produce Fatigue and Strife

Here are the workplace conditions that stress and fatigue Blue/Red Extroverts:

- Incompetence in others; fear of incompetence in self; being unfairly questioned
- Pressures to provide detailed plans
- Little freedom; mandatory rules/procedures; micromanagement
- Dealing with small talk, emotional reactions, or office politics
- Closed-minded coworkers who cling to the past
- Seeing a solution you cannot implement

If you are under extreme stress, you'll likely become stubborn, rebellious, and critical. Detail obsession, tunnel vision, and excessive eating, drinking, sleeping, or exercising are attempts to regain control. If these pursuits fail, energy and criticisms escalate. At worst, you'll shut down all emotions and avoid situations where you feel incompetent; this breeds uncontrolled outbursts. For coping mechanisms, see "Strategies to Improve Effectiveness When Challenged.")

Self-Coach Your Way to More Productive Work Relationships

The primary focus of the Blue/Red Extrovert who wants to self-coach for career advancement should be on how to handle others' emotional issues, rules, and practical demands.

Problem Solving and Decision Making

The Blue/Red Extrovert has these strengths:

‣ Constantly scans the universe for new or unusual opportunities, ideas, solutions, and processes

‣ Brainstorms multiple options and tolerates ambiguity

‣ Can analyze copious data and discover connections others miss

‣ Learns from similar situations

‣ Analyzes added-value well

Strategies to Improve Effectiveness When Challenged

Interpersonal challenges detract from productivity. Here are self-coaching activities to cope with your biggest challenges:

‣ *Fear of your own incompetence.* This fear is very strong in you. You'll avoid situations where you feel like a newbie. Avoidance, however, breeds incompetence. Identify Red colleagues and ask how they handle new challenges; learn the difference between amateur and incompetence. Carefully select projects to maximize successful completion.

‣ *Having to work alone.* Delegate these tasks to Introverts (who'll thank you for the alone time!) or else negotiate working with others.

‣ *Diminishing cooperation from others.* Do you make glib comments or hog the limelight? These tendencies can offend important colleagues. On a low-risk situation, step back and let other people do it their way. Express appreciation for their skills. Analyze their reactions and results.

▸ *Emotional reactions that cloud reality and logic.* It is important to acknowledge different types of intelligences. Feelings can be valuable, make-or-break inputs. Find a Green to mentor you about emotional logic. Handle emotions as "if . . . then" equations (e.g., "if he feels this, then he'll likely do that").

▸ *Being disorganized.* You live in a theoretical world; practicalities are secondary. (Blow too many deadlines and commitments, however, and you'll be theorizing a new resume.) At 9:00 a.m., take ten minutes to prioritize your day. It will greatly improve your follow-through.

When facing challenges, rely on your cool-headedness and ability to innovate. Avoid jobs dealing primarily with routine. Blue/Red Extroverts are tough-minded and strategically brilliant, but become unsettled in the face of strong emotion and need a Green ally.

CASE STUDY 2: **When a Career Isn't Working**

Blue/Red Extrovert Martin Cormun was proud of his job as director of the Museum of Science and Technology in his city. He had contact with some of the biggest names in the field, and he really enjoyed the many evening networking events to which the museum played host annually.

But during the day, working alone in his thickly carpeted office made him feel restless and irritable. All thirteen of his assistants had quit because he had micromanaged them out of sheer boredom.

His frustration peaked after a board meeting where members waxed poetic about protocols of the past. Blue/Red Extroverts chafe when asked to continue doing things as they have always been done.

At a networking event, Martin met young, entrepreneurial Suzanne Pielski. She was brimming with ideas for a start-up that would apply existing industrial technologies in new ways. Martin had solid connections for both venture capital and technologies. Suzanne begged him to come on board; in typical Blue/Red fashion, Martin evaluated and seized the exciting opportunity.

Today he serves as the new consultancy's strategic director. He took a temporary cut in pay, but sees a big future for the company. His twelve-hour days are energizing, and his assistant shows no sign of quitting.

Political Savvy—Making Your Words Count

A valuable part of the Color Q system lies in learning how to harness the Green's marketing and people skills, the Gold's detail thinking and administrative talent, and the Red's crisis management capabilities to your advantage. Utilize irritating coworkers as powerful political allies.

Greens. *"I'm not going to lay off Harry. I'm going to cut the budget and take a voluntary pay cut instead," announced Theresa (a Green). Alfonso (a Blue), her boss, is astonished and asks, "Why retain dead wood whose productivity has gone steadily downhill?" Theresa answers: "Because his wife has just been diagnosed with breast cancer."*

The Green is the most people-oriented of the four primary Color Q personalities. Their understanding of people may seem a puzzling, secondary focus, but it's a vital balance to your logical, strategic orientation. Your style can irritate a Green. You critique too quickly, criticize bluntly, and play devil's advocate. In turn, Greens irritate you by needing emotional handholding. Harmony with others is not that important to you; you don't understand why Greens care. Why explore values when you could be exploring alternatives? You find the ensuing conflict a waste of time. However, you both share the ability to surprise, delight, charm, and have fun. Grit your teeth and give some positive feedback. Explain that discussing emotions is difficult for you because they are deep and overwhelming, and a Green will instantly support you.

Negotiating Strategies

▸ Find common ground with Greens and their long-term thinking, spontaneous delight, and sense of fun. Use their people skills to increase buy-in for your ideas.

▸ Ask them how you're perceived. Their feedback will be gentle and tactful.

▸ Show respect and appreciation for their people skills and marketing abilities.

▸ To ensure their political buy-in, factor in their values when formulating strategies and making decisions.

▸ Explain that your love of exploring objective alternatives and critiquing is just your process and should not be taken personally. They'll have a hard time understanding, so reiterate often.

Golds. *"We see some promising opportunities for our robotics division if we pursue surgical applications, so we're going to shut down and reassign the manufacturing group," explained (Blue) Stuart, the start-up's owner. "No, we can't support such a radical directional shift," replied Aston (a Gold), the company's venture capital supplier.*

Golds are the rule makers and procedure setters of the world. Their administrative talents relieve you of pesky details. They may irk you by resisting new ways, but in order to be effective, Golds need structure. You irritate Golds by testing limits and bending rules. Find common ground with Gold/Blues, who also prefer logic and linear thought. To make Gold coworkers allies, focus on less risky solutions that allow them to slowly become comfortable with your more unusual ideas. When formulating business plans, express appreciation for their grasp of facts and accuracy. You may ignore even positive parts of the past; they'll incorporate these details in ways that can make or break your plans.

Negotiating Strategies

▸ To ease tensions, use words like "facts," "tradition," "respected," and "proven."

▸ Explain that your critiques and rule-bending are not intended to be personal; they are just ways to find the "right" answer.

▸ Acknowledge and flatter their superior detail management.

‣ Make a consistent effort to include them when you are formulating strategic plans or proposing product innovations. They can point out and prevent implementation issues.

Reds. *"Chris, what are we going to do about replacing packaging machine A? It's failed three times in the past two weeks," asks Millie (a Red). "I'm thinking about upgrading the entire line over the next three years with new machines from Apex," replies Chris (a Blue). Millie, in turn, demands: "But what about machine A now? Next time it fails, it could be decommissioned. Then what?"*

Your style can irritate a Red by being picky about semantics and abstract ideas. Reds live in a here-and-now world of practicalities. They want to do, not strategize. You need them to quantify how much implementation your ideas require; you also need their ability to contribute concrete steps for business plans. Luckily, you both like to find fun in work, bend a few rules, refine plans along the way, and discover opportunity even in the face of disaster.

Negotiating Strategies

‣ Use action words and phrases with a Red—*move, stimulate, expedite, "let's get some real work done"*—and evaluate the response.

‣ Forget about talking strategically. Using concrete words, discuss specifically what needs to be done *now* to accomplish desired ends.

‣ Curb tendencies to argue semantics and abstract points.

‣ Solicit their opinions during strategy sessions. Reds formulate real-world implementation plans that avert future problems. They'll also simplify your intellectual complexities.

‣ Find common ground through your mutual tolerance for ambiguity and uncertainty.

Extrovert vs. Introvert

If the previously described strategies are still missing the mark, your coworker may be an Introvert. If so:

▸ Respect, don't challenge, their need to recharge their batteries with privacy—it's not personal. Just accept that it will be difficult for you to understand why they shun interaction and prefer working alone.

▸ Tone down your enthusiasm; listen more.

▸ Invite them to speak, but don't force them until they've thought things through.

▸ Do not fill their pauses.

Recognize any coworkers in the preceding descriptions? Find more negotiating strategies in each Color Q personality's overall chapter and in Chapter 25, "Adjusting to the Workplace Styles of Others."

▸ ▸ ▸

In summary, Blue/Red Extroverts live in their imagination and, when absorbed in their latest project, think of little else. Your tireless energy is sometimes exhausting to others.

Your commitment and self-confidence is infectious. You may find yourself a guru to others who lack your talents, perseverance, and personal drive. In your search for new experiences, you continually discover that a goal loses its fascination when it's accomplished or becomes routine.

Well suited to be a leader, you instinctively motivate others and appreciate their unique qualities. This acceptance wins you many friends.

Diversity is the key to your happiness. You collect an amazing variety of interests, challenges, and admirers. To be truly successful and leave a lasting impact, however, you need to attend to details and complete mundane commitments.

blue/backup
red introverts

YOU'RE NOT ONLY a Blue; you also have strong secondary character-istics of the Red personality. And you have tested as a Color Q Introvert, which means you recharge your batteries by being alone rather than with people. Blue/Red Introverts are natural skeptics who may think this chapter is all about "feelings." It isn't; it's about being effective. The Color Q system is based on the Myers-Briggs Type Indicator. which has been researched world-wide for over seventy years. (Please read Chapter 4, "The Color Q Personality System: Its Foundation and History," if you require in-depth background.)

Here's the cost-benefit analysis of reading this material:

> ▸ *Cost.* Twenty to thirty minutes of your time to read (ten to fifteen
>   minutes to skim).

▸ *Benefit.* Gain mastery over the outcomes of your interactions with all coworkers. Develop stronger core competencies for interacting with people who irritate or drain you; transform them into helpful allies.

Top Motivators

Let's test the system. Are these your strongest motivators?

▸ Intellectual freedom

▸ Ideas and abstract thinking (the more unique the better)

▸ Thinking "outside the cube"

▸ Rigorous intellectual application

▸ Solving the seemingly unsolvable

If that's on track, read on.

As an Introvert, you're less productive in open office settings. It's critical that your complex mental modeling not be uninterrupted. Blue/Red Introverts form only 2 percent of the world's population, but without your ability to envision new solutions, we'd likely remain in the Stone Age.

Corporate Culture—Finding the Optimal Fit

It's the responsibility of every personality to find or create their optimal work environment. Optimal cultures differ among Color Q personality types. Strengths in one company may be unneeded elsewhere. The corporate culture itself may not be dysfunctional; for instance, Blues hate what Greens love. Conflict, sapped strength, resentment, and feelings of defeat are symptoms of poor cultural fit and can be avoided by understanding your preferences.

The Blue/Red Introvert's **most preferred work environment** emphasizes:

▸ Focus on intricate problems and unique solutions

▸ Start-up, not maintenance, of projects/systems (strong administrative support available)

- Minimal meetings, procedures, deadlines, and noise
- Working alone or with small groups of coworkers who are intellectual, independent, motivated, and informal
- Tolerance for open time frames, physical disorganization, and blunt critiques
- Rewards for creating/improving ideas, competence, and risk-taking

If these points seem obvious, it means you've tested correctly. (Compare with a Green/Gold Extrovert's ideal environment.)

The Blue/Red Introvert's **least preferred environment** is characterized by:

- Having to handle lots of details, routines, and/or people's feelings
- Tight deadlines and strict schedules
- Mandated tidiness
- Rewards for following procedure and being risk-averse
- Too much focus on past protocols
- Overly sensitive coworkers and office politics

Leveraging Executive Presence and Building Personal Brand

One of the critical tasks of a Blue/Red Introvert manager is to build one's personal executive reputation or "brand." As one of the most talented strategists of all the Color Q personalities, you'll ace this task. Your brand enables you to set organizational direction and market yourself externally when necessary. Here is an executive summary of the Blue/Red Introvert leadership brand:

> *A master strategist, you are the first to identify new or unusual ideas, strategic advantage, and added-value.*

People count on you to develop innovative solutions, looking beyond the expected. Although you'd rather work on your own, you're often invited into upper management. Your long-term thinking and radar for cutting-edge ideas makes you obvious executive material (and the financial rewards are tempting). You make quick decisions under pressure and instinctively know how to delegate. However, you make a better visionary than administrator.

CASE STUDY 1: *The Successful Blue/Red Introvert*

James G. Squyres, Buyside Research

Squyres owns a Darien, Connecticut, firm that applies technology to conduct investment analysis studies for Wall Street firms. Because the company develops unique computer programs for each client's requirements, "We walk on beaches where there're no footprints," he says.

Although not a household name, Squyres's innovative work has quietly revolutionized Wall Street. In the 1960s he was one of the first people to apply computer programming to investment research. Writing programs for war games while in the army developed the skills he needed in the emerging global banking field. "At that time, I was unique on Wall Street," he recalls. Also at Citibank, his team worked with the Federal Reserve to eliminate paper certificates for Treasury bonds. He was involved as the New York Stock Exchange embraced technology for high-volume order processing. Squyres designed the technology to close the NYSE on triple-witching days.

Squyres has been successful because he understands the necessity of gaining support. "Change cannot be dictated," he says. "We cannot expect an enthusiastic workplace response to change without explaining, without educating. . . . By her example, my wife, Amy, has been showing me how to get something done, how to identify and appreciate people's values, how to deal with decision-making systems."

His Red side views strategy as dependent on necessity. "If something wasn't working and I thought it could be fixed," he says, "I asked to work on it."

Participating In and Managing Productive Teams

Blue/Red Introverts work best independently. You are most valuable during the initial design/strategy phase when you enjoy debating options.

Here's what you bring to the table: logic; sharp analysis of complex problems; ability to challenge conventional wisdom; high standards; a calming influence when emotions flare. Your in-depth knowledge provides visionary perception of marketplace trends.

Communications Style

Adjusting one's vocabulary to align with another Color Q personality's style can elicit powerful positive responses. Empathetic vs. objective analysis, theoretical vs. practical, structured vs. adaptable—these clashes fuel most workplace conflicts. Being able to "style shift" creates strategic advantage in negotiations, managing, and interviewing.

Blue/Red Introverts are businesslike and reserved. In your areas of interest, you communicate with speed, enthusiasm, and banter. You prefer written materials before meetings and are comfortable with theoretical jargon, statistical data, and technical terms. Reds, with whom you share some personality traits, prefer concrete words and action verbs like "move," "stimulate," and "expedite." Golds respond to "facts," "tradition," "respected," and "proven." Greens focus on abstract concepts and metaphors, emphasizing words like "values," "relationship," "feel," and "friendly." (The "Political Savvy" section includes tips for style shifting.)

Blue/Red Introverts are basically skeptical and do not require the agreement, understanding, or support of others for their visions (until the implementation phase). Conflict is handled with frankness and logic. At work, you are more likely to express concerns than appreciation.

Blind Spots

These blind spots are prevalent in Blue/Red Introverts; only some will apply to you:

- ▸ Relying on logic; exploring objective alternatives rather than feelings

- Initiating too many projects, then missing deadlines and commitments
- Setting complex goals and experiencing "analysis paralysis"
- Being overly critical, blunt, impatient, and competitive
- Intimidating those less quick-witted than you
- Being uncertain of how to achieve buy-in from others

Stressors That Produce Fatigue and Strife

Here are the workplace conditions that particularly stress and fatigue Blue/Red Introverts:

- Being constrained by details, procedures, and deadlines (limited options)
- Lack of autonomy
- Mandated group interaction
- Coworkers who cannot grasp the ideas you present
- Emotional outbursts of others or illogical arbitrariness
- Success that's measured by actual implementation

Blue/Red Introverts under *extreme* stress are prone to defensive outbursts. You can be cynical, resistant, resentful, or withdrawn. When you lose clarity, you'll obsess over minor inconsistencies until you get your footing. You may shut out all emotions as "irrelevant." Stubbornness and sarcasm are used to mask challenges to your competence and self-confidence.

Self-Coach Your Way to More Productive Work Relationships

The primary focus of the Blue/Red Introvert who wants to self-coach for career advancement should be on how to improve practical and emotional components of your strategies.

Problem Solving and Decision Making

The Blue/Red Introvert has these strengths:

» Constantly scans for the new, then critiques and redesigns

» Evaluates possibilities by objective standards; generates many options

» Reviews both traditions and new systems using critical logic

» Uses debate and skepticism when creating models or theories

» Focuses on errors in logic, improvements, and long-term consequences

Strategies for Improving Effectiveness When Challenged

Although Blue/Red Introverts bring tremendous strategy and vision to today's workplace, interpersonal challenges may distract focus. Here are self-coaching strategies for your biggest challenges:

» *Resistance to structure, rules, and bureaucracy.* You believe, rightly, in the value of applying strategic, logical solutions to long-range problems, and you become impatient with bureaucratic obstacles. Work within the system; develop upper-echelon allies.

» *Having to work in large teams or open offices.* Ask to work primarily on smaller subcommittees. Negotiate a private work space because you'll never feel comfortable without one.

» *Defeating buy-in to your solutions by ignoring the impact on people.* It's difficult for you to understand why humans irrationally resist your logical strategies. Hurt feelings develop for unknowable reasons. Find a Green mentor to help you master "emotional intelligence." Analyze what wins people over; use "if . . . then" equations.

» *Difficulty with details and practicalities.* Details are the strength of Golds, practicalities of the Reds. If you are not yet in a position to delegate to them, you soon will be. Meanwhile, form alliances through mutual respect of abilities. When realities conflict with theories, let others lead.

▸ *Obsessive searches for truth.* If your sense of competence is challenged, you'll work until it's regained. You may ignore your physical needs for so long that you become ill. Competence requires stamina, supported by nutritious food, adequate sleep, and exercise.

▸ *Lack of competence in others.* How quick are you to dismiss nonintellectual competencies? Can you rescue a stalled negotiation like your Green colleague? Handle practical implementation like a Red? Keep an organization running as smoothly as a Gold? When you sense a lack of competence in yourself, you withdraw (which is self-defeating). Keep yourself in the game and garner needed support from the other Color Q types through mutual respect.

When dealing with challenges, try physical activity that disengages your overstimulated mind. Doing nothing may be your best battery recharger, or try activities like card games, chess, travel, lectures, and reading. Values clarification exercises are useful, giving you thought-processing time to make sense of things and reconnect with your sense of competence. Prioritize your real need for privacy.

- -

CASE STUDY 2: When a Career Isn't Working

Hired as an electronic technician, within six months Alan Case proposed a strategic system redesign for Barnett & Cole Tooling that saved the company more than $2 million in the first year. He was promoted to manage this new system's unit at double his entry salary. He was twenty-three years old.

Initially, Alan hired three staff members. His Blue/Red eye for competence helped; he gave his team much autonomy. Blue/Reds enjoy analyzing problems, taking risks, and exceeding targets. Alan's staff had great respect for their young, capable boss. They formed an insular group at the local pub after work, often making fun of "incompetent," "flighty," or "rule-bound" coworkers.

One of those rule-bound coworkers, Howard, overheard the group laughing at the pub and decided to teach them a lesson by slowing down delivery of needed system parts. After several months, Alan's analysis uncovered the resentful administrative employee. He gave Howard a public tongue-lashing, then complained to his supervisor.

"You need to learn how to work with Howard," the supervisor said. "I'm not firing my best employee of twenty years."

Alan consulted Grace, the human resources director. She walked Alan through some style shifting behaviors, including how to apologize with sincerity. Although Alan will never be entirely comfortable with the "touchy-feely stuff," he now recognizes personality-based interaction skills are important to his success.

Political Savvy—Making Your Words Count

A valuable part of the Color Q system lies in learning how to harness the Green's marketing and people skills, the Gold's administrative talent, and the Red's practical implementation to your advantage. Engage irritating coworkers as powerful political allies.

Greens. The Green is the most people-oriented of the four primary Color Q personalities. Their understanding of people and emotions seems soft and secondary, but it's a vital balance to your logical, strategic orientation. Your style can irritate Greens; you don't need their agreement or support and treat social pleasantries as optional. Greens are often intimidated by your attitude, and they sense your low opinion of them. You prefer to solve problems in relationships; Greens need to feel emotionally honest. They avoid your debate and challenges because they dislike conflict. But challenge their values and you'll be handed your head! You see displays of emotion at work as unprofessional, dismissing those that challenge mental models; to Greens, this reaction seems cold. They won't confront you, but they'll become distant and unsupportive. Explain that you find it difficult to discuss possibly overwhelming emotions, and a Green will instantly support you.

Negotiating Strategies

‣ Find common ground through your mutual ability to identify future trends.

‣ Ask them how your behaviors affect others. Their feedback will be gentle and tactful.

‣ Show respect and appreciation, even if it's irritating, for their people skills and marketing abilities. This gesture increases their buy-in for your strategies and ideas, and they will bring in others, too.

‣ To ensure their political support, factor in their values when formulating strategies and making decisions.

‣ Explain that debating and critiquing is just your process and should not be taken personally. They'll have a hard time understanding this about your personality, so reiterate often.

Golds. Golds are the rule makers and procedure setters of the world. Their administrative talents relieve you of pesky details. They may irk you by refusing to consider new ideas, but in order to be effective, Golds need structure and stability. Appreciate Golds when they provide critical administrative support. To make Golds your allies, work with them about the details of how your ideas and strategies will work, and keep at it until they're in agreement. When formulating business plans, invite their input; they're brilliant with procedural details.

Negotiating Strategies

‣ To ease tensions, use words like "facts," "tradition," "respected," and "proven."

‣ Bond with Gold/Blues through your mutual preference for logical thinking.

‣ Explain that your critiques and debates are not personal, just ways to find "the truth." They will resist when you try to "improve" their structures, so pick your battles carefully.

▸ Acknowledge and flatter their superior detail management, especially when they perform these tasks for you.

▸ Make a consistent effort to include them during strategic planning or product innovation. They'll point out implementation issues that might otherwise sideline a project.

Reds. Your style can irritate a concrete-thinking Red with its abstractions, complex explanations, and overanalysis of problems. The Red's strength is to address implementation issues that can derail "the strategy." You also need Reds to create needed rapport with others. You want to point out logical flaws; Reds (who operate completely in the here-and-now) reply, "Does the 'flaw' matter at this moment? Let's get on with it."

Negotiating Strategies

▸ Find common ground in your mutual ability to get around problems and limitations and make quick decisions.

▸ Use these words and ideas with a Red—*move, expedite, stimulate, "let's get some real work done"*—and evaluate the response.

▸ Forget about talking strategically or theoretically. Simplify. Using concrete words, discuss specifically what needs to be done *now* to accomplish desired ends. Do a three-point "elevator pitch," then wait for questions.

▸ Solicit their opinions during initial strategy sessions. They'll simplify your intellectual complexities and point out practicalities that can make or break a venture. Step aside from making revisions and refinements; let your Red colleague "get on with it." Do not micromanage.

▸ Let a Red mentor demonstrate the difference between abstract "solutions" and real-world problem solving.

Extrovert vs. Introvert

If the aforementioned strategies are still missing the mark, the colleague may be an Extrovert. If so:

▸ Respect, don't challenge, their need to recharge their batteries by interacting with others—they need this the way you need private time. It will, however, be difficult for you to understand why they must constantly be around people and how they can prefer noisy environments.

▸ Engage in thoughtful debate; ask neutral questions.

▸ Interject verbally often, to keep them on point.

▸ Volunteer to handle tasks for them that require working alone. Benefit from their gratitude—and the solitude.

Recognize any coworkers in the preceding descriptions? Go in-depth by reading each Color Q personality's overall chapter and then Chapter 25, "Adjusting to the Workplace Styles of Others."

▸　▸　▸

In summary, Blue/Red Introverts are intellectual, analytical, and reflective. You value ideas and intellect above anything else. You seek to explain the universe, not control it! Lifelong learning is of highest importance, and you tend to acquire degrees and certifications more than most, particularly in abstract or theoretical subjects.

Whatever field you choose, you become the visionary, scientist, or architect; but you usually prefer to make your contributions from relative solitude. The mundane details of life may be neglected, as you frequently become lost in your intellectual pursuits. Often appearing aloof to others, you may have to give extra attention to your personal relationships. Overall, you are capable of outstanding creative achievements.

golds overall

GOLDS REPRESENT 46 percent of the overall world population, by far the largest percentage of the four primary Color Q personalities. If you are not a Gold but want to learn how to identify or improve communications with one, go to "How to Recognize a Gold Colleague" at the end of this chapter.

Sonia Sotomayor, Associate Justice of the Supreme Court of the United States

Perhaps one of the most "Gold" jobs in the United States is that of associate justice on the United States Supreme Court. And one of the women who fills this position exemplifies the Gold personality—Sonia Sotomayor. (This well-known Gold was tested by author Shoya Zichy in 1999.)

In her long journey from a South Bronx housing project to the bench of America's highest court, Sotomayor's step-by-step achievement style is characteristically Gold. Her father, a Puerto Rican tool and die maker, died when she was nine. Her mother was a strong and capable practical nurse who put Sonia and her brother through Catholic school.

In their housing development apartment, there was always a big pot of rice and beans on the stove or bacon-and-egg sandwiches prepared by her mother, Sotomayor recalls. It was their mother's way of keeping their friends at home and away from drug-infested stairwells.

Here, Sotomayor came into contact with many of the urban disadvantaged. There were "the working poor, the despairing poor, or the addicted poor," she recalls. "And you saw different kids making different choices."

Sotomayor's choice? To improve her English, she read all the Nancy Drew books, dreamed of becoming a detective, and devoured the TV show *Perry Mason*. On one episode she noticed that Perry Mason usually had to ask a judge for permission to do what was needed. "Suddenly, the lightbulb popped in my head," she recalls with a grin. "I realized that the judge was the most important character in the show. Somehow I made the connection, and at the age of ten, I decided that would be my life path."

Through mentoring and scholarships, she made it into Princeton University. The girl from the projects felt little in common with her fellow students, but it didn't stop her. "First, I found that my vocabulary and writing skills were poor, and I didn't know anything about the classics," she recalls objectively. "So during college summers, I retaught myself basic grammar, learned ten new words a day, and set up a program reading all the books I had missed." The step-by-step Gold effort turned her life around. She graduated summa cum laude and Phi Beta Kappa[1] from Princeton and made it into Yale Law School. There she served as editor of the *Yale Law Journal*. (Golds are naturally good editors.)

With these credentials, she joined the Manhattan district attorney's office, and after five years as a prosecutor, went to the law firm of Pavia & Harcourt. Here, she immersed herself in real estate, employment, banking, contracts, agency law, and intellectual property.[2] In 1992, her childhood dream became a reality—she became a federal district judge. Six years later, the U.S. Senate confirmed her appointment to the U.S. Court of Appeals for the Second Circuit, making her the first Puerto Rican woman to reach the nation's second highest court.

On August 8, 2009, Sonia Sotomayor became the Supreme Court's 111th justice, its first Hispanic justice, and its third female justice.[3]

Her leadership strengths, Sotomayor claims, are due to being highly organized. "I find the most direct and quickest route to accomplish things," this Gold says. "I just look at someone doing something and immediately think of how it could be done more efficiently." Sotomayor readily admits to a typical Gold blind spot: "Sometimes I make decisions too quickly, or I may get caught up in the pure logic of the situation and forget to consider how others will react."

Investor Warren Buffett, Berkshire Hathaway

Another highly respected Gold personality (as regarded by the Myers-Briggs community) is investor Warren Buffett. His Gold reliance on past performance and established companies has lifted the value of his Omaha, Nebraska-based firm Berkshire Hathaway from $19.00 a share in 1955 to $116,914 a share in 2012. He sees himself as merely the steward of his $45 billion fortune.[4]

Ray Linder, chief executive officer of Goodstewardship.com, describes Buffett's investment philosophy as one very typical of a Gold. "His great skill," says Linder, "is not about predicting the value of the future better than others, but rather understanding the value of the past better than others."

Buffett meticulously combs balance sheets of (typically blue chip) firms ten years and older for clues that the company is worth more than its current share price. His large investments in companies like IBM, Coca-Cola, Procter & Gamble, and Burlington Northern Santa Fe Railroad carried him through the recent recession with fewer losses than most.

Like most Golds (but on a grander scale), Buffett eschews debt and leverage, keeping up to $20 billion liquid[5] and ready for good investment opportunities. Linder summarizes: "It is said he reflects a practical, down-to-earth attitude in investing and personal lifestyle."

Golds are the backbones of corporate and public institutions. Society's administrators, you are naturally talented at protecting others and directing the logistics of people, goods, schedules, and services. You value detail and procedures, are recognized for your follow-through, and can mobilize others to achieve well-defined goals. Golds shine when establishing policy; you aim for status, respect, and power. "Let's do it right," summarizes the Gold mentality.

As a Gold, you may be skeptical reading a book like this, preferring instead to deal with things more concrete and less abstract. To optimize this book's value to you, study the "Negotiating Strategies" section of your particular personality chapter. Here you will find concrete tips for effectively dealing with even the most unfocused and disorganized coworkers. These strategies will help when all your best efforts have failed. Also study the "How to Recognize. . ." sections of Chapters 5, 10, and 15, which give an overall profile of the other Color Q personalities, and apply the suggestions to difficult coworkers. Then evaluate the results.

How to Recognize a Gold Colleague

External Environment Clues

- Usually an administrator or manager
- Maintains a clean desk
- Favors no-frills decor
- Has well-organized files

Personal Mannerisms—Personal Behavior

- Always on time
- Solid-seeming personality
- Dresses conservatively with quality clothing
- Devises and follows rules and procedures
- Detail-oriented
- Logistically skilled
- Accountable
- Responds to recognition and appreciation

Personal Mannerisms—Verbal

▸ Thinks/speaks in concrete, linear fashion

▸ Skeptical and cautious

How to Communicate with a Gold—"Style Shifting" Tips

- ▸ Acknowledge this person's title and achievements
- ▸ Make your points sequentially or chronologically
- ▸ Be factual and accurate
- ▸ Be precise and down-to-earth
- ▸ Avoid broad ideas and abstract theories
- ▸ Be reliable and prompt; honor promises and commitments
- ▸ Prepare for meetings; don't "wing it" (presentations must run smoothly)
- ▸ Follow procedures and respect the hierarchy
- ▸ Prioritize conserving resources
- ▸ Use concrete words and phrases like *costs, return on investment, time line, proven,* and *"first, second, third."*

21

---

gold/backup
blue extroverts

YOU'RE NOT ONLY a Gold; you also have strong secondary characteristics of the Blue personality. And you have tested as a Color Q Extrovert,
which means you recharge your batteries by being with people rather than
alone. Logic defines you; also stability, efficiency, structure, and belonging.
You are proficient at creating schedules and systems.

Top Motivators
As an Extrovert, you find working alone for long periods draining and
unproductive. Negotiate working in open environments. You need to be
around people (who work as diligently as you). Gold/Blue Extroverts form
9 percent of the world's population; without you the business world would
grind to a halt.

Negotiate, during hiring or review, for the following Gold/Blue Extrovert motivators:

▸ Power and authority

▸ Compensation that's commensurate with mastered skills

▸ A recognizable position in the organization's hierarchy with predictable advancement opportunities

▸ Stability through commitment to tried-and-true methods and traditions

▸ Opportunity to improve systems efficiency

Corporate Culture—Finding the Optimal Fit

It's the responsibility of every personality to find or create their optimal work environment. Optimal cultures differ among Color Q personality types. Strengths in one company may be unneeded elsewhere. The corporate culture itself may not be dysfunctional; for instance, Golds simply hate what Reds love. Conflict, sapped strength, resentment, and feelings of defeat are symptoms of poor cultural fit and can be avoided by understanding your preferences.

The Gold/Blue Extrovert's **most preferred work environment** emphasizes:

▸ Working for a respected and well-established institution

▸ Stability and predictability, with clear rules and reporting hierarchy

▸ Rewards for precision, dependability, administrative skills, and loyalty

▸ Sticking to "the plan" (i.e., preferred use of tried-and-true methodologies)

▸ Participating on teams with businesslike, hardworking coworkers

▸ Expectable progress up an identifiable corporate ladder

If these points seem obvious to you, it means you've tested correctly. (Compare with a Red/Green Introvert's ideal environment.)

The Gold/Blue Extrovert's **least preferred environment** is defined by:

- Constant change and ambiguity, and a lack of clear goals
- Unreliable, irresponsible, disorganized, or overly sensitive coworkers
- Uncertainty about the future, especially during business or project start-up (i.e., no "tried-and-true" procedures)
- Little sense of belonging (e.g., people working alone)

Leveraging Executive Presence and Building Personal Brand

One of the critical tasks of a Gold/Blue Extrovert manager is to build one's executive reputation or "brand." The opportunity cost of ignoring this task is the same as investing in a high-risk stock. Don't do it . . . unless you can afford to lose everything. Your brand allows you to do the right things with internal power and market yourself externally when necessary.

> *The Gold/Blue Extrovert's leadership brand should be built around your bold drive to map out what needs to be done: assigning tasks to the strongest staff, setting goals, and controlling schedules. Your image is one of being able to get the job done.*

You are a natural leader—a pillar of your community—with a strong sense of duty. With your outstanding logistical skills, you define needed actions, then implement efficiently.

Staff and clients describe you as cool-headed and reliable. You give precise instructions to achieve clear and measureable goals. A cautious risk taker, you are capable of making tough, unpopular decisions when necessary. You believe if you want the job done right, tackle it with tried-and-true methods.

CASE STUDY 1: **The Successful Gold/Blue Extrovert**

Martha Clark Goss, Board Member

She is one of those behind-the-scenes super-competent people who actually run the world. A professional board member, Martha Clark Goss currently serves on three high-profile corporate boards for American Water Works, Neuberger Berman Mutual Funds, and Allianz Life of New York. Her fields of expertise encompass investment management, auditing, governance, and internal controls.

"I am clear," Martha says, "on how important the internal control environment and processes are to a company's success."

Martha became treasurer of the Prudential Insurance Company of America at age 33—a position usually occupied by professionals in their fifties at the top of their game. The Gold/Blue Extrovert talent for analysis and reorganization was particularly pronounced in Martha, and she used it. "I took the treasury from a back-office, cash management operation to a worldwide financial function. I had a lot of input on how the corporate financial structure was managed," she explains.

This success led to the opportunity to organize an industry-specific investment group as president of Prudential Power Funding Associates. Focusing specifically on electric and gas utilities and alternative energy power projects, Martha managed a $7 billion portfolio. She also served as chief financial officer of Booz Allen Hamilton, Inc., where she restructured the company's worldwide financial organization, saving the firm $40 million a year. In typical Gold/Blue Extrovert style, she describes herself as "highly focused—I get to the core of a situation quickly and have outstanding logistical abilities."

Today, her financial analysis and restructuring expertise is in high demand by global corporations who need to integrate and improve their financial and business operations.

Participating In and Managing Productive Teams

Cream rises, so you often find yourself leading the team. Collaboration increases your productivity. Bringing order during start-up is your first priority (but pay attention to diplomatic niceties as you organize details and operations). Resources go where they should; progress is evaluated fully; no detail falls through the cracks under your watch. You achieve goals on time and under budget.

At times, though, you'll need to remind yourself that diplomacy is just as important as schedules and deadlines.

Communications Style

Adjusting vocabulary to align with another Color Q personality's style elicits powerful positive responses. Empathetic vs. objective analysis, theoretical vs. practical, structured vs. adaptable—these clashes fuel most workplace conflicts. Being able to "style shift" brings major strategic advantages in negotiations, managing, and interviewing.

Bottom line is that for you, it's about choosing the logical right way over the many illogical wrong ways. You're a simple, clear, direct thinker and communicator. You unhesitatingly share your opinions, think on your feet, and reply quickly. You respond to words like "facts," "tradition," "respected," and "proven." By contrast Blues (with whom you share some personality traits) prefer theoretical jargon, statistical data, and technical terms. Reds like active words—"move," "stimulate," and "gusto." You are uncomfortable with Greens, who prefer metaphors and feelings, emphasizing words like "values," "relationship," and "friendly."

Gold/Blue Extroverts prefer to be businesslike and favor direct talks with business colleagues over written communications. Conflict is something to deal with logically and impersonally, with quick closure. You avoid small talk and personal disclosures, focusing instead on schedules and deadlines. Style shifting for you means accommodating the emotions and abstract ideas of others.

Blind Spots

These blind spots are prevalent in the Gold/Blue Extrovert (some of them will apply to you):

▸ Decides what's "right" and pressures others to follow

- Interrupts others to critique their logic; may be too abrupt or confrontational

- Takes charge without being asked

- May rely too heavily on past experiences and miss current opportunities (i.e., weak at foreseeing or responding to marketplace shifts)

- Can stall the process by picking out flaws

- Prematurely dismisses the nonlogical or nonlinear thinking of intuitive types as "incompetent"

Stressors That Produce Fatigue and Strife

Here are specific workplace conditions that stress and fatigue Gold/Blue Extroverts:

- Those who flaunt customs and rules

- The job not being done "right" the first time

- Uncertain goals or deadlines

- Working alone for too long

- Self-doubt when handling chaos or leading through a crisis

- Being asked to disregard deeply rooted principles

- Inadvertently hurting others in pursuit of goals

If you are under *extreme* stress, emotions may threaten to overwhelm you. When your actions fail to correct a problem, you're at a loss. You may start to attribute unrealistic, negative meanings to other people's words or actions and become detached or cold. It may be difficult to control your urge to be verbally aggressive, interruptive, and judgmental. During leisure hours you might experience self-pity, depression, physical symptoms, or outbursts fueled by ignored feelings.

Self-Coach Your Way to More Productive Work Relationships

The primary focus of the Gold/Blue Extrovert who wants to self-coach for career advancement should be on how to handle the emotional issues and abstract ideas of other people.

Problem Solving and Decision Making

The Gold/Blue Extrovert has these strengths:

▸ Uses what's learned from past experiences

▸ Controls the process with logical, cause-and-effect analysis

▸ Absorbs and assesses lots of statistics and empirical data

▸ Organizes projects and people effectively; devises systems, procedures, and schedules

---

Strategies to Improve Effectiveness When Challenged

Interpersonal challenges detract from productivity. Here are self-coaching activities to help solve your biggest challenges:

▸ *Having to work alone.* Delegate these tasks to Introverts (who'll thank you for the alone time!) or negotiate working with peers.

▸ *Emotional reactions that cloud reality and logic.* There are different types of intelligences. Feelings can be valuable, make-or-break inputs. Find a Green to mentor you through emotional logic. Try this technique: View emotions as "if . . . then" equations; for example, "If he feels this, then he'll likely do that."

▸ *People rejecting your contributions because you haven't factored in their needs.* Accommodate the needs of Reds and Blues for less structure. Ask Greens for their input about the human impact of your plans. Acknowledge, with appreciation, other people's contributions before proposing your own.

▸ *Doubting your ability to cope—with a situation or with your own emotions.* In order to achieve, you often ignore your emotions. Emotions build up and may feel explosive. This is especially true when you've done your best and nothing is working. Try these coping mechanisms: Identify a Red colleague and ask for help with midcourse corrections or crises. Calm pent-up feelings with physical exercise.

▸ *Pushing through to closure by dismissing others' opinions.* You've performed logical analysis in order to identify the "right" direction; you've no use for those who go "with the gut" or gravitate "toward new ways." To overcome this challenge, pick one low-risk situation and then step back and let others do it their way. Then analyze the outcomes.

When dealing with challenges, slow down. Revisit facts and details. Add inputs (e.g., the impact on people, the long-term strategy) that require extra effort. Sort through your emotions with any of a number of tools; for example, take up journaling, painting, even jogging. Reestablish order by arranging books by author or cataloging a collection. Reemphasize your need for structure and belonging.

- -

CASE STUDY 2: When a Career Isn't Working

The dog under veterinarian Roland Petty's care was howling, and wouldn't stop. It set every nerve in the Gold/Blue Extroverted doctor on edge. He had used several tried-and-true methods for calming the animal to no avail.

After sedating the dog, Dr. Petty stepped out for air. He'd just confronted the part of veterinary medicine that was his weakness—cases that didn't respond to set protocols. It made him want to abandon the small animal practice he recently inherited from his dad, only that was not a realistic option for a tradition-minded Gold/Blue.

He was planning expansion—into pet accessories and feed, or perhaps opening an exotic animal practice. But he'd have to hire—maybe hand over his patients—to another vet.

This pleasant Gold/Blue daydream was interrupted by the vet tech reporting an emergency intake. The dream became a reality ten months later, when Dr. Petty handed over his last patient chart to one of his recently hired veterinarians and promptly made the first order for a newly completed feed and accessory annex. He has since undertaken some private consulting with exotic pet owners (e.g., treating a chimpanzee's skin disorder) and plans further improvements to the practice's computer system to accommodate its new employees and ventures. The administrative challenges have energized him.

- -

Political Savvy—Making Your Words Count

A valuable part of the Color Q system lies in learning how to harness the Green's marketing and people skills, the Blue's long-term strategizing, and the Red's crisis management capabilities to your advantage. Learn to utilize irritating coworkers as powerful political allies.

Greens. *Gold/Blue Bob, the recently promoted head of new product development, called his first meeting of Green/Reds to brainstorm the top two projects for the coming year. He gave them twenty minutes, not understanding their process required far more time. The productivity of the demoralized group plummeted. After studying Color Q, Bob now calls meetings at 9:00 a.m. and has lunch brought in. He asks everyone to brainstorm all day until his 4:00 p.m. return. The options the group now generates are innovative and exciting, and Bob gains back his whole day.*

Greens are the most people-oriented of the four primary Color Q personalities. Their understanding of people and change may seem like a soft and secondary focus, but it's a vital balance to your logic. Your style can irritate a Green by overlooking social niceties while trying to achieve your goals. The Green's unusual manner of dress can offend your appropriate tastes. You want to focus on getting the job done today; Greens want to understand how the market will shift tomorrow. Make a blunt comment or dismiss their values as not logical enough to consider, however, and your potential Green ally will become cold and distant. Explain that you find it difficult to discuss emotions because they might be overwhelming, and a Green will instantly support you.

Negotiating Strategies

▸ Use these words with a Green and evaluate the response: *feel, relationship,* and *warm.*

▸ Emphasize that you don't want to inadvertently hurt anyone and need their help.

▸ Show respect and appreciation for their people skills and substantial marketing acumen.

▸ To ensure their political buy-in, factor in their values when making plans and decisions.

▸ Don't interrupt to critique their logic or to pick flaws. Greens talk nonsequentially, and their logic is completely different from yours. They will circle back to the point if you give them time.

Reds. *"I was just about to fire Asanti (a Red). He was always laughing and throwing paper airplanes around the office; but the day we had the fire in the computer room, his quick actions saved data and lives. I see him differently now," says Quentin (a Gold/Blue).*

Your style can irritate a Red with its emphasis on sticking to the plan. The Red's strength is to expect, even welcome, midcourse corrections; Reds like to see how things play out in the real world. Your detailed schedules may not seem realistic enough to a Red, who will challenge with on-the-ground scenarios. To the Gold/Blue Extrovert, the Red's style appears to be barely controlled chaos; in fact, it seems to be mostly play, little work. This is a setup for chronic conflict with an achievement-oriented Gold/Blue Extrovert. But if a crisis looms, send in a Red, who'll be energized by it.

Negotiating Strategies

▸ Evaluate a Red's response to words and phrases such as *move, stimulate, expedite, "let's get some real work done."* Don't argue semantics.

▸ Forget about talking strategically. Using concrete, factual words, discuss specifically what needs to be done *now* to accomplish desired ends.

- Solicit their opinions during strategy sessions. Reds can create contingency plans on the spot when needed.

- Do not micromanage; let them handle delays, ambiguities, and unforeseen changes.

- Find common ground in your mutual focus on the issues.

- Invite input from Reds during business planning. They'll minimize your intellectual complexities and add necessary concrete steps.

Blues. *"What do you mean, you don't like ANY of my ideas?!"* Robert (a Blue) exclaimed. *"Couldn't you at least have considered what has worked elsewhere, instead of wasting time starting from scratch?"* replied exasperated Kent (a Gold/Blue).

To a Gold/Blue Extrovert, Blues appear to put all their formidable mental energy into creating strategies that may ignore what has worked in the past. Your style can irritate a Blue by dismissing the possible benefits of change; besides, how can you respect someone whose office has so many paper piles? All is not lost, however, because you can bond over your mutual love of using systems to accomplish goals.

Negotiating Strategies

- Be verbally short and concise.

- Use "if . . . then" sentences, which are very effective.

- Tell them you'll support them if they allow you to do the implementation planning. Blues need you to find workable solutions.

- Adjust your vocabulary and use theoretical jargon, statistical data, and technical terms. To prove a proposal's worth, point out several long-term benefits. Use ingenuity, logic, and wit to make the case.

Extrovert vs. Introvert

If the previously described strategies are still missing the mark, your coworker may be an Introvert. If so:

▸ Accept that it will be difficult for you to understand why they shun interaction and prefer working alone. Respect, don't challenge, their need to recharge their batteries with privacy—it's not personal.

▸ Tone down your enthusiasm; listen more.

▸ Invite them to speak, but don't force them until they've thought things through.

▸ Do not fill their pauses.

Recognize any of your coworkers in the preceding descriptions? Find more negotiating strategies in each Color Q personality's "overall" chapter and in Chapter 25, "Adjusting to the Workplace Styles of Others."

▸　▸　▸

In summary, Gold/Blue Extroverts are assertive, loyal, opinionated, and decisive. You are a take-charge type who gets things done. Respectful of tradition, you support established practices and channels of authority. Outgoing and direct, you are basically easy to know—"what you see is what you get."

While some people may find you too blunt, you express your concern by looking after the needs of those under your care.

22

gold/backup blue introverts

YOU'RE NOT ONLY a Gold; you also have strong secondary characteristics of the Blue personality. And you have tested as a Color Q Introvert, which means you recharge your batteries by being alone. Gold/Blue Introverts may think a chapter about "feelings" is a waste of time. However, this chapter is actually about preferences. The Color Q system is based on the research of the Myers-Briggs community, which has conducted studies worldwide for more than seventy years.

Here are the four main advantages of reading this material: 1) Gain mastery over coworker interactions. 2) Develop stronger core competencies for dealing with irritations and energy drains. 3) Identify the roots of ongoing conflicts. 4) Understand the exact steps to achieving buy-in for your procedures and plans.

Top Motivators

Research has proven that the Gold/Blue Introvert's strongest motivators are:

▸ Setting goals and making plans

▸ Establishing and maintaining order, structure, and control

▸ Undertaking responsibility

▸ Being appropriate

▸ Belonging

▸ Achieving bottom-line results

A final motivator is that, as an Introvert, you need a workplace where your intense concentration will be uninterrupted. Always negotiate for private space.

Gold/Blue Introverts account for 9 percent of the world's population, but without your orderliness, society would be less civilized.

Corporate Culture—Finding the Optimal Fit

It is the responsibility of every personality to find or create their optimal work environment. Optimal cultures differ among Color Q personality types. Strengths in one company may be unneeded elsewhere. The corporate culture itself may not be dysfunctional; it's just that Golds hate what Reds love. Conflict, sapped strength, resentment, and feelings of defeat are symptoms of poor cultural fit and can be avoided by understanding your preferences.

The Gold/Blue Introvert's **most preferred work environment** emphasizes:

▸ Tangible projects/products and measurable results

▸ Clear chain of command and advancement opportunities

▸ Working on one task at a time without interruptions

▸ Neat, orderly surroundings, with appropriate decor and dress code

> Diligent coworkers who follow rules and procedures

> A stable, well-respected institution that offers long-term security

If these points seem obvious, it means you've tested correctly. (Compare with a Red/Green Extrovert's ideal environment.)

The Gold/Blue Introvert's **least preferred environment** is characterized by :

> Unclear goals

> Open-endedness, loose controls, and noise

> Little privacy with many interruptions

> Coworkers who are inefficient and casual about deadlines

> People who hold grudges or waste time discussing personal issues

> Rewards for intuition over facts

Leveraging Executive Presence and Building Personal Brand

One of the critical tasks of a Gold/Blue Introvert manager is to build one's personal executive reputation or "brand." Objectively speaking, this communicates your achievements, skills, and honors; in short, your hierarchical status. Your brand enables you to implement organizational structure and promote yourself externally when necessary. Here is an executive summary of the Gold/Blue Introvert leadership brand:

You are among the best at setting goals, making plans, and getting the job done. Gifted at implementing well-defined policies, you honor "the system," trust contracts, and organize work around procedures.

You are naturally decisive and adroit at time planning. With these strengths, you rise to power quickly. Rewarding subordinates who play by the rules, you earn respect and a reputation for fairness. You provide security and stability for your staff; by midcareer, you often are recognized as a pillar of your community.

CASE STUDY 1: *The Successful Gold/Blue Introvert*

Steven Brill, The Lighting Design Group

You have seen Steven Brill's work. You probably were unaware of it, because he's so good at it. Brill is the president and founder of The Lighting Design Group in New York, the largest television lighting design firm on the East Coast.

Gold/Blue Introvert Brill is the reason actors and sets look good. He has more than twenty years of broadcast lighting design experience and multiple Emmy awards. He has done lighting design work on The Cosby Show, *CBS's* The Late Show with David Letterman, *CNN's* Anderson Cooper 360, *and dozens of Olympics and presidential debates.*

Keeping things on track and orderly during projects such as timed television shows are natural strengths of the Gold/Blue Introvert. Brill is stimulated by the chance to work independently, with efficiency and accuracy. "I am extremely determined; I manage to work through failure and turn it into a success," he says.

His Gold/Blue managerial preferences are evident and help him excel under pressure. He says: "It's difficult getting the team to work productively under stressful conditions. I try to handle conflict by breaking down the stressful issues into component parts; I find that people are more able to handle the stress when they can look at the situation from that point of view."

Participating In and Managing Productive Teams

Gold/Blue Introverts work best independently. You consistently deliver on time within budget. "I analyze what the client needs are, and modify our response appropriately," says Steven Brill. You're a reality check for others' abstract ideas, analyzing procedures and costs. Focusing on one thing at a time, you implement plans even under pressure. "I am good at organizing an effective team that is appropriate to our clients' needs," says Brill.

You contribute efficiency, accuracy, predictability, thoroughness, and responsibility. While recognizing the core of problems and how to get things done, you need to guard against procedural rigidity.

Communications Style

Adjusting one's vocabulary to align with the style of another Color Q personality can elicit powerful positive responses. Empathetic vs. objective analysis, theoretical vs. practical, structured vs. adaptable—these clashes fuel most workplace conflicts. It has been proven that being able to "style shift" provides substantial benefits during negotiations, managing, and interviewing.

Gold/Blue Introverts are outwardly composed and businesslike; they are quiet observers with an inward, wry sense of humor. You prefer written materials and want to think before replying. You respond to words like "facts," "tradition," "respected," and "proven." Blues (with whom you share some personality traits) prefer theoretical jargon, statistical data, and technical terms. Reds like concrete words and action verbs like "move," "stimulate," and "expedite." Greens (with whom you are least comfortable) prefer abstract concepts and metaphors, emphasizing words like "values," "relationship," "feel," and "friendly." (The "Political Savvy" section lists step-by-step suggestions for style shifting.)

Your communication style is clear and direct, asking for specifics and talking sequentially. You handle conflict logically, objectively, and impersonally. When the discussion's over, it's over. Logic rules. You are uncomfortable discussing personal matters at work.

Blind Spots

Certain blind spots are prevalent in Gold/Blue Introverts (only some of them will apply to you):

- Prioritizing present efficiency and dismissing new ideas prematurely
- Ignoring marketplace shifts and avoiding plan modifications
- Relying too heavily on past experience
- Overanalyzing causes of conflict and pushing too hard for closure

> ▸ Pointing out flaws and disregarding the need for rapport building

Stressors That Produce Fatigue and Strife

The workplace conditions that stress and fatigue Gold/Blue Introverts include:

- ▸ Seeing well-laid plans fail to correct a problem

- ▸ Doubting your ability to handle a situation

- ▸ Having to endure interruptions and last-minute changes, or being asked to "wing it"

- ▸ Seeing things "fall through the cracks"

- ▸ Working with thoughtless, overly casual coworkers

- ▸ Being taken for granted

Under *extreme* stress you may exhibit the emotional outbursts you dislike in others. If you fear losing control, you'll withdraw, freeze, or barrage others with facts. Long-term stress can cause physical pain. "I had fifteen years of back troubles," says Gold/Blue Introvert Elizabeth D. "When I got divorced, they disappeared."

Self-Coach Your Way to More Productive Work Relationships

The primary focus of the Gold/Blue Introvert who wants to self-coach for career advancement should be on improving how you handle change, emotions, and abstract thinking.

Problem Solving and Decision Making

The Gold/Blue Introvert has these strengths:

- ▸ Identifies and analyzes key facts

- ▸ Develops existing ideas

▸ Concentrates on improving efficiency

▸ Plans ahead, sets goals, and controls the schedule

▸ Implements what has worked elsewhere

▸ Measures costs before proceeding

Strategies to Improve Effectiveness When Challenged

Interpersonal challenges detract from productivity. Here are step-by-step self-coaching strategies for your biggest challenges:

▸ *Challenges to the status quo.* You believe that power resides in structure and hierarchy. Some does, but there also are other kinds of power. Feelings and innovative ideas contain power, too. Learn how they might be utilized to improve current procedures. Keep an open mind; offer planning assistance to maintain control. Remember, today's tried-and-true methods started as innovative ideas.

▸ *Having to work in large teams or open offices.* Ask to work primarily on smaller subcommittees. Bring physical order to your space. Negotiate private work space for greater productivity.

▸ *Foreseeing/responding to marketplace shifts.* Departing from the plan is uncomfortable, but sometimes necessary. Cultivate a Blue you can turn to for strategic help and a Green for people/marketplace intelligence. Be prepared to "style shift."

▸ *Defeating buy-in to your plans by ignoring emotional components.* You often don't understand why others irrationally resist your logical procedures. Find a Green mentor to help you master "emotional intelligence." Use "if . . . then" equations. Focus on appreciation to win people over and to soften your bluntness.

▸ *Being asked to lead through a crisis.* This situation raises inner doubts, preventing you from moving forward with full capability. Delegate to a Red, who will find the crisis energizing. If you can't delegate, follow a Red colleague's advice even (or especially) if it goes against your grain.

▸ *Working alongside lazy, gossipy coworkers.* This is a "style shift" challenge. Reds might seem lazy, but they're like firefighters waiting for the next call. Greens foster relationships, through which they identify needs that translate to sales. The best solution to these differences? Acknowledge and laugh appreciatively about them, and use them as necessary.

When dealing with challenges, prioritize your need for privacy. Imagine all worst-case scenarios and plan step-by-step responses, but focus on one task at a time. Communicate to your boss that, to be most effective, you need structure and a sense of belonging. During leisure hours mix business with pleasure. Volunteer, watch or coach sports, design a garden, or plan a holiday.

CASE STUDY 2: When a Career Isn't Working

Brent Samuels loved the law. As a boy, he always played policeman, telling people what to do and what was right. Gold/Blues believe people should behave properly and be held accountable if they don't.

After high school he was accepted into the police academy. He learned how to make arrests, use firearms, and render attackers powerless. A diligent student, he especially enjoyed the simulation exercises and graduated top of his class.

Then he beat the odds. While getting coffee, he interrupted a convenience store holdup. In the split second it took Brent to remember appropriate firearms use, the perpetrator shot him and shattered his right femur.

Months of medical care followed. His supervisor expressed concerns about Brent's fitness to continue with police work—not only physically, but also because of Brent's hesitation in a crisis. Brent became deeply depressed; his sense of belonging with his police family was as shattered as his leg. X-rays revealed slow, steady healing, but his career crisis left him frozen.

In this low place, Brent observed the radiologist performing his X-rays. Gold/Blues find set procedures and attention to detail soothing and engaging. After a few weeks Brent was on a first-name basis with Curt; after two months, the pair had mapped out a plan for Brent to enter radiology training. The police department picked up the costs of retraining. Today, Brent enjoys doing things right—at his own pace.

- -

Political Savvy—Making Your Words Count

A valuable part of the Color Q system lies in learning how to harness the Green's marketing and people skills, the Blue's strategic talents, and the Red's crisis-handling strengths to your advantage. Engage irritating coworkers as powerful planning and implementation allies.

Greens. *"You're really going to make Karen and all her clients angry if you impose penalties on all accounts unpaid after thirty days," warned Lisa (a Green). "I don't think we need to factor in feelings. This is just a bottom-line issue," replied Jared (a Gold/Blue). But Lisa replied, "Yeah? What happens to the bottom line if Karen jumps ship and takes all those clients with her?"*

Greens are the most people-oriented of the primary Color Q personalities. Their understanding of emotions may appear soft and secondary, but it's also a vital balance to your logical, structured orientation. Your style can irritate Greens; you are obvious in your disapproval of their colorful dress style, and you test them on facts and details. Abstract-thinking Greens are often intimidated by your sequential logic; they immediately sense your low opinion of them. You prefer to do things for others to show affection; Greens lead with their emotions all the time. You dismiss values that challenge rules and procedures as highly unprofessional. To Greens, your style seems blunt and critical. They won't confront you, but they'll become distant and unsupportive. Explain to them that you find it difficult to discuss emotions at work because those emotions might be overwhelming, and a Green will instantly support you.

Negotiating Strategies

▸ Find common ground with Greens, especially in midcareer, as you become more open to considering people's emotions.

▸ Ask Greens how to develop emotional patience. Their feedback will be gentle and tactful. When they use metaphors, ask them to "style shift" and speak more concretely to you.

▸ Show patience, respect, and appreciation (even if it irritates you) for their substantial people and marketing skills. This effort will increase buy-in for your plans and procedures.

▸ To ensure their support, factor in their values.

▸ Explain that your love of details, questioning, and critiquing is just your process and should not be taken personally. They'll have a hard time understanding this part of your personality, so reiterate often.

Blues. *"Why are you rejecting this product improvement? It's got a guaranteed 22 percent profit margin, possibly as high as 50 percent," asked Doug (a Blue) heatedly. Max (a Gold/Blue) replies: "We've never risked implementing any improvement that didn't bring in at least a 30 percent return."*

To a Gold/Blue Introvert, Blues appear to put all their formidable mental energy into creating strategies that may ignore the details of implementation. Although you share some traits, your style can irritate a Blue by emphasizing details, procedures, and cost analyses rather than overall strategy. In the Blue's mind, your desire to stick with the tried-and-true must be challenged with criticism and questions. You won't take the challenge personally. Remember, it's actually a compliment, so bond over the show of interest.

Negotiating Strategies

▸ Be verbally short and concise.

▸ Use "if . . . then" sentences, which are very effective.

▸ Relate your procedures to their strategies. For instance: "In order to introduce this new product by August, you'll have to line up X, Y, and Z," or "I'll research the legal and patent ramifications, so they don't trip you up."

‣ Adjust your vocabulary to use theoretical jargon, statistical data, and technical terms. To prove a proposal's worth, point out long-term benefits. Use ingenuity, logic, and wit to make the case.

‣ Accept that the Blue/Red's workspace may have many piles on it. Ignore the neat-and-tidy stuff; choose other battles.

‣ Bond with Blues over your mutual desire to innovate. You improve existing products/services; Blue starts from scratch. You innovate when needed; Blue innovates constantly.

Reds. *"We need to suspend work on store 322. The tornado damaged the street and half the town's population has been relocated," reports Blythe (a Red). But Tory (a Gold/Blue) replies: "Move ahead as scheduled. Our builders say they can get local workers in. I'm not going to be the first project manager to miss a completion deadline."*

Your style can irritate Red by limiting their autonomy and enforcing established procedures. The Red's strength is to handle midcourse corrections, last-minute changes, and those stressful crises that derail "the plan." You also need Reds to create team rapport. You point out logical flaws; Reds (who operate in the here-and-now) ask, "Does the 'flaw' matter at this moment?"

Negotiating Strategies

‣ Use words and phrases like *move, expedite, stimulate, "let's get some real work done"* with a Red, and evaluate the response.

‣ Rein in the tendency to criticize "lazy" Reds. They are coiled springs waiting to jump on the next crisis. Downtime (which they fill with gadget play and camaraderie) keeps them on top of their game.

‣ Find common ground in your keen observation of details, working with tangible items and trusting your own experience.

‣ Invite Red input into a business plan. When midcourse corrections are needed, Reds will be up to speed.

Extrovert vs. Introvert

If the aforementioned strategies are still missing the mark, the colleague may be an Extrovert. If so:

▸ Respect, don't challenge, their need to recharge their batteries by interacting with others—they need this the way you need private time. But expect that it will be difficult for you to understand why they must be constantly around people and why they prefer noisy environments.

▸ Ask as many questions as you want, but be neutral, not challenging.

▸ Interject verbally often; keep them on point.

▸ Volunteer to handle tasks for them that require working alone. Benefit from their gratitude—and the solitude.

Recognize any of your coworkers in the preceding descriptions? Further advance your understanding of the other Color Q personalities by reading their overall chapters and then Chapter 25, "Adjusting to the Workplace Styles of Others."

▸　▸　▸

In summary, Gold/Blue Introverts are responsible, patient, loyal, and steadfast. Often you serve as anchors in your work or personal communities. Your strength is creating and enforcing policies, procedures, schedules, and deliverables. You naturally adapt to the roles assigned to you—be it leader or follower—ensuring that your organization remains efficient and on track. Decisive and duty-bound, you get things done and are fair with others. You need to be needed and readily take on parental roles in your professional and personal relationships.

gold/backup
green extroverts

YOU'RE NOT ONLY a Gold; you also have strong secondary characteristics of the Green personality. And you have tested as a Color Q
Extrovert, which means you recharge your batteries by being with people.
As a Gold/Green Extrovert, you are one of the friendliest, most outgoing,
and engaging types. Traditions, harmony, and cooperation are prominent
for you. Whether as leader or team member, you carefully utilize both
human and tangible resources.

Working alone for long periods is draining and unproductive, however.
As an Extrovert, you need to work with people. Negotiate working in open
environments. Gold/Green Extroverts form 14 percent of the world's population; of all the personality types, only Gold/Green Introverts also form

this large a percentage. Your most notable contribution to the world is a critical combination of resource-handling and people skills.

Top Motivators
Negotiate, during hiring or review, for these Gold/Green Extrovert motivators:

- A values-based mission
- Opportunities to help others accomplish goals
- An environment that's respectful of traditions
- Predictability
- Harmonious interaction
- Recognition of your contributions

Corporate Culture—Finding the Optimal Fit
It's the responsibility of every personality to find or create their preferred work environment. Optimal cultures differ among Color Q personality types. Strengths in one company may be unneeded elsewhere. The corporate culture itself may not be dysfunctional; for instance, Golds hate what Reds love. Conflict, sapped strength, resentment, and feelings of defeat are symptoms of poor cultural fit and can be avoided by understanding your preferences.

The Gold/Green Extrovert's **most preferred work environment** emphasizes:

- Stability, organization, predictability, rules, and procedures
- Achievable expectations
- Control over delivery of a tangible product or service
- Frequent interaction with customers and cooperative coworkers; friendly administrative interface
- Inclusion in decision making

> Rewards for efficiency, loyalty, and amicability

If these points seem obvious, it means you've tested correctly. (Compare with a Red/Blue Introvert's ideal environment.)

The Gold/Green Extrovert's **least preferred environment** is characterized by:

> Emphasis on abstract theories

> Competition and/or unreliable, unprepared coworkers

> Unresolved conflicts

> Constant change, uncertainty, and chaos

> Instructions to ignore your values

> Future focus

Leveraging Executive Presence and Building Personal Brand

One of the critical tasks of a Gold/Green Extrovert manager is to build one's executive reputation or "brand." A brand communicates your strengths in a memorable way to others. Your brand gives you the power to establish values, procedures, and harmony internally and market yourself externally when necessary.

> *The Gold/Green Extrovert's leadership brand should be built on your strength for anticipating needs, handling details, and organizing resources and procedures. Building on what already exists and conserving resources are your strengths.*

Schedules, calendars, and lists are your preferred tools. Staff would describe you as loyal, attuned, and responsive; you excel at motivating others to cooperate and achieve goals. Subordinates feel important because you keep them in the decision-making loop. You also are highly observant; employees know they'll be held accountable. But you show little tolerance for those who misuse resources or question your authority.

CASE STUDY: *A Successful Gold/Green Extrovert*

Martha Sloane, Certified Nursing Assistant

A typical Gold/Green Extrovert has natural talents for working with people, planning/development, and budgeting. These are the exact skills Martha Sloane listed as her top three. Currently, Martha is a retired executive recruiter who has trained to be a certified nursing assistant. In both these positions, Martha's core talents come to the fore.

"My strengths are the ability to listen and talk with people of all ages," Martha says. "It was during my father's illness that I became interested in caring for the elderly. But I am most proud of the recruiting business I developed and ran. It was fulfilling whenever I was able to place a candidate at a firm where they were successful. I also enjoyed coaching candidates on how to interview and rewrite their resumes."

Martha's major stressors are deadlines and short time frames, which may force her to produce work not in accordance with her own high standards. "I handle those times by taking short breaks and [doing] deep breathing," she says. Sometimes she will "put the deadline or short time frame on hold and work on something else" to regain her sense of control.

"My firm was successful and well known until the 2008 financial crisis," Martha recounts. Facing the future, this typical Gold/Green Extrovert wants to continue helping others. "It is hard to strategize for the future considering the many changes that have occurred over the past ten years," says Martha. "I try to plan, make budgets, and follow through on my plans and budgeting. For now, I enjoy working with the elderly, helping them to feel well cared for, and that their life is still important."

Participating In and Managing Productive Teams

Team collaboration is inspiring for you, if the team is harmonious. You resolve conflict by promoting win-win solutions. During chaotic start-ups, you create order with structure, schedules, systems, agendas, budgets, and records; then you apply conscientious follow-through.

Teammates find themselves rising to your standards, being more accurate and on time than usual. Mobilizing others is particularly satisfying to a Gold/Green Extrovert.

Communications Style

Adjusting vocabulary to align with another Color Q personality's style elicits powerful positive responses. Empathetic vs. objective analysis, theoretical vs. practical, structured vs. adaptable—these clashes fuel most workplace conflicts. Learn how to "style shift" to create harmony and cooperation during negotiations, managing, and interviewing.

Gold/Green Extroverts are warm and attentive, preferring face-to-face interaction over writing or texting. You ask questions, know your facts, think on your feet, and reply quickly. Your preferred vocabulary includes words like "facts," "tradition," "respected," and "proven." Greens (with whom you share some personality traits) prefer metaphors and analogies, emphasizing words like "values," "relationship," "feel," and "friendly." By contrast, Blues prefer theoretical jargon, statistical data, and technical terms. Reds use active words such as "move," "stimulate," and "expedite."

Gold/Green Extroverts seek similarities with others, often sharing stories of others who've faced similar challenges. Be alert to your listener's capacity to absorb, especially the nonlinear thinkers.

Blind Spots

Certain blind spots are prevalent in Gold/Green Extroverts; some of them will apply to you:

- Prefer established ways and the resulting efficiencies to innovation and future thinking

- Dislike engaging in confrontation or corrective feedback

- Avoid giving bad news

- See criticism as a personal, not professional, challenge

- Allow people problems to delay task completion

- Ignore own needs; may have unclear limits on demands

Stressors That Produce Fatigue and Strife

Here are specific workplace conditions that stress and fatigue Gold/Green Extroverts:

- Uncooperative teams

- Challenges to your values

- When others are hurt, despite best efforts to show personal concern for others

- Overwhelming responsibilities and chaos

If you are under *extreme* stress, you've likely suppressed negative emotions. You may focus on others, overburdening yourself. You can become critical or bossy. Worrying about the worst creates gloom and self-doubt. Overanalysis and relying too much on experts are tools that become crutches.

Self-Coach Your Way to More Productive Work Relationships

The primary focus of the Gold/Green Extrovert who wants to self-coach for career advancement should be on how to handle other people's innovations, abstract or nonlinear thinking, and midcourse corrections.

Problem Solving and Decision Making

The Gold/Green Extrovert has these strengths:

- Defining the problem, then applying best practices

- Asking, "What does the past teach? What are the costs? What matters to relevant parties? Who has to sign off?"

- Listening to each party's concerns

- Making present task decisions quickly and longer-term decisions slowly

Strategies to Improve Effectiveness When Challenged

Interpersonal challenges detract from productivity. Here are self-coaching activities to help solve your biggest challenges:

- *Having to work alone.* Delegate these tasks to Introverts, who'll thank you for the alone time! Negotiate working with others for increased productivity.

- *Dealing with those who question authority.* Listen carefully, because people who feel they are heard become more cooperative. What do they suggest to accomplish the goal more effectively?

- *Enduring rather than confronting difficult people.* Harmony and cooperation provide valuable productivity, but overextending yourself creates resentment that saps your energy. Study how your Blue colleagues confront others impersonally; role-play the iron-fist-in-velvet-glove approach before confronting a difficult colleague.

- *Handling necessary innovation.* You are a "best practices" professional, overanalyzing "new" practices that provoke uncomfortable uncertainty. Try allowing conservative innovation to proceed while providing input on costs, implementation, and human resources.

- *Taking criticism personally.* Criticism feels like disharmony to you; emotions overwhelm content. When a coworker offers criticism, acknowledge your discomfort, thank your coworker, then reiterate your concerns. For example: "Thanks, Clara. Just so I'm clear, you're saying I'm interrupting your train of thought by prematurely focusing on costs?" Make sure the other person agrees with you; then propose win-win solutions.

- *Dealing with abstract or nonlinear thinkers.* Blues use abstract "if . . . then" strategic thinking. Offer your implementation capabilities after they've conceived a plan. Nonlinear Greens stay on track by focusing on people's responses. All of you will have to do some "style shifting."

When dealing with challenges, you will usually attempt to reestablish harmony and belonging. Accept your need for belonging and structure rather than trying to get attention by falling into depression or reacting with overprotectiveness. Make needed life adjustments. Release strong emotions by exercising with friends.

- -

CASE STUDY 2: **When a Career Isn't Working**

Peter McIvor felt lucky to get the purchasing agent position at a factory only two miles from his house, saving him commute time and gas. Gold/Green Extroverted Peter knew he could quickly build relationships with the vendors and make fast decisions.

He enjoyed meeting vendors at the company's holiday party and got off to a good start by negotiating for lower piece prices on several critical components. But, after three months, Extroverted Peter started feeling stressed sitting alone in his small office.

He compensated by calling vendors. The frequency of his calls irritated some of his vendors and made others hesitant to return his messages.

Then one of his key vendors unexpectedly went bankrupt, leaving the factory short of $150,000 worth of key components. Peter offered to visit affected clients with the sales manager. Peter explained the details of the problem; together, they worked on solutions with each client.

"You're terrific with customers, Peter," the manager remarked. "I'd like you to consider joining our client retention team."

Peter made the move. He now works in an open office and spends his days on the phone or at client meetings. His energy has skyrocketed, and his Gold/Green diplomatic skills have earned him several raises.

- -

Political Savvy—Making Your Words Count

A valuable part of the Color Q system lies in learning how to harness the Green's marketing and people skills, the Blue's innovative and strategic thinking, and the Red's crisis-management capabilities to your advantage. Learn to utilize irritating coworkers as powerful political allies.

Greens. *"We need to get that budget off to Howard today. Oh, did you talk to Marta about her insurance questions? I've got some, too . . . so we should conference call . . . and if we get Jake on the line with us we can solve his hiring problem," said Sarah (a Green) in one breath. Colter (a Gold/Green) struggled to keep up with all the steps these four sudden, nonlinear demands required. "Slow down, Sarah! One thing at a time!" he finally interjected.*

Greens are the most people-oriented of the four primary Color Q personalities. They are also the most nonlinear thinkers; as you converse with them, you struggle to sort out details and step-by-step procedures. Instead of following procedures, they want to "get creative." You want to focus on getting the job done efficiently today; they want to sense how the market will respond tomorrow. Don't "guide" them with a barrage of details, however; your potential Green ally will become cold and distant. But explain that you find it difficult to deal with intense emotions or being taken for granted, and a Green will instantly support you.

Negotiating Strategies

▸ Use words like *feel, friendly,* and *relationship* with a Green and evaluate the response.

▸ Ask them how your plans will be perceived; emphasize that you don't want to inadvertently hurt anyone.

▸ Show respect and appreciation for their ability to identify marketplace shifts.

▸ To ensure their political buy-in, factor in their values when developing schedules and plans.

▸ Do not interrupt them (even when they talk nonsequentially). Take notes. You'll find they address all the necessary points, just not in sequential order.

Reds. *"The citizens' committee has halted our expansion plans; they say we're threatening that indigenous species. Let's explore expanding in the opposite direction," says Margaret (a Red). In reply, Hanson (a Gold/Green) observes, "We'll get behind. It's twice as expensive to do that. Let's look at accommodating the needs of the species in question first."*

Your style can irritate a Red with its emphasis on sticking to rules and procedures. The Red's strength is to expect, even welcome, midcourse corrections. Your detailed schedules may not seem realistic enough to a Red, who will challenge with on-the-ground scenarios. To the Gold/Green Extrovert, the Red's style appears to be either lazy or sprinting off to a crisis. This is a setup for chronic conflict with the Gold/Green Extrovert, who thrives on stability and predictability. But if a crisis looms, call upon a Red, who'll be energized by it.

Negotiating Strategies

▸ Use words and phrases like *move, expedite, stimulate,* and *"let's get some real work done"* with a Red and evaluate the response.

▸ Bond over your mutual focus on the present. Using the concrete, factual words you both prefer, discuss specifically what needs to be done *now* to accomplish desired ends.

▸ Invite Red input into a business plan. If a crisis arises, Reds will be well-informed allies.

▸ Do not micromanage; let them handle delays, ambiguities, and unforeseen changes.

▸ Curb insistence that rules and procedures be followed without exception.

Blues. *"Here's the solution to declining enrollment in our credit card business: Lower penalties and lengthen the grace period,"* says Chang (a Blue). But *Brandon (a Gold/Green) replies: "That's not an option. It would shave our profit margins relative to competitors. Senior management will never approve."*

To a Gold/Green Extrovert, Blues appear to put all their formidable mental energy into creating strategies that may ignore the details of implementation. It becomes Blue innovation vs. Gold/Green best practices. Your style can irritate a Blue by overanalyzing implementation and emphasizing the human impact. Emotions are irrelevant distractions to a Blue; to you, emotions are a central concern. However, you can bond over your mutual love of designing systems to accomplish goals.

Negotiating Strategies

▸ Be verbally brief and concise.

▸ Use "if . . . then" sentences, which are very effective.

▸ Try offering your support, provided they allow you to do implementation planning. Blues need you to structure the details and get others' cooperation. In this case, you may just create tomorrow's best practices together.

▸ Adjust your vocabulary and use theoretical jargon, statistical data, and technical terms. To prove a proposal's worth, point out several long-term benefits. Use ingenuity, logic, and wit to make the case.

Extrovert vs. Introvert

If the strategies described are still missing the mark, your coworker may be an Introvert. If so:

▸ Accept that it will be difficult for you to understand why they shun interaction and prefer working alone. Respect, don't challenge, their need to recharge their batteries with privacy—it's not personal.

▸ Tone down your enthusiasm and desire for chitchat, and listen more.

▸ Invite them to speak, but don't force them until they've thought things through.

▸ Do not fill their pauses.

Recognize any coworkers in the preceding descriptions? Find more negotiating strategies for dealing with each Color Q personality type by reading the overall chapters and then Chapter 25, "Adjusting to the Workplace Styles of Others."

▸ ▸ ▸

In summary, Gold/Green Extroverts are outgoing, practical, and organized. You pride yourself on your abilities to create harmony, nurture others, and remember important details. You have firm opinions and like to be in environments that are decisive and settled.

Loyal to established institutions, you need to be active and productive. Often volunteering on committees, you are highly represented in charitable, social, and civic organizations.

You have little tolerance for those who hurt the feelings of others, and you are apt to let the offender know! You also need frequent expressions of appreciation for your efforts. If these acknowledgments are not forthcoming, you can become touchy and irritated.

24

gold/backup
green introverts

YOU'RE NOT ONLY a Gold; you also have strong secondary characteristics of the Green personality. And you have tested as a Color Q Introvert, which means you recharge your batteries by being alone rather than being with people. You perform a constant balancing act in your life—you are deeply motivated to provide for the welfare of others but need lots of alone time to recharge your inner batteries. Being highly observant allows you to target what's needed and provide it, while still having enough time to yourself. Today's demands, however, challenge the balance.

Top Motivators
Here are the Gold/Green Introvert's strongest motivators:

> ‣ Predictability and stability

- Ensuring the welfare of those around you

- Fulfilling personal commitments and honoring traditions

- Harmony

- Being needed and included

- Following a vision based on your inner values

A final motivator is that, as an Introvert, you need to work in private where you can think and reflect. Gold/Green Introverts account for 14 percent of the world's population; but without your ability to meet others' needs, everyone would be less productive.

Corporate Culture—Finding the Optimal Fit

It is the responsibility of every personality to find or create their optimal work environment. Optimal cultures differ among Color Q personality types. Strengths in one company may be unneeded elsewhere. The corporate culture itself may not be dysfunctional; for instance, Golds hate what Reds love. Conflict, sapped strength, resentment, and feelings of defeat are symptoms of poor cultural fit and can be avoided by understanding your preferences.

The Gold/Green Introvert's **most preferred work environment** emphasizes:

- Focus on one thing at a time with minimal interruption

- Applying mastered skills to tangible products

- Widely accepted procedures, standards, clear rules, and achievable expectations

- Friendly, cooperative, organized atmosphere

- Predictable rewards for accuracy, follow-through, and end results

- Long-term security at a stable, well-respected institution

If these points seem obvious, it means you've tested correctly. (Compare with a Red/Blue Extrovert's ideal environment.)

The Gold/Green Introvert's **least preferred environment** is defined by:

‣ Constant change, ambiguity, tension

‣ Little privacy, many interruptions

‣ Frequent communication in metaphors

‣ Highly competitive coworkers

‣ Reward system that favors intuition over factual accuracy

‣ Rewards far in the future

Leveraging Executive Presence and Building Personal Brand

One of the critical tasks of a Gold/Green Introvert manager is to build one's personal executive reputation or "brand" that immediately conveys your achievements, skills, honors, and reliability. Your brand enables you to create stability and structure internally and introduce yourself externally when necessary. Here is an executive summary of the Gold/Green Introvert leadership brand:

> *You are practical, detail-oriented, and gifted at anticipating what employees and customers need. Your follow-through and logistical capabilities are exceptional.*

Harmony and stability are top priorities. Naturally decisive, you assign tasks to those well suited to perform them; at crunch time, you pitch in with your highly developed work ethic. Everyone on your team is well informed. Leadership is seen as a way to serve others inconspicuously. You prefer being second-in-command—out of the spotlight and focused on your obligations.

CASE STUDY 1: *Successful Gold/Green Introverts*

Dr. Silvester Lango, Orthopedic Surgeon

Born in Slovenia, Dr. Lango survived the Nazis, fascists, and communists; then he studied medicine in Switzerland and the United States. Today he is an orthopedic surgeon treating degenerative conditions of the bones and joints in New York City. Despite his early hardships, his Gold/Green ability to build a practice team triumphed. "My office is not run as a business, but as an extended family," Dr. Lango says. "I cherish my relationship with the staff."

He is proud of his accomplishments. "I was able, without much help and [encountering] many hurdles, to achieve a reasonable emotional and professional well-being," he says modestly.

His greatest challenges are insurance paperwork and demanding people. But his Green side prevails: "I most enjoy work in my own practice, interacting with patients, helping them reduce stress and pain," he says.

George Yarocki, Author and Indian Motorcycle Restorer

Despite founding three successful manufacturing businesses in his long career, George Yarocki insists, "I never wanted to be a boss." Like most Gold/Green Introverts, George prefers to lead inconspicuously.

At age 21, George opened his first business—a metalworking shop. He was challenged by two employees who openly defied him. "As 'prima donnas' do, they had made themselves indispensable," George recalls. "But firing them would have been a definite loss to the business." George tolerated their behavior for the sake of profits until he sold the business, "partly to rid myself of these two for good."

He then founded a business making backhoe and loader attachments. He carefully selected his new staff with advice from a management professor who said: "You must surround yourself with people you look forward to being in the company of, each and every day."

"I did exactly [that]," says George, "and enjoyed twenty-nine years of peace and comfort as my business prospered."

Pursuing a lifelong passion, today George runs an antique motorcycle restoration business. He has also written five publications on

antique Ace and Indian motorcycles. Showing the Gold/Green prefer-
ence for tradition, stability, and family, he is located less than a mile
from his childhood home.

Participating In and Managing Productive Teams

Gold/Green Introverts are true team players. Practical, conscientious, detail-oriented . . . the team counts on you. You pride yourself on efficiency and reliability—never missing a deadline. Achievement means following rules, upholding procedures, anticipating needs, attending to details. You'll assert yourself only to enforce harmony and stability.

As team leader you are organized, caring, patient, and conscientious, supporting the team both with positive feedback and necessary resources. Although a cautious innovator, you encourage other people to express their views and ideas.

Communications Style

Adjusting one's vocabulary to align with the style of another Color Q personality can elicit powerful positive responses. Empathetic vs. objective analysis, theoretical vs. practical, structured vs. adaptable—these clashes fuel most workplace conflicts. It has been proven that being able to "style shift" provides substantial benefits during negotiations, managing, and interviewing.

Although quiet and reserved, Gold/Green Introverts are also warm and people-oriented. One-on-one communication is preferred, with written materials and time to prepare before going face-to-face. You ask specific questions and listen attentively, responding to words like "facts," "tradition," "respected," and "proven." Greens (with whom you share some personality traits) prefer metaphors and abstract concepts, emphasizing words like "values," "relationship," "feel," and "friendly." Blues prefer theoretical jargon, statistical data, and technical terms. Reds like concrete words and action verbs such as "move," "stimulate," and "expedite." (The upcoming "Political Savvy" section lists step-by-step suggestions for style shifting.)

Getting to know people personally, but appropriately, is the Gold/Green Introvert style. While affirming others, you tend not to share your own feelings. Focusing on others puts them quickly at ease; but you do enjoy sharing opinions and advice. Personal influence is exercised behind the scenes.

Blind Spots

These blind spots are prevalent in Gold/Green Introverts (although only some of them will apply to you):

- Can get discouraged if unappreciated and become overburdened
- Underestimate your own value and ability; shy away from the spotlight
- Overreact to challenges like new concepts, competition, and political infighting
- Avoid conflict to ensure harmony; may not be assertive about your own needs
- Have difficulty arguing logically; need time to formulate

Stressors That Produce Fatigue and Strife

Here are specific workplace conditions that stress and fatigue Gold/Green Introverts:

- Noisy, discourteous, unreliable coworkers
- Being the focus of conflict or criticism
- Too much interaction with people or, conversely, a lost sense of belonging
- No clear sense of direction (e.g., when changes happen with no prep time)
- Feeling used, underappreciated

Gold/Green Introverts under *extreme* stress experience gloom and self-doubt, imagining the worst and doubting their ability to cope. You may become cold, snappy, and critical or turn into a rigid defender of the status quo. Like George Yarocki, you might leave a difficult situation rather than confront or express your needs.

Self-Coach Your Way to More Productive Work Relationships

The primary focus of the Gold/Green Introvert who wants to self-coach for career advancement should be on how to improve your abilities to handle or adapt to change, innovation, and abstract thinking.

Problem Solving and Decision Making

The Gold/Green Introvert has these strengths:

▸ Goes step-by-step using past experience

▸ Seeks evidence of prior success to minimize turmoil of change

▸ Absorbs, assesses, and organizes cost and scheduling data

▸ Evaluates effects of change on self and others

▸ Vigilant about things "falling through the cracks"

Strategies to Improve Effectiveness When Challenged

Interpersonal challenges detract from productivity. Here are step-by-step self-coaching strategies for your biggest challenges:

▸ *Challenges to the status quo.* You believe that power resides in structure and hierarchy. It does, but there also are other kinds of power. If someone believes in the power of a feeling or an innovative idea, for example, ask how past experiences demonstrate effectiveness. Offer to help implement the idea.

▸ *Having to work in open offices.* Organize your space and negotiate for privacy (you'll never feel comfortable without it).

▸ *Foreseeing/responding to marketplace shifts.* Departing from the plan is uncomfortable, but sometimes necessary. Cultivate a Blue for strategic help and a Green for people/marketplace intelligence. Be prepared to "style shift."

▸ *Having to lead through change or crisis.* This situation raises inner doubts, reducing effectiveness. Delegate the crisis, if you can, to a Red, who will find it energizing. Or follow a Red peer's advice even—or especially—if it ignores procedure.

> ◆ *Coworkers who insist on constant innovation or sharing emotions at work.* These are "style shift" challenges. Blues are hardwired to innovate. Greens read clients' needs well in advance of marketplace shifts. The best response to these differences? Recognize, appreciate, utilize.

When dealing with challenges like criticism, remember such feedback is usually professional, not personal. If situations escalate into conflict, respond ASAP; avoidance breeds resentment. Schedule free time to prevent burnout; refuse to complete other people's assignments. Call attention to your very real achievements to get the appreciation you deserve. When forced to work with strategic or intuitive thinkers, take calculated risks.

- -

CASE STUDY 2: When a Career Isn't Working

Gold/Green Introvert Elaina Montez started her career as a secretary for one of America's largest executive recruitment firms. After three years she was promoted to recruiter, specializing in the Latino market. Fluent in Spanish, Elaina became well known in the upper echelons of Latino executives.

During her twenties and thirties, Elaina made frequent international trips to high-profile events. Instead of pursuing marriage and children, which Golds desire, she found it increasingly difficult even to date. Introverted Elaina started feeling drained in ways sleep couldn't fix.

It took a long, hard fight against breast cancer to get Elaina off the merry-go-round. After breaking down with no one to comfort her, she decided to live whatever life she had left with completely different priorities.

Elaina quit her job, opening her own recruitment firm and hiring two recruiters. She discovered her natural Gold/Green managerial talents. Giving up travel and dealing with just two people instead of 200, she felt her old energy flowing back. She dated frequently, making up for lost time.

Flash-forward three years. Elaina now makes 85 percent of her previous highest income. She is grooming one of her employees to take over the majority of her duties so that she can join her husband for three months of maternity leave when they have their first child. Her cancer has been in remission for two years. She now works with, instead of against, her Gold/Green Introvert needs for alone time, stability, predictability, and family—all the things her old position denied her.

Political Savvy—Making Your Words Count

A valuable part of the Color Q system lies in learning how to harness the Green's marketing and people skills, the Blue's strategic and innovation talents, and the Red's crisis handling to your advantage. Engage irritating coworkers as powerful allies.

Greens. *"My coleader Tripp (a Green) always asked me how I felt about something in the middle of a meeting. When I pulled out my spreadsheet, he'd interrupt me, saying 'Forget the facts, what does your gut tell you?' With all those people looking at me, my gut told me to check the facts! I finally told him I didn't like dealing with emotions at work because they could get overwhelming. He was great—now he asks me before the meeting, in private. That works,"* recalls (Gold/Green) Bruce L.

Greens are the most people-oriented of the four primary Color Q personalities. How they handle people and emotions may be uncomfortably nonlinear, but it balances your factual, step-by-step style.

Negotiating Strategies

- Find common ground in your shared concern for people.

- When Greens use metaphors or analogies, ask them to "style shift" and speak more concretely to you.

- Show patience, respect, and appreciation (even if it's irritating) for their nonlinear people skills and marketing abilities. You'll get more buy-in for your plans and procedures as a result.

- Explain that you need the structure of details and procedures, but it's not meant as a personal affront to them. They'll have a hard time understanding this about you, so reiterate often.

Blues. *"It takes me hours to make my finance people (Golds) consider any new idea that will make the company money!" Jason M. (a Blue) complains.*

To a Gold/Green Introvert, Blues appear to put their formidable mental energy into creating innovations that may disrupt procedures and ignore implementation details. Your style can irritate a Blue by challenging strategy with details, procedures, and cost analyses. Stand your ground: A Blue's criticism is not personal. It's actually a compliment; it means the Blue is interested in what you're saying.

Negotiating Strategies

▸ Be verbally short and concise.

▸ Use "if . . . then" sentences, which are very effective.

▸ Relate your detail orientation to their strategies: "In order to introduce this new product by August, you'll have to line up X, Y and Z," or "I'll research the legal and patent ramifications, so they don't trip you up."

▸ Adjust your vocabulary and use theoretical jargon, statistical data, and technical terms. To prove a procedure's worth, point out several long-term benefits. Use ingenuity, logic, and wit to make your case.

▸ Don't take offense when Blues see warmth as work distraction. Blues don't always respect social niceties, especially when engrossed in a fascinating project. This is not meanness; just different priorities.

Reds. *"I need $5,000 from petty cash to purchase a used injection molder at the bankruptcy auction of our competitor. It's happening this afternoon, and it will save us tens of thousands," insists Dirk (a Red). But Camille (a Gold/Green) says, "I'm afraid $5,000 cash is beyond my limit to authorize. You'll need my boss's signature." Dirk answers, "He's out of town! This can't wait! Just do it!"*

Your style can irritate Reds by limiting their autonomy and insisting they conform to procedures. The Red's strength is to handle midcourse corrections and crises that can derail "the plan." You want to keep things stable and predictable; Reds reply, "Real life isn't like that!"

Negotiating Strategies

▸ Use these words and phrases when dealing with a Red: *move, stimulate, expedite,* and *"let's get some real work done."*

▸ Refrain from calling Reds disorganized. They require regular crises; if there are none, they'll create them out of lost keys and misplaced documents! Don't help—they need the stimulation.

▸ Find common ground in your keen observation of details, interest in working with tangible items, and trusting your own experience.

▸ Invite input from Reds when doing business planning. Then, if mid-course corrections are needed, they'll be up to speed.

Extrovert vs. Introvert

If the aforementioned strategies aren't enough, the colleague may be an Extrovert. If so:

▸ Accept that it will be difficult for you to understand why they must constantly be around people and prefer noisy environments. Respect, don't challenge, their need to recharge their batteries by interacting with others—they need this the way you need private time.

▸ Ask questions; share more of yourself.

▸ Volunteer to handle tasks for them that require working alone. Benefit from their gratitude—and the solitude.

Recognize any of your coworkers in the preceding descriptions? Go in-depth by reading each Color Q personality's overall chapter and then Chapter 25, "Adjusting to the Workplace Styles of Others."

▸ ▸ ▸

In summary, Gold/Green Introverts are conscientious, sensible, and private. You enjoy being needed. Highly observant, you have a superior memory for details. You also are extremely loyal.

Very accurate and thorough, you can be counted on to get things done. You lend stability and order to your family, workplace, and volunteer organizations. Because you are not normally assertive, you may feel taken advantage of and must work on expressing your needs to others.

adjusting to
the workplace
styles of others

Jane (a Green) heads the client-servicing area at a major Chicago insurance company. She needs to make a presentation to her boss, Rich (a Blue), to obtain more staff. Rich is ambivalent; he acknowledges that Jane's excellent client relationships have significantly increased the firm's business but that she has difficulty managing conflict. As a manager, she is weak at giving her staff clear and concise feedback. Rich wonders if she could handle more people, but he knows that he can be too blunt and critical; he wants to make sure he addresses the situation well.

PEOPLE TEND TO leave jobs because of their bosses and coworkers, not the job itself. "If it weren't for my manager, I'd really love my work." "If my boss would just stay out of my hair, I'd be able to complete my projects on time." Sound familiar?

There are reasons—and solutions—for such jarring relationships. Certain Color Q personalities clash with others; they don't recognize each other's strengths. If you want your managers to actually make your life easier, your first step is learning to identify their personality color. Then you can use these insights to your advantage. As you will see here, it's possible to learn how to speak another's language, or make a "style shift."

Often it's not feasible to give someone else—like your boss—the self-assessment test in Chapter 2. This is where Color Q detective work comes in. The tips outlined in this chapter will help you assess someone else's Color Q personality. (These tips also work outside the office when trying to improve relations with your dates, spouse, parents, in-laws, even your children!)

Once you've assessed someone's Color Q personality, you can begin to change the way you communicate with that person. Then, two things will happen: 1) You will get more help (even respect) from adversaries and troublesome associates, and 2) you will come to appreciate their strengths (and perhaps even come to like them).

Rich has learned about personality differences and recognizes he needs to change the way he deals with Jane, a major revenue producer for the company. Instead of his usual quick, twenty-minute meeting, he takes her out to lunch and spends a little time at the beginning of the meal asking about her son's chess skills, a game he enjoys, too. Then he asks her to explain staff conflicts, without jumping in to provide immediate solutions. Together they brainstorm various ways of handling the issues. Jane is relaxed and ready to admit that sometimes she avoids dealing with her team's disagreements. She agrees to seek his advice when she feels overwhelmed and to take managerial-communications training. Rich is energized by his success at coaching a valued employee. He gives Jane permission to hire two people, half of her request, with a possible increase later.

How to Assess Someone Else's Color Q Personality

Determining someone's style takes time and close observation. But if you can assess their primary Color Q personality and Introvert/Extrovert preference, it will go a long way toward improving communications.

Let's simplify: Everyone has either a Gold or a Red component, as well as a Blue or a Green component. In addition, remember that everyone is either an Extrovert or an Introvert.

To find clues that will reveal these components, first look at the person's work space. Scan it in the morning, at noon, and after the individual has gone home for the day. Then assess the person's communication style.

- *If People Have a Gold Component:* Their desk is usually uncluttered with no piles of papers; everything is neatly filed. Golds begin and end projects before starting new ones. They are serious, formal, and always on time. (Find more in-depth tips in Chapter 20, "Golds Overall.")

- *If They Have a Red Component:* The desk is a mess of papers and piles. Everything is a work in progress. Other clues: Reds are loose, relaxed, and humorous (often sitting with their feet up on the desk), but they are also time-pressured or late. (Find more in-depth tips in Chapter 10, "Reds Overall.")

- *If They Have a Green Component:* Their office decor may be colorfully chic or bohemian, with many pictures of family and friends. They'll often engage in a lot of small talk in an effort to personalize the relationship and put you at ease. (Find more in-depth tips in Chapter 5, "Greens Overall.")

- *If They Have a Blue Component:* Their office will be filled with research studies, business references, and awards. Blues create a sense of distance and have a desire to keep the relationship on a professional basis. Typically they will be brief, terse, and constantly appraising you. Chitchat is limited. (Find more in-depth tips in Chapter 15, "Blues Overall.")

Jean (a Gold), an advertising executive, is calling on a new prospect, Henry. She first calls on his boss, Cathy, to learn their group's needs. Jean notices many personal photos of family and friends in Cathy's office. Cathy greets her warmly, offers coffee, and inquires about her years with the advertising firm. Before long they discover that they both take classes at the Art Students League, and make plans to meet for coffee after their next class. When Jean turns to business, Cathy is quick to provide the needed information. Then Jean continues to Henry's office for her formal appointment. Henry has several achievement awards on his walls and a significant reference library. He looks at Jean, waiting for her presentation. Jean hands him the appropriate material and makes her pitch, then asks for his input. When he makes a series of critical comments about her presentation, she does not take it personally. She knows it's actually his way of showing interest. For the time being she seeks only to convince him of the superior professionalism of her company's services. Jean recognizes that Cathy is a Green and Henry is a Blue. Reading both individuals properly has gone a long way toward helping Jean land this new account.

Everyone is also either an Introvert or an Extrovert. Both have good people skills but express them in different ways. Here are clues that will reveal this component of someone's personality:

- *Extroverts* are more talkative, speak in a louder voice, and gesticulate more. They may speak before thinking and later change their mind.

- *Introverts* listen more, tend to have more subdued energy, and gesticulate less. They think before answering and rarely change their minds.

Observe people's style while they are speaking and adjust your behavior accordingly. They will become more comfortable and actually listen to what you have to say.

Getting Along with Other Colors at Work

Whether you are managing, selling to, motivating, or working with others, Color Q helps hone your approach. Use the tips offered here with troublesome bosses, colleagues, or staff members and note the results. If you've accurately assessed one or both color components (i.e., primary and backup colors), the effects will be significant. You will see a dramatic change in how you work with and motivate others. Now, here's how to work best with each Color Q personality.

Communicating Smoothly with Golds

Diane (a Green) is a vice president of marketing for a chain of home-goods stores. She is known for her innovation and creativity. She likes to spend time with her staff and encourage ideas (even crazy ones!). But she is having trouble working on a project with Patrick, the vice president of sales (a Gold). Under his management, his department has exceeded company sales goals for two years. Diane and Patrick have been ordered to link marketing and sales efforts. Patrick is a stickler for details; Diane sees the big picture. Patrick is clearly impatient with Diane and wants to see a budget and sales projections. She thinks ideas are more important than numbers in the planning stage and refuses to work on projections until the big picture is clarified. The tension between the two is growing. Both are under pressure from their bosses to develop a major campaign.

When Managing Golds. Tell them your precise expectations; then provide a stable environment with clear channels of communication and authority. You need to be decisive and organized, emphasizing firm procedures and deadlines. Then get out of their way and respect their unique ability to "get things done."

When Selling to, Persuading, or Working with a Gold. All presentations and meetings must run smoothly. Be reliable, on time, and follow requested procedures. At all costs avoid vagueness; be factual, accurate, precise, and down-to-earth. Avoid words like "feel" and "believe." Use words like "proven," "traditional," and "respected." Respect the hierarchy of their department or company; if they say you have to talk to someone else, they normally mean it and are not putting you off.

Upon studying Color Q, Diane saw that Patrick had all the character-istics of a Gold. She began using his "language." She was more precise and organized and made sure she was on time for meetings. Patrick began paying attention to Diane's ideas and was impressed with her cre-ative vision. Together, they developed an innovative, highly successful campaign strategy and now often work to devise new programs.

Communicating Smoothly with Reds

John (a Gold) is vice president of finance for a major product-design firm. He thinks the new company president, Donald (a Red), is difficult and too informal. Donald is action-oriented, wanting quick results. He doesn't pay attention to John's detailed reports and proposals, or even read his memos. Instead, Donald wants John to give him final results while walking down the hall. Donald gets impatient if John describes all the information leading to his conclusions. He often tells John to "cut to the chase."

Meanwhile, colleagues in other departments are more enthusiastic about their work. Creativity is up and projects are completed faster. John can't understand why his boss is so popular and successful when John feels his own hard, detail-oriented work has gone unappreciated. He is angry that Donald hasn't promoted him or given him a raise.

When Managing a Red. Talking face-to-face is always better; memos and e-mails do not engage Reds. They need stimulation, fun, freedom, and inde-pendence to be on top of their game. They are most productive in a flexible and self-paced environment. Not only do Reds enjoy crises; they will create them if they are bored. Reds are difficult to control and impossible to micromanage, but they will not disappoint you if you give them freedom. Avoid meetings, rules, and lengthy memos wherever possible. Allow them to follow their instincts.

When Selling to, Persuading, or Working with a Red. Be brief and use action verbs like *stimulate, liven up, challenge, enjoy,* or *confront.* Use hands-on demonstrations instead of computer slideshows. For Reds, timing is every-thing. Don't continue if they're distracted. Acknowledge the distraction (such as picking up the phone) and ask to meet again later that day. Get to the point, avoid theories, and stress the immediacy of your solutions. Be very flexible, open-ended, and ready for their "fly by the seat of the pants" decisions and fast closes.

> *Gold John didn't belong in Donald's Red world. Human resources tried to counsel John. He refused to edit his information and believed he was entitled to proper meetings with Donald, complete with PowerPoint presentations. John also refused to upgrade his computer for faster results, as Donald had been telling him to do for months. (Donald had no patience for people who couldn't or wouldn't keep up with him.) John was finally asked to leave. He is now a vice president at a bank, where his boss requires detailed reports and strict procedures. John thrives in this job.*

Communicating Smoothly with Blues

> *Bob (a Blue) and Mary (a Green) are colleagues in the wealth-management unit of a major bank in Cincinnati. They have worked in adjacent cubicles for the past five years, yet they continuously quarrel over priorities and client-management strategies.*
>
> *Bob is knowledgeable about finance and uniquely gifted in handling complex investment issues. He gets irritated, however, by his customers who want to meet frequently. Mary takes great pride in her ability to grow her client base through frequent referrals. Unlike Bob, she enjoys taking client phone calls and meeting with them regularly. Discussions of market performance are more problematic. She feels she doesn't know enough about investment trends to provide high-level advice. Bob finds the interruption of Mary's constant telephone conversations irritating and makes snide comments about the personal nature of her conversations.*

When Managing a Blue. You need to be strategically visionary to capture the interest of Blues. Explain to them the future implications of what you're doing and how it might even have global consequences. Above all, provide them an autonomous environment with minimal guidelines. Establish demanding goals or else they'll get bored and distracted. Debate with them and don't take their challenges personally; it's a sign you've got their interest. Listen to their insights and analytical skills; they'll make you a lot of money.

When Selling to, Persuading, or Working with a Blue. Be highly competent and innovative or Blues will disregard your message. Present the "big picture" and long-term potentials first; limit the facts. Don't become personally offended by anything they say—instead, counter with wit, ingenuity, and logic. Avoid words such as "feel" and "believe"; substitute words like "think" and "know."

> *Mary and Bob attended a personality-style seminar suggested by their boss. After the session, they realized they made different yet equally valuable contributions to the success of their unit. They began jointly managing their shared clients. Bob enjoys the investment expert role, while Mary is the relationship manager who helps families set goals. Company business has grown by 40 percent. Even more important, they recognize each other's value and actually enjoy discussing their different perspectives.*

Communicating Smoothly with Greens

When Managing Greens. Green employees like Mary (from the previous example) need a harmonious environment with opportunities for personal growth. They become troubled and distracted by competition and conflict. Personalize your work relationship; ask about the Green's family, hobbies, and pets in appropriate ways. Be inspiring and positive. Establish a shared vision and allow Greens creative freedom to address it. Give frequent feedback, but keep it diplomatic. Harsh criticism and fear tactics destroy their productivity, as do strict hierarchies; they prefer to work collaboratively.

When Selling to, Persuading, or Working with a Green. Ask Greens what they need, then listen with empathy. Expect nonsequential conversation and allow them time to return to the original point, which they will. When presenting your product or solution, give the big picture and show the future impact on people.

> *Bob learned to speak in Mary's "people" language while Mary learned to speak to Bob in "numbers." The result: a win-win relationship.*

Introvert vs. Extrovert

Often you will be communicating with an Extrovert. These individuals tend to be energetic. They are more talkative and gesticulate more than other people. They frequently speak before thinking and later change their mind. Being with people further energizes them. Extroverts are the networkers of the world.

Introverts listen more, tend to have a more subdued energy, and gesticulate less. They think before answering and rarely change their minds. If you are an Extrovert speaking with an Introvert, bring your energy level down a notch. Lower your voice and control your hand gestures. Whenever possible, send an e-mail ahead of time about what you want to discuss. *Never* jump in to fill an Introvert's silence, no matter how uncomfortable it makes you.

> *One time I was asked to organize a panel for a major financial services conference. I called an executive vice president at Bank of America to invite him to speak and also to get his suggestions for other panelists. I knew he was a deep Introvert and was prepared for a lengthy silence on the call.*
>
> *For seven minutes, I sat quietly without making any comments while he mentally constructed an entire panel for me, including topic, speakers, and copy, without saying a word! After he finally spoke, he shared his ideas, offered to make the phone calls to invite the other panelists, and thanked me for not interrupting his thinking. By honoring his style, I completed what would have normally been a three-day project in less than fifteen minutes!*

If you are an Introvert speaking with an Extrovert, you may experience uncomfortable lulls in the conversation. Ask a lot of questions to keep the dialogue going. Raise your energy level by nodding and smiling appropriately.

▸　▸　▸

When you learn how to adjust your workplace style, you should see an immediate improvement in your dealings with anyone whose Color Q personality you've assessed correctly. Relationships improve, work goes more smoothly, and teams experience fewer conflicts. You may even get a promotion, salary increase, or discover you already have the job of your dreams!

approach to innovation
the primary styles

Lily Klebanoff Blake, Board Member
with Emerging Markets Expertise

GREEN/REDS ARE some of Color Q's most innovative personalities, as Lily Klebanoff Blake's career illustrates. Blake says she is most proud of "moving into markets when they were just emerging and being able to navigate effectively through those untested and often undefined shoals."

The Soviet Union imploded in the 1990s, breaking into fifteen independent states. Blake "was at the forefront of business development in a number of the former Soviet Republics as they were moving from a planned to a market economy. It was a time of abrupt change where old commercial systems were shattered, effective new ones had not yet been put into place, and one had to negotiate and navigate in uncharted territory to get things done." Despite these challenges, Blake was able to navigate complex tax and legal issues and get access to land and local approvals for a hotel-and-office-complex developer in Kazakhstan.

Blake also has been at the forefront of America's health care evolution. Working for the New York City Office of Management and Budget, she represented the city in negotiations with state and federal authorities on health care and legislative issues. She has served on the Bellevue Hospital Advisory Board and helped staff the capital committee of the Health and Hospitals Corporation.

"There has never been a roadmap or template for any of the positions I've undertaken," remarks Blake. "Often I was the first person in a newly defined role."

Webster's *New World Dictionary* defines the word innovate as "to introduce new methods, devices, etc.; to make changes." Authors Mark Dodgson and David Gann, in their book *Innovation: A Very Short Introduction,* shorten the definition even more: "Ideas, successfully applied."[1] Innovation, they write, "is found in what organizations produce: their products and services. It is found in the ways in which organizations produce: in their production processes and systems, work structures and practices, supply arrangements, collaboration with partners, and very importantly, how they engage with and reach customers."[2]

It is clear that innovation encompasses a vast array of behaviors. Introducing a new method requires strengths and skills very different from introducing a new device. When companies ask employees to innovate, four different responses immediately occur.

1. Golds *(the procedure and resource managers)* get nervous and concerned.

2. Greens *(the ideas/client experiences/marketing specialists)* inventory the dissatisfaction they've been hearing expressed and try to find answers.

3. Blues *(the knowledge and strategy specialists)* inventory performance shortfalls and strategize improvements.

4. Reds *(the practical skills and crisis managers)* get excited and look around for the first material thing they can lay their hands on to improve.

Each Color Q personality (and yes, especially the nervous Golds) has unique contributions to make to the process of innovation. Companies that utilize Color Q personality strengths can harness their people for more successful responses.

Here's how. Let's break innovation into two types: conceptual and concrete.

Conceptual Innovation

Innovation of this type is about creating new ideas, customs, trends, regulations, or professional organizations ... anything that is based in the mental rather than material world. Let's anchor this definition with an example: You work for fictional Upstart Software Company. Its goal is to develop a word-processing program that will outsell Microsoft's. Here's how to make your strongest contribution at the conceptual stage:

Golds. Sit back and relax. Your contributions will come later, figuring out how to administer the new employees and procedures it will take to make the final concept work. Rein in your tendency to express administrative concerns about every fielded idea. Wait until the final three are on the table, and then express only your biggest concerns. However, if the innovation involves government regulation, your contribution will be critical.

Your Strength: *Making the administrative details work.*

Greens. Make a list of all the frustrations you've had and all the things you like best about word processing. Talk to other people and gather their input. How people feel about using the new product will be a key component in both the marketing effort and the product's eventual acceptance in the marketplace. Address the question: How do we create word-of-mouth that says this product is really (great, easy, fun, hip) to use? Share this input with the Blues on your team, so they can incorporate it into their technical thinking. Nominate yourself to attend relevant professional meetings (especially if you're an Extrovert).

Your Strength: *Identifying the "wow" factor that makes people like the product enough to buy it and recommend it.*

Blues. Evaluate all key and secondary components of the competing product. Address questions such as: What are the future trends? What's antiquated?

Where are the flaws? What can be improved? How can we make a product that is technically better overall? Make sure you work with Greens and include components that people respond to on an emotional as well as a technical level. It's going to take both those inputs to knock your competitor out of the water.

Your Strength: *Strategizing the best new concepts and improvements to start the process off right.*

Reds. Strategizing a long-term future concept is not your strength; hands-on, concrete, short-term problems are. Like the Golds, at this phase you should sit back and relax; maybe play with the rival software to see how it could be made more fun to use. Share any findings with Greens and Blues. When the final three concepts are on the table, discuss any concrete, practical steps that will be needed to make it happen, and contribute contingency plans for the real-world scenarios that might possibly arise. Address the question: How can we make sure our new concept doesn't get bogged down?

Your Strengths: *Keeping the user-friendly factor uppermost in people's minds and/or dealing with midcourse corrections.*

Material or Product Innovation

Innovation of this type involves creating new raw materials, new products, new distribution chains . . . anything that is based in the material rather than mental world. Fictional Upstart Software Company has determined that in order to develop a word-processing program that will outsell Microsoft's product, it has to invent a fun, new type of computing device to deliver it. Here is how to make your strongest, best contribution to this challenge at the material stage:

Golds. Work closely with Blues and Reds when the final three designs reach the table. Your resource-management abilities will help determine which design is most economically feasible. Research prices, vendors, availabilities of all key components; if manufacturing on premises, research raw materials, manufacturing components, and human resource needs. Address the question: What resources will need to be provided, and how will the company administer employee needs, payments, deliveries, and space needs?

Your Strength: *You are a key contributor among the four Color Q personalities with regard to resource allocation.*

Greens. The mechanical world is not your preferred arena. Your contribution to the invention process is communicating how people will likely respond to any given feature of the new computing device. Is it fun to use? Can you intuitively figure out its function without a manual? Is the device attractive and nicely designed? Address the question: How will people interact with this new device?

Your Strengths: *An intuitive understanding of what people want, and how they will interact with a new device, both as buyers and users.*

Blues. Among the four Color Q personalities, you are the most naturally able to build detailed models of things in your head. Sequester yourself so that you won't be interrupted. Doodle, scribble, draw on the computer ... get the ideas down before they're lost. Your inventing reverie may last days—so prepare your coworkers for a communications blackout. But don't skip update meetings, or you'll find yourself out of the loop and all your hard work ignored at final decision time. Answer the questions: What's never been done before? Why hasn't anyone tried XYZ? What could we make this device do that would blow users away?

Your Strength: *Going where no one has gone before.*

Reds. You are never happier than when in mechanical, hands-on tinkering mode. This is your time: —Build miniature models, make sparks fly, blow things up . . . above all, make sure the device feels good to the hand, is fun, is easy to master, or does something that will make the user's life easier and better. Work with Blues and Greens—they're the idea people, you're the practical person. But you all contribute when it comes to improving something. Answer the questions: How can we make this product work? How can we make it easy to use? How can we make this fun to use?

Your Strengths: *Mechanical aptitude, ability to solve short-term problems on the fly without getting flustered or frustrated.*

When innovation fails, it's usually because corporations assign the wrong personalities to the wrong parts of the process. Upstart Software will fail in its bid to unseat Microsoft if it:

‣ Asks a mechanically gifted Red to create a long-term technical strategy (use a Blue).

‣ Asks a marketing gifted Green to objectively quantify the potential audience (use a Gold).

‣ Asks an administratively gifted Gold to accept or reject abstract concepts (use a team of all four Color Q types).

‣ Asks a strategically gifted Blue to plan step-by-step implementation of the concept (use a Red/Gold team).

The more diverse a team is, the better the solutions generated. The key is to balance both the concrete and the abstract thinkers and to ask all to contribute only from their strengths. Team conflict can be minimized by allowing the colors best suited for each project stage to lead the way, then having them step aside when that stage is complete.

A "Best Business Book for 2011" recognized by CIO Insight, *Breaking Away: How Great Leaders Create Innovation That Drives Sustainable Growth—and Why Others Fail*, defines four levels of innovation.[3] They coincide neatly with the four primary Color Q personalities. Transformational innovation, which changes societies, is the province of the visionary Blue. Category innovation, which recognizes and meets customer needs sometimes before customers are aware of them, is driven by the intuitive Greens. Marketplace innovation that engages customers in new, fun ways requires the practical, fun-loving input of the Red; and operational innovation, which makes internal organizational improvements, is the bailiwick of the administrative Golds.

Bottom line: If you are going to innovate, put the right people to the task. Failure is a certainty if you try to innovate from a core of human weakness rather than strength; breathtaking transformations occur when you get your people doing what they were born to do.

27

negotiating compensation

EACH COLOR Q personality has its own strengths and weaknesses when it comes to money. But notice that the name of this chapter isn't "negotiating salary." Compensation for work takes two forms—*monetary* and *nonmonetary*. Each Color Q personality needs to feel adequately compensated, but the kinds and levels of each type of compensation differ by personality.

Monetary rewards include salary, bonuses, and perks, including vacation, sick time, education, health insurance, pension contributions, club memberships, and the like. Nonmonetary rewards include appreciation, mentoring, creative freedom, prestige, power, or control. With the exception of appreciation, you must negotiate to obtain most nonmonetary rewards, so negotiating skills blend with what you value to form your "compensation style."

The personalities most comfortable with compensation negotiations are the Blues, Reds, and Gold/Blues. You leave nothing on the table and often walk out with the table, too! The Gold/Greens are in the middle. The least comfortable are the Greens. Arguing about money destroys the harmony you value. You'd almost rather quit a job than negotiate compensation beyond what is offered.

Here are two case studies of two workers in the same office:

Jake (a Blue/Red) strides into his boss's office for his annual work evaluation. He has three things to work harder on and several areas that show improvement. "That's cause for a celebration!" Jake says brightly to his boss. "How about a 15 percent raise to reward those improvements and incentivize me through next year's challenges?" The boss has been green-lighted to give 7 percent raises across the board to all staff members; higher raises are to be given only in special cases to retain top talent. "Jake, I don't think we're in the ballpark for 15 percent," he says. "I had a 5 percent raise in mind."

"You and I both know that's the mandatory lowball offer," says Jake, warming to the challenge. "Give me your real numbers."

"Well, I might discuss 6 percent, but I'd want to hear more about how you're going to tackle these three areas where improvement is needed first," says the boss.

Jake now has an idea where the real numbers lie. "You can see I've made all last year's improvements. Plus you've said that you depend on me because I can solve problems quickly. Remember in February how I saved the Royster account? For that alone I deserve 10 percent."

The boss pauses; the Royster account has contributed 5 percent to the bottom line of the firm this year. That would make his 10 percent an easy sell. "You're right, Jake. I think I can coax 8 percent out of the budget for you."

Jake frowns. "That only brings me up to $73,000. My college buddy over at LMN Company gets $80,000 for the same position, and he's told me he's being promoted this year and they'll need someone. He says they'd start me at $75,000. I don't want to leave here, but I have to do what's best for me and my family. What can you do for me? Maybe pay my out-of-pocket health insurance premiums?"

His boss answers, "I can't set that kind of precedent with the health insurance. But I think we can do $75,000."

"Great, boss!" Jake says. "Gonna start those improvements today. By the way, the Royster people have invited me to their brainstorming retreat in March. It's in Maui. Will the company pay for my wife to attend? She's friends with Royster's sister."

"Of course, Jake."

Tony's evaluation is next. A Green/Red, Tony has a glowing report, with improvement in all areas and outstanding performance in one. He only needs to work on giving clearer critical feedback, a small item. Tony deflates. He had planned to ask the boss for a 3 percent raise; now his hopes of deserving it are dashed.

The boss starts with his opening gambit. "We'd like to give you a 5 percent raise this year."

Tony is elated. His hard work has been appreciated, after all, he thinks. After his boss's comment about his feedback abilities, he wasn't sure he was going to get anything. "Five percent! That's great, boss! Thank you so much! My family will be thrilled!" Tony sits back, hoping this will be the year they offer him a company car, which he really needs for his fieldwork.

"You're welcome, Tony. Keep up the good work." The boss stands and extends his hand, feeling good that the money he saved on Tony will help cover Jake. In the coming year, Tony hears snippets about the 7 percent raises others got, but thinks his lower raise is due to his inability to give good critical feedback.

It isn't. Tony's lower raise is due to his unhoned negotiating skills. Tony could have gotten at least 7 percent (or even more, because of his outstanding performance) and a company car with no problem . . . if he had just asked. But arguing about his worth makes him so uncomfortable that he relies on passive recognition instead. Tony needs to role-play to recognize what his outstanding performance is worth.

If you compare the Blue/Red with the Green/Red, you'll see extremes—one goes for the whole enchilada, while the other just gets a little lettuce. Most Color Q personalities are in between.

The Green Compensation Style

Money motivates Greens less than other colors. It's a means to support their personal development, aesthetic surroundings, and those they love. Greens are more motivated by nonmonetary compensations—creative freedom, personal improvements, appreciation, connection with coworkers, and belief in the company's mission. Money produces tensions; Greens have a deep need for harmony. "My coworkers are like family," says Theresa W. "The pay isn't great here, but I would really grieve if I had to leave."

Your preferred nonmonetary compensation is harmonious work relationships, creative expression, and ability to improve the world. Negotiate for education courses and additional time off for personal development.

Green/Gold Negotiating Tips. You usually don't push hard enough for your raises. Recognize that the company isn't withholding compensation as a reflection on you; the company is driven by the bottom line. This is one time to value money above a relationship.

Green/Red Negotiating Tips. Yes, we picked on you already (in the case study), but for your own good. Negotiate! You'll be surprised by how much more you can get. If you can't bring yourself to ask for money, request more vacation time, more skills improvement courses, or a senior-level mentor. Role-play with a Blue or Red, if possible. Focus on the value of your contributions and how to improve your negatives. Everyone else does.

The Red Compensation Style

Reds don't worry about money—it comes, it goes; you'll make more tomorrow. It's the experiences it buys today that matter! "What good is money," says Red Terence P., "if you can't spend it on the better things in life, especially the fun?" Your savings account, if it exists at all, is frequently tapped to fund the next big thrill. Lucrative investments keep you afloat, because your keen observations lead you to be first in line. This helps the savings account situation, as does your easy ability with salary negotiations.

Your preferred nonmonetary compensation is collegiality, physical freedom, project independence, and excitement. Negotiate for project control, flexible hours, and travel.

Red/Blue Negotiating Tips. Do what you're doing and be generous with your time to mentor other Color Q personality types, especially Greens. You're one of the best.

Red/Green Negotiating Tips. You're a good negotiator, perhaps more relaxed than Red/Blues, and you'll leave them smiling as you walk out the door with every last possible dollar and perk. You, too, should mentor other colors.

The Blue Compensation Style

For you, money is validation of competence and accomplishments. You recognize money as a flow rather than a stagnant resource. Your superior strategic skills make you a more capable investor of your earned assets, but you can go wrong by being overconfident. Money mirrors emotion, and investments often act irrationally. Fortunately, your expertise and high achievements ultimately attract equally high compensation, as do your negotiating strategies. "To leave money on the table is simple incompetence," says Martin O. "It's unconscionable, especially if you want to send your kids to college."

Your preferred nonmonetary compensation is underwritten education, prestige, and administrative support. Negotiate for an assistant, education, and time to write professional articles or make speeches at industry-recognized events.

Blue/Gold Negotiating Tips. You've researched your worth down to the penny before negotiating. You understand strategic give-and-take and never accept an initial offer. No money or benefit ever goes unclaimed; if it's available, you'll get it. Be careful not to let your confidence sound arrogant, or to ignore the human side. If the boss is tired or preoccupied, pressing the case could work against you.

Blue/Red Negotiating Tips. You know what you're worth, what's available, and how to get it. You are talented at compensation negotiations, combining strategy, innovation, and initiative. You are very likely to get more than the boss planned to give you, often including perks no one has thought of before. If the boss balks, use your substantial wit to blunt the tension of negotiation impasses.

The Gold Compensation Style

Your group was named the Golds for its ability to handle money. For you, money is security. Meticulous records are kept. Budgets are detailed. Statements are reconciled . . . promptly. Cash flow is accurately controlled, perhaps daily. Impulse purchases are forbidden; your "rainy day" fund always covers emergencies while preventing debt. Golds often achieve early retirement.

"About two months before job evaluations are due, I inventory all my accomplishments of the past year. Then I look at the company's perform-ance, especially compared to our competitors," says Sarah A. "I have facts at my fingertips when I speak to my boss."

Your preferred nonmonetary compensation includes titles that reflect your ability to handle details and the power to control all areas for which you are responsible. Negotiate for promotions that put you in charge and extra staff to oversee all procedures adequately.

Gold/Blue Negotiating Tips. You are tough negotiators, driven by fear of falling short and letting your family down. You do your homework and understand your value to the penny. You may come across more demanding or desper-ate than necessary; if your boss tries to give you a 5 percent raise rather than 7 percent, you may feel your security is on the line.

Gold/Green Negotiating Tips. Your Green component seeks harmony; arguing about money makes you uncomfortable. You research your worth, but may leave the bargaining table feeling that you didn't get everything possible. You won't accept the first offer, but will likely accept the second as discom-fort with the process grows. Your highly developed work ethic deserves top-tier compensation, and your family is depending on you. Role-play with a Blue or Red friend to learn how to get more than expected.

▸ ▸ ▸

The bottom line—know your personality type, work its strengths, and face its weaknesses. The word to remember when it comes to compensation is *maximize.*

generation conflict or personality conflict?

THERE HAVE BEEN conflicts between the generations, seemingly, since recorded times. How many of these might be clashes of personality rather than age? Color Q tools can analyze these communications barriers.

Worldwide, the percentages of each color type in all populations remain fairly constant—Greens at 17 percent; Reds at 27 percent; Blues at 10 percent; and Golds at 46 percent. (These findings are according to my research and that of parts of the temperament community, which is an offshoot of the Myers-Briggs Type Indicator.) But each generation has overarching values and patterns of behavior that can be described by these primary Color Q personalities as well. For example, baby boomers as a group have embraced and emphasized Gold-type values and behaviors . . .

more on that shortly. While Gold baby boomers feel a natural fit with their times, the other colors have to adapt to be successful.

Characteristics of the older generation—conservative, invested in stability, cautious about new ways—are typically found in the Gold personality. Golds are the most populous of the four personality types (46 percent) and hold the most managerial positions. The Gold personality is the primary "boss" role model.

The characteristics of the younger generation—interested in the "now," wanting to balance play and work, seeking constant stimulation—are typically found in the Red personality. It's Reds who excel at the high-pressure, high-performance jobs of the world—firefighter, police officer, and military. These positions are mainly filled by the young generation of the day.

Consider the following case study, and try to guess what the source of the conflict is.

- -

Red vs. Gold or Young vs. Old?

Jim, a Gold managing director at a well-known bank, has called his Red assistant Will into his office and told him to shut the door.

Jim begins by saying, "Will, I've got to see some performance improvements from you, starting now. Making your own hours will have to be curtailed; there have been too many details falling between the cracks because you've been out. Two-hour lunches will no longer be acceptable, even if you do stay late to make up the time. And I'm uncomfortable not knowing whether you're on Facebook or doing the research I've requested. I'm going to need more reporting of your activities and less feeling that the ends justify the means. What do you suggest you might do about this?"

Will feels blindsided. Up to this point, Jim has done nothing but praise his performance and results, albeit only occasionally. Will frowns, shifting defensively in his now-hot seat. "I get all the work done, and I've never missed a deadline," Will says. "I don't know what details have fallen through the cracks, because this is the first I've heard of anything like this—can you give me an example?"

Jim falters. He had just assumed that things were falling between the cracks as they normally do when an employee isn't at their desk. Now he frowns.

"Well . . . for example, I almost missed that conference call Tuesday because you didn't tell me about it until ten minutes before it happened."

Will is confused. A ten-minute warning seems like ample time to him . . . and Jim didn't actually miss the call . . .

Is this a case of Red vs. Gold or young vs. old?

It's both. It's a work/life balance Gen Y Red (Will) trying to under-stand a workaholic baby boomer Gold (Jim). And although the issues are modern (work/life balance, Facebook vs. face time), all the sources of conflict in this case study are personality-oriented—namely, Red (spontaneous, adaptable, crisis-oriented) vs. Gold (predictable, stable, procedural).

- -

Below the surface of cultural references, today's workplace conflicts are usually more personality-type clashes. These most typically are Red vs. Gold (as described in the case study) or Green vs. Blue (people and feelings vs. detachment, strategy, and logic). To a lesser degree, there's Gold vs. Blue conflict (stability vs. innovation) and Red vs. Green conflict (practical and concrete vs. intuitive and abstract).

There are four major generations now operating in the workplace:

1. *Traditionalists were born between 1925 and 1945.* As described by Rita M. Murray and Hile Rutledge in *Generations: Bridging the Gap with Type*, this group endured two World Wars and the Great Depression, leaving them valuing security, community, hierarchy, and authority. Their work model was the military structure.[1] These are Gold personality values.

2. *Baby boomers, born between 1946 and 1964, are a generation 80 million strong.* Competition for jobs has been fierce among boomers, breed-ing a generation of workaholics who put in sixty-hour weeks just to stay in the game. Boomers are competitive, seeking visible signs of accomplish-ment, whether trophies, corner offices, or salary increases; they define themselves by their work.[2] The boomers, like their parents, emphasize Gold values. Although the percentages of the four color groups remain the same as the worldwide population at large in every generation, baby boomers who were Golds excelled; other Color Q personalities adapted.

3. *Generation Xers came right behind the boomers.* Born between 1965 and 1979, they reject the boomers' work-centered life in favor of work/life balance. Intergenerational challenges expert Phyllis Weiss Haserot of Practice Development Counsel has done extensive studies on the current four generations of workers. Now reaching their peak earning years, Gen Xers, according to Haserot, have amassed considerable expertise, still use face-to-face communication as well as electronic communications, are more flexible in work style, have greater acceptance of workplace diversity, and have thrown off the "entitled" label of their youth to become today's hard workers.[3] Generation X exhibit Blue values, favoring as role models people such as Bill Gates, who are innovative and visionary.

4. *Millennials (also referred to as Generation Y) were born between 1980 and 2000.* They are noted for their ambition and will work hard for recognition. Bea Fields, coauthor of *Millennial Leaders: Success Stories from Today's Most Brilliant Generation Y Leaders,*[4] lists work/life balance, information, speed, fun, creativity, and simplicity as their group values. In 2011, they constituted 28.8 percent of the work population and in 2016 will be at 28.3 percent. Millennials as a group exhibit Red patterns of behavior, rewarding spontaneity and the ability to take things as they come.

At work, the generations usually relate to each other either through mentor/mentee or boss/subordinate relationships. Since the dot-com days, these relationships do not always have the older worker in the mentor or boss role. "The model that interests me," says Christine Birnbaum of human resources at New York Life Investments, "is the Facebook one—Mark Zuckerberg paired up with an experienced manager, Sheryl Sandberg."

Lois Zachary, author of *The Mentor's Guide,* says Gen Yers are particularly interested in being mentored for career advancement, but also in helping older generations develop social media and technology skills.[5] Megan Atkinson, an energy-efficiency professional and member of Gen Y, says, "My most valuable assets have been mentors that recognize my generation's need for a long-term vision."[6]

Two prime examples of "intergenerational" conflict are older workers having to report to younger bosses and the adoption of communications technologies. How do these conflicts play out between Color Q personalities?

Gold vs. Red

Example 1: Gold younger boss, Red older worker. The Gold will insist that the Red adhere to Gold's structure and will be intolerant of the Red's casual, freewheeling (and misperceived, on the Gold's part, as seemingly defiant and disrespectful) attitude. The Red may rebelliously not adopt the Gold's technology immediately, at least until they try it and find it to be fun.

Example 2: Red younger boss, Gold older worker. The Gold will keep asking the Red boss for procedural guidance, and the Red will become impatient with the Gold subordinate's seeming inability to "wing it." The Red will typically be at the upper end of tech savvy, while the Gold may find it difficult to transition into new communications. (To reiterate—these are not generational conflicts, they are Color Q personality conflicts.)

Gold vs. Green

Example 1: Gold younger boss, Green older worker. The Gold will insist that the Green adhere to the Gold's structure. The Green will have a hard time adhering to linear, step-by-step procedures and will constantly bring up emotional responses or ideas that will cause customers to respond more favorably. The Gold younger boss may begin the relationship more tech savvy, but the Green will soon see and propose potential new uses for technology that the Gold may find irritating and may not wish to adopt.

Example 2: Green younger boss, Gold older worker. Green bosses will try to relate warmly to their older Gold workers and prioritize making them comfortable with the relationship. This approach may boomerang and make the Gold uncomfortable. The Green will spend a lot of time working with Golds to get them to feel comfortable using new technology, giving lots of praise when the Gold masters a skill. Golds will grit their teeth until their tech skills become standard operating procedure, or else they will ask for an interdepartmental transfer to get away from their eccentric, stream-of-consciousness, overly friendly boss—attributes the Gold will blame on their boss's youth but instead belong to their Green personality type.

Gold vs. Blue

Example 1: Younger Gold boss, older Blue worker. The Gold will insist that the Blue adhere to the Gold's structure. Blues will do the minimum that is required to keep their younger boss off their back so that they can strategize and innovate wherever possible. It is likely that Blue workers will come to the relationship equally or more tech savvy than their younger Gold boss, and may even use their innate love of technology to subtly imply their Gold boss isn't as competent as the Blue would be in the senior position.

Example 2: Younger Blue boss, Gold older worker. This is almost a classic textbook case of what people perceive to be a generational difference; but it is, in fact, entirely personality-based. The younger Blue boss will be the most highly tech savvy of all; the Gold older worker the least willing to adopt technology. This combination will be painful for both parties. The Blue will have no patience for the Gold's resistance to tech adoption; the Gold will find having a younger boss a difficult adjustment at best, since it is an untraditional arrangement. The pressure to adopt not only new technologies but all the latest permutations will stretch the structured and stability-oriented Gold to the brink (again, a personality, not a generational, conflict).

Red vs. Green

Example 1: Younger Red boss, older Green worker. This is a combination that can work rather well. The younger Red boss will adopt technology enthusiastically for its practical as well as entertaining applications. The Green older worker will be eager to form a good relationship and will respond well to technology's ability to surprise and delight. Most of their conflicts will occur when concrete, factual, linear Reds try to communicate with abstract, metaphoric, nonlinear Greens. Younger Red bosses will be alternately amused or annoyed by their older Green workers, saying things such as, "What the hell are you talking about? Say it in English."

Example 2: Younger Green boss, older Red worker. Green bosses will go out of their way to make the older Red feel comfortable. The Red will want to be left alone to "get on with it." The Green is likely to feel undermined by the Red over time (although Reds may just be trying to get things done without the burden of having to deal with their boss's feelings all the time). The Red and the Green are likely to be equally tech savvy, or willing to bring one another up to speed with little conflict. Reds will use technology to get the job done; Greens will explore its more artistic and marketing potentials.

Red vs. Blue

Example 1: Younger Red boss, older Blue worker. This is a relationship where it will be difficult for the older Blue to respect the younger Red. The older Blue is logical, strategic, highly achievement-oriented, and quite tech savvy. Younger Reds are spontaneous, collegial, fun-loving, and enjoy crises (which, if bored, they will create). Crises are anathema to Blues, who think proper strategic planning should prevent them. Blues will disrespect younger Reds who don't seem to "control" projects; Reds will disrespect the Blue's inability to make needed midcourse corrections without complaint and criticism. Blues will think they are better at seeing and exploiting more of technology's potential than their younger but more practical Red boss.

Example 2: Younger Blue boss, older Red worker. The highly tech-savvy Blue boss will attribute the Red's resistance to adopting the latest technology to the Red's age, but it is actually due to the Red's preference for tools that have practical rather than theoretical uses. Younger Blue bosses will perceive Reds as being insubordinate when they put their feet up on the desk and chat or play with gadgets instead of putting nose to the grindstone. This is not insubordination, merely a style difference, since Reds are more casual and spontaneous. (The Blue will realize this during the next crisis, which the Red will excel at handling.)

Green vs. Blue

Example 1: Younger Green boss, older Blue worker. Green bosses will go out of their way, at first, to make the Blue worker comfortable with the relationship. The Blue will be critical of how everything is done, challenging the

Green. The Blue will likely be equally or more tech savvy than the Green and may actually offend the Green with challenging remarks. (Blues are hardwired for nonpersonal criticisms, but Greens take it personally.) While Greens are the most emotionally savvy Color Q personality, Blues often ignore social niceties (especially when engaged in a project). Young Green bosses may feel this is insubordination by their older Blue worker when it is actually a style difference.

Example 2: Younger Blue boss, older Green worker. The older Green worker, eager to connect, will work very hard to meet the younger Blue's expectations. The Green will try diligently to be as tech savvy as the boss, but will become highly discouraged when the Blue's (impersonal) critical remarks never seem to stop. If the Green goes in with emotional complaints, the Blue's response may be a detached "Live with it."

> ▸   ▸   ▸

Although there are some cultural references and worldviews that create communications gaps between today's generations, it is more likely that conflicts are personality style–based. If addressed with a "style shifting" approach (such as those described in this chapter, and in Chapters 5, 10, 15, 20, and 25), such conflicts can transform into increased intergenerational understanding and cross-generational support. "Style shifting" can build the needed bridges that productively blend each generation's unique experience.

self-coach your
way to success

THIS CHAPTER SUMMARIZES the main ways to use Color Q for self-coaching, to learn new skills, and resolve workplace (and personal) conflicts.

BLUES: Use this chapter to determine content validity and the value of applying strategies listed in other chapters.

GOLDS: Use this material as a study guide to summarize your learning.

GREENS: Use it as a quick refresher before "style shifting" to deal with a difficult colleague.

REDS: If all you read in this book is one chapter, make it this one.

Go to your personality color section below.

Blues

William (a Blue) addresses his budget committee teammates: "Our budgeting process is antiquated. We need to incorporate this state-of-the-art software now," he says.

"No!" cries Ella (a Gold). "That can't be done in the time frame we have."

"Yes!" says John (a Red). "I beta-tested it, it's great!"

"Maybe," says Terry (a Green). "What do the department heads think?"

Blues self-coach best by:

▸ Harnessing your desire for competence and expertise.

▸ Seeking instructors who are logical, tough, top-of-their-game experts who can present accurate information straightforwardly.

▸ Being open to debate, competition, and critical feedback.

▸ Being free to explore in depth, evaluate material, set goals, measure your progress.

Blues may come into conflict with others by:

▸ Critiquing in ways that sound like excessive criticism (Greens)

▸ Emphasizing logic over emotions (Greens)

▸ Constantly trying to innovate and "improve" (Golds)

▸ Disregarding details and procedures (Golds)

▸ Focusing on strategy rather than practicalities (Reds)

▸ Arguing semantics and abstract theories (Reds)

Golds

Camille (a Gold) is in charge of the petty cash window at a large corporation. Robert (a Green) asks: "I need $500 traveling money and also $150 for a client breakfast; and do you think I'll need to up my corporate credit-card limit?"

"Bring me three separate request slips," says Camille.

"I'll need $12,000 for the third quarter's research materials," says Quentin (a Blue). "My limit is $500, and it's only July. Submit individual requests," she replies.

"I gotta have $1,000 now, Camille. I'm off to the airport," says Louie (a Red) with a grin. Camille rolls her eyes. "Only with a request slip, you rogue. Here. Make it out."

Golds self-coach best by:

> Learning and practicing until excellence is achieved.

> Finding competent instructors who provide abundant data, one-on-one feedback, realistic deadlines, and clear expectations.

> Reviewing materials before class, then questioning and critiquing.

> Using checklists for achieving step-by-step improvement.

> Employing real-life demos, case studies, labs, and simulations. Practical experience must precede theory.

Golds may come into conflict with others by:

> Emphasizing procedures over intuitions (Greens and Blues)

> Preferring concrete, step-by-step planning over long-term strategizing (Blues)

> Resisting change and innovation; favoring efficiency and tradition (Blues and Reds)

> Focusing on rules rather than responding to change (Reds)

> Insisting that procedures be followed (Reds)

> Showing irritation with nonsequential discussion (Greens and Blues)

Greens

Stacey (a Green) is team leader for her firm's office move. "Let's start by asking what each employee's needs are," she says.

"Alternatively, let's research square foot rental predictions for the next twenty years," says Olson (a Blue).

"Make a step-by-step To Do list," says Rita (a Gold).

"Just get the cheapest space and make it work!" says Carl (a Red).

Greens self-coach best by:

▶ Using your time management talent and setting achievable goals.

▶ Working with a study group (Extroverts) or working alone with manuals and references (Introverts).

▶ Using alphabetical lists, metaphors, or analogies.

▶ Grasping the big picture first, then embellishing with details.

▶ Seeing how material will improve self or better others.

Greens come into conflict with others by:

▶ Using stream-of-consciousness rather than sequential communications (Golds)

▶ Emphasizing intuition over step-by-step procedures (Golds)

▶ Placing values before logic and detached analysis (Blues)

▶ Emphasizing human responses over long-term strategy (Blues)

▶ Showing empathy rather than taking action (Reds)

▶ Avoiding communicating in concrete terms (Reds)

Reds

"Fire!" yells Alex (a Red), who runs to get the computer room's extinguisher.

Dolores (a Gold) frantically searches for the emergency procedures manual. Harry (a Blue) immediately envisions the location of each fire exit and strategizes the one least likely to be overcrowded. Lilly (a Green) grabs her cell phone so that she can call her husband and races over to help a wheelchair-bound coworker.

Reds self-coach best by:

▶ Keenly observing details and being involved, hands-on, in solving immediate problems.

▶ Linking facts to personal experience, trial-and-error experimentation, and stories about people.

▶ Seeking experienced sources who can provide immediate feedback.

- Using labs, demos, field trips, and interactive multimedia.

- Being alone with your manual (Introverts); learning through cause-and-effect.

- Being flexible about rules, structures, and deadlines.

- Keeping it fast and fun!

Reds come into conflict with others by:

- Making midcourse corrections rather than sticking to "the plan" (Golds)

- Emphasizing spontaneity over step-by-step procedures (Golds)

- Preferring practical thinking over abstract strategy (Blues and Greens)

- Challenging innovative strategy with real-world scenarios (Blues)

- Taking action rather than showing empathy (Greens)

- Preferring concrete communication to metaphors and analogies (Greens)

▶   ▶   ▶

If you are in leadership role, it is imperative to develop conflict-resolving skills. This book has been designed as a self-coaching resource to use at the start of any miscommunication. Give it to all your employees. Even if you've inherited an employee conflict of long standing, Color Q's "style shifting" techniques break down barriers and make people receptive again.

The cost for improving communications in your workplace? Minimal. The cost of not doing it? Billions of dollars annually in lost productivity alone in the United States. Do happier people work harder? We leave you with a quote from a *New York Times* article that examined that very question: "Workers' well-being depends, in large part, on managers' ability and willingness to facilitate workers' accomplishments—by removing obstacles, providing help, and acknowledging strong effort."[1]

You hold in your hands all the tools you need for long-term success.

NOTES

Chapter 3: How to Use This Book for Fast Results
1. Teresa Amabile and Steven Kramer, "Do Happier People Work Harder?" *New York Times,* September 3, 2011.

Chapter 4: The Color Q Personality System: Its Foundation and History
1. Norman Winski, *Understanding Jung* (Los Angeles: Sherbourne Press, 1971), p. 10.
2. Teresa Amabile and Steven Kramer, "Do Happier People Work Harder?" *New York Times,* September 3, 2011.

Chapter 5: Greens Overall
1. Daneen Skube, "Become a Wizard of Multitasking!" *Chicago Tribune,* September 12, 2010

Chapter 8: Green/Backup Red Extroverts
1. Megan Bungeroth, "East Sider of the Year," *Our Town,* March 29, 2012, p. 20.

Chapter 10: Reds Overall
1. William Stadiem, *Too Rich* (New York: Carroll & Graf, 1991), p. 3.
2. Donald Trump with Tony Schwartz, *Trump: The Art of the Deal,* (New York: Random House, 1987), p. 43.
3. Ibid.

Chapter 11: Red/Backup Blue Extroverts
1. Department of Justice Office of Public Affairs, "Attorney General Holder Names Sheila L. Birnbaum as Special Master of September 11th Victim Compensation Fund," news release, May 18, 2011.

Chapter 15: Blues Overall
1. Evan Thomas, "Bill and Hillary's Long, Hot Summer," *Newsweek,* October 19, 1998, p. 41.
2. U.S. Department of State, www.state.gov/r/pa/ei/biog/115321.htm.
3. Ibid.

Chapter 20: Golds Overall

1. Nico Pitney, "Sonia Sotomayor, Supreme Court Nominee: All You Need To Know," June 1, 2009; www.huffingtonpost.com/2009/05/01/sonia-sotomayor-supreme-c_n_194470.html.
2. White House news release, May 26, 2009; www.whitehouse.gov/the_press_office/Background-on-Judge-Sonia-Sotomayor.
3. "Sonia Sotomayor Overview," *New York Times,* February 1, 2010, p. A17.
4. Rana Foroohar, "Warren Buffett Is on a Radical Track," *Time,* January 23, 2012, pp. 34 and 38.
5. Ibid., p. 34.

Chapter 26: Approach to Innovation: The Primary Styles

1. Mark Dodgson and David Gann, *Innovation: A Very Short Introduction* (New York: Oxford University Press, 2010), p. xi.
2. Ibid.
3. Jane Stevenson and Bilal Kaafarani, *Breaking Away: How Great Leaders Create Innovation That Drives Sustainable Growth—and Why Others Fail* (New York: McGraw-Hill, 2011), pp. 15–26.

Chapter 28: Generation Conflict or Personality Conflict?

1. Rita M. Murray and Hile Rutledge, *Generations: Bridging the Gap with Type* (Norman, OK: Performance Consulting Publishers, 2009), p. 4.
2. Cam Marston of Generational Insight, presentation at the LOMA Financial Forum, 2011; www.generationalinsight.com.
3. "Gen X and Y Advantages in the Business Development Game" E-Tips by Phyllis Weiss Haserot, Practice Development Counsel, www.pdcounsel.com, June, 2011.
4. Bea Fields, Scott Wilder, Jim Bunch, and Rob Newbold, *Millennial Leaders: Success Stories from Today's Most Brilliant Generation Y Leaders* (Buffalo Grove, IL: Writers of the Round Table Press, 2008).
5. Allison Cheston, "How to Find the Right Mentor," *Globe and Mail,* November 18, 2011.
6. Ibid.

Chapter 29: Self-Coach Your Way to Success

1. Teresa Amabile and Steven Kramer, "Do Happier People Work Harder?" *New York Times,* September 3, 2011.

RECOMMENDED RESOURCES FOR PROFESSIONAL DEVELOPMENT

Business Coaching

Coaching and Career Reports: www.ColorQPersonalities.com.

Coaching for High Potential Women: **Lynne Morton**, www.pisols.com, lmorton@pisols.com.

Cross-Cultural Consulting and Transition Coaching: **Susanne Mueller**, www.susannemueller. biz, smueller4@nyc.rr.com.

Emerging and High Potential Leader Coaching: **Kathryn C. Mayer**, www.kcmayer.com, mayer@kcmayer.com.

Executive Image Coach: **Anna Wildermuth**, www.personalimagesinc.com, anna@ personalimagesinc.com.

Leadership Coach: **Robert W. Cuddy**, rwcuddy.com, rwcuddy@aol.com.

Leadership Training and Coaching: **Bea Fields**, http://beafields.com, bea@beafields.com.

Small Business Coach: **Craig Jennings**, www.craigjennings.com, craig@craigjennings.com.

Career Coaching

Career Coach: **Laura S. Hill**, www.careersinmotionllc.com, laurahill@cimllc.com.

Career and Job Search Strategist: **Cynthia Shapiro**, www.CynthiaShapiro.com, Cshapiro@CynthiaShapiro.com.

Communications Coaching and Training

Business Communication Coach: **Nancy Ancowitz**, www.NancyAncowitz.com, Nancy@NancyAncowitz.com.

Media Training and Presentation Coaching: **Diane DiResta**, www.diresta.com, diane@diresta.com, www.speechmakersite.com (Speech Maker online template for crafting a speech).

Organizational Development

Consultant to Corporate Wellness Programs: **Suzanne Brue**, www.the8colors.com, suzanne@the8colors.com.

Executive Training and Business Workshops: **Andrea R. Nierenberg**, www.NierenbergGroup.com, andrea@NierenbergGroup.com.

Management Consultant: **Mary Lippitt**, www.enterprisemgt.com, mlippitt@ enterprisemgt.com.

Management Consultant: **Rob Toomey**, www.Type-Coach.com, rob@type-coach.com.

Organization Development and Training: **Hile Rutledge**, www.oka-online.com, hrutledge@oka-online.com.

Organizational Trainer and Consultant: **Ray Linder**, ray@goodstewardship.com.

Strategy Implementation, Organizational Effectiveness, and Leadership Coaching: **Mary Graham Davis**, www.davisbatesongroup.com, mgdavis@davisbatesongroup.com.

Team-Building Training and Coaching: **Jane Maloney**, www.interaction-inc.com, jane@interaction-inc.com.

Workplace Inter-generational Solutions Consultant: **Phyllis Weiss Haserot**, www.pdcounsel .com, pwhaserot@pdcounsel.com.

Social Media, Online, and Technology Resources
Social Media Writer and Project Manager: **Jeannette Paladino**, http://writespeaksell.com, jpaladino@writespeaksell.com.

The Small Business Website Guy: **John Sawyer**, http://chonresources.com, sawyerjw@gmail.com.

Web and Online Technologies Project Management Consulting: **Janet Handal**, http://janethandal.com, janet@handal.com.

Recommended Business Books
Ancowitz, Nancy. *Self-Promotion for Introverts: The Quiet Guide to Getting Ahead*. New York: McGraw-Hill, 2009.

Baber, Anne and Lynne Waymon. *Make Your Contacts Count: Networking Know-How for Business and Career Success*. New York: AMACOM, 2007.

Butler, Susan. *Women Count: A Guide for Changing the World*. West Lafayette, IL: Purdue University Press, 2010.

Carson, Nacie. *The Finch Effect: The Five Strategies to Adapt and Thrive in Your Working Life*. Hoboken, NJ: Jossey-Bass, 2012.

DiResta, Diane. *Knockout Presentations*. Worcester, MA: Chandler House Press, 2009.

Fields, Bea. *Millennial Leaders: Success Stories from Today's Most Brilliant Generation and Leaders*. Buffalo Grove, IL: Writers of The Round Table Press, 2008.

Hammerness, Paul and Margaret Moore. *Organize Your Mind, Organize Your Life, Train Your Brain, and Get More Done in Less Time*. Buffalo, NY: Harlequin, 2011.

Haserot, Phyllis Weiss. *The Rainmaking Machine: Marketing Planning, Strategies, and Management for Law Firms*. Eagan, MN: Thomson Reuters/West, 2012.

Kay, Andrea. *Life's a Bitch and Then You Change Careers*. New York: Stewart, Tabori and Chang, 2005.

King, Patricia. *Monster Boss*. Avon, MA: Adams Media, 2008.

Mayer, Kathryn. *Collaborative Competition: A Woman's Guide to Succeeding by Competing*. New York: Collaborative Competition Press, 2009.

Nelson, Audrey, Ph.D. and Claire Brown, Ph.D. *The Gender Communication Handbook: Conquering Conversational Collisions Between Men and Women.* Hoboken, NJ: Pfeiffer/Wiley, 2012.

Nierenberg, Andrea. *Million Dollar Networking: The Sure Way to Find, Grow, and Keep Your Business.* Herndon, VA: Capital Books, 2005.

Sedlar, Jeri. *Don't Retire, REWIRE! 5 Steps to Fulfilling Work That Fuels Your Passion, Suits Your Personality, and Fills Your Pocket,* 2nd ed. Indianapolis, IN: Alpha/Penguin Group, 2007.

Shapiro, Cynthia. *What Does Somebody Have to Do to Get a Job Around Here!* New York: St. Martin's Griffin, 2008.

Wildermuth, Anna Soo. *Change One Thing.* New York: McGraw Hill, 2009.

Zichy, Shoya with Ann Bidou. *Career Match: Connecting Who You Are with What You'll Love to Do.* New York: AMACOM, 2007.

Books on the Myers-Briggs and Temperament Models

Baron, Renee. *What Type Am I, Discover Who You Really Are.* New York: Penguin 1998.

Berens, Linda and Dario Nardi. *The 16 Types: Descriptions for Self Discovery.* Huntington Beach/Los Angeles: Telos Publications, 1999.

Brue, Suzanne. *The 8 Colors of Fitness: Discover Your Color-Coded Fitness Personality and Create an Exercise Program You'll Never Quit!* Delray Beach, FL: Oakledge Press, 2008.

Dunning, Donna. *10 Career Essentials.* Boston: Nicholas Brealey Publishing, 2010.

Hammer, Allen. *Introduction to Type and Careers: Career Management and Counseling.* Mountain View, CA: Davies Black Publishing, 1993, 1996.

Hirsh, Sandra and Jean Kummerow. *Introduction to Type in Organizations.* Mountain View, CA: Davies Black Publishing, 1998.

Keirsey, David. *Please Understand Me II.* Del Mar, CA: Prometheus Nemesis Book, 1998.

Kise, Jane. *Intentional Leadership: 12 Tools for Focusing Strengths, Managing Weaknesses, and Achieving Your Purpose.* Bloomington, IN: Triple Nickel Press, 2012.

Kroeger, Otto and David B. Goldstein. *Creative Differences: Using Your Personality Type to Thrive at Work and at Play.* New York: Simon & Schuster, 2013.

Kroeger, Otto, Janet Thuesen, and Hile Rutledge. *Type Talk at Work.* New York: Dell Publishing, 2002.

Linder, Ray. *What Will I Do with My Money? How Your Personality Affects Your Financial Behavior.* Chicago: Northfield Publishing, 2000.

Murray, Rita and Hile Rutledge. *Generations: Bridging the Gap with Type.* Norman, OK: Performance Consulting Publishers, 2009.

Myers, Isabel Briggs with Peter Myers. *Gifts Differing.* Mountain View, CA: CPP, 1995.

Myers, Katharine D. and Linda K. Kirby. *Introduction to Type Dynamics and Development.* Palo Alto, CA: Davies Black Publishing 1987, 1998.

Nash, Susan. *Let's Split the Difference: Your Guide to Clarifying the Differences Between Similar Types.* Los Angeles: Radiance House, 2009.

Nardi, Dario. *Neuroscience of Personality: Brain Savvy Insights for All Types of People.* Los Angeles: Radiance House, 2011.

Pearman, Roger and Sarah Albritton. *I'm Not Crazy, I'm Just Not You.* Boston: Nicholas Brealey Publishing, 1997.

Quenk, Naomi L. *Was That Really Me?* Boston: Nicholas Brealey Publishing, 2002.

Segal, Marci. *A Quick Guide to the Four Temperaments and Creativity: A Psychological Understanding of Innovation.* Huntington Beach, CA: Telos Publications, 2006.

Tieger, Paul D. and Barbara Barron-Tieger. *The Art of SpeedReading People.* Boston: Little, Brown, 1998.

For additional books and resources on the MBTI and Temperaments, check out:
Center for Application of Psychological Type (CAPT)
www.capt.org; 1-800-777-CAPT
CAPT offers training, publishes type-related materials, compiles research to advance the understanding of type, and maintains the Isabel Briggs Myers Memorial Library.

Consulting Psychologist Press (CPP)
www.cpp-db.com;1-800-624-1765
CPP is the publisher and distributor of the MBTI Indicator and related materials.

The Myers & Briggs Foundation
www.myersbriggs.org
A not-for-profit foundation established by the Isabel Briggs Myers family.

Keirsey Temperament Theory
www.keirsey.com
Publishes and represents the work of David Keirsey and others specializing in the temperament theory.

INDEX